Managing the
Euro Area
Debt Crisis

Managing the
Euro Area
Debt Crisis

William R. Cline

Peterson Institute for International Economics
Washington, DC
June 2014

William R. Cline, senior fellow, has been associated with the Peterson Institute for International Economics since its inception in 1981. During 1996-2001, while on leave from the Institute, he was deputy managing director and chief economist of the Institute of International Finance. From 2002 through 2011 he held a joint appointment with the Peterson Institute and the Center for Global Development, where he is currently senior fellow emeritus. Before joining the Peterson Institute, he was senior fellow, the Brookings Institution (1973-81); deputy director of development and trade research, office of the assistant secretary for international affairs, US Treasury Department (1971-73); Ford Foundation visiting professor in Brazil (1970-71); and lecturer and assistant professor of economics at Princeton University (1967-70). His numerous publications include *Resolving the European Debt Crisis* (coeditor, 2012), *Financial Globalization, Economic Growth, and the Crisis of 2007–09* (2010), *The United States as a Debtor Nation* (2005), and *International Debt Reexamined* (1995).

**PETERSON INSTITUTE FOR
INTERNATIONAL ECONOMICS**
1750 Massachusetts Avenue, NW
Washington, DC 20036-1903
(202) 328-9000
FAX: (202) 659-3225
www.piie.com

Adam S. Posen, *President*
Steven R. Weisman, *Vice President for
   Publications and Communications*

Cover Design by Barbieri & Green
Cover Photo by © Thinkstock, IStock

Library of Congress Cataloging-in-Publication Data
Cline, William R.
   Managing the euro area debt crisis / William R. Cline.
      pages cm
   ISBN 978-0-88132-687-1
   1. Debts, Public—European Union countries. 2. Monetary policy—European Union countries 3. Currency crises—European Union countries. 4. European Union countries—Economic policy. I. Title.
   HJ8615.C55 2014
   336.3'4094—dc23

                                    2014009202

This publication has been subjected to a prepublication peer review intended to ensure analytical quality. The views expressed are those of the author. This publication is part of the overall program of the Peterson Institute for International Economics, as endorsed by its Board of Directors, but it does not necessarily reflect the views of individual members of the Board or of the Institute's staff or management. The Peterson Institute for International Economics is a private, nonprofit institution for the rigorous, open, and intellectually honest study and discussion of international economic policy. Its purpose is to identify and analyze important issues to making globalization beneficial and sustainable for the people of the United States and the world and then to develop and communicate practical new approaches for dealing with them. Its work is made possible by financial support from a highly diverse group of philanthropic foundations, private corporations, and interested individuals, as well as by income on its capital fund. For a list of Institute supporters, please see www.piie.com/supporters.cfm.

Contents

Preface

The financial calamity that devastated Southern Europe over the last four years has legitimately challenged some basic assumptions of the recent economic thought and even more rightly undermined the complacency of many an economic policymaker. In the two years or so since the European Central Bank's (ECB) commitment to purchase sovereign bonds of troubled countries—the so-called Outright Monetary Transactions (OMT)—the risks for the currency union's future appear to have receded. As William R. Cline makes clear in this book, *Managing the Euro Area Debt Crisis*, there are good prospects that the longer-term fiscal aspects of the euro area crisis can be managed on an orderly basis in coming years as well. Cline makes clear that this management is a matter of could (and should), however, and not a certainty. Most importantly, Cline offers a new methodology for assessing the sustainability of government debt that will be broadly applicable to all market economies.

The euro area sovereign debt crisis discussed in this important and globally relevant volume started in early 2010 in Greece, which by early 2012 became the first industrial country since the 1930s that was forced to restructure government debt and seek deep reductions in claims by creditors. Contagion from the Greek debt crisis soon swept Ireland and Portugal, forcing them to seek official support from the IMF and European partners. Credit risk spreads on government bonds spiked to dangerous levels in the far larger economies of Italy and Spain. As of spring 2014, Ireland has successfully completed its official support program and returned to market access. Portugal is on the verge of completion of its program as well, as this book goes to press, and sovereign bond spreads have dropped significantly for Italy and Spain.

Cline's unconventional assessment of future long-run solvency for Italy and Spain is consistent with his prescient working papers published by the Peterson Institute for International Economics in February and August 2012 forecasting this stabilization, despite panic. Back then, when the crisis was still overly threatening European stability, his view was controversial. Today his independent views on debt sustainability may prove equally ahead of the curve. The biggest factor contributing to this trend, in his view, was the decision by the ECB to become an effective lender of last resort through the launching of its OMT program for purchasing government bonds if needed, subject to conditionality through adjustment programs. Cline considers maintenance of the OMT as crucial, even though so far it has not had to make any purchases.

In preparing this book, Cline drew on his extensive experience in past analyses of sovereign debt and financial crises, notably in Latin America in the 1980s (*International Debt: Systemic Risk and Policy Response*, 1984, and *International Debt Reexamined*, 1995) and in East Asia and other emerging markets in 1997-98 in his capacity as chief economist of the private sector's Institute of International Finance (while then on leave from PIIE). For this study, he has developed a new method to assess the probability distribution of future paths for the sovereign debt burden. The method goes beyond the usual enumeration of scenarios by taking account of likely correlations between good and bad scenarios for each of five key macroeconomic variables (GDP growth, primary or noninterest fiscal balance, sovereign risk spread in the interest rate, bank recapitalization costs, and privatization earnings). The resulting array of future debt trajectories and their likely probabilities enables him to diagnose whether or not the sovereign is likely to become or remain solvent. Cline's operationalization of the insight that financial crises tend to drive correlated downturns in most factors determining debt sustainability is a true breakthrough.

Cline's new method leads to original views on European debt. His model indicates that Ireland, Portugal, Italy, and Spain all show future debt paths reflecting solvency, although achieving and maintaining that solvency will require strong and persistent political will to sustain the sizable primary surpluses needed. The prospects for Greece are less sanguine. Cline concludes that, despite many strides, Greece may face continued reluctance by investors to restore its sovereign credit reputation, raising the possibility of a need for further relief from official creditors in the future.

In this rigorously analytical book, Cline considers the argument that austerity in Europe has been excessive. He judges that the Southern European economies under severe sovereign debt stress not only had zero access to large-scale private financing but also could have precipitated further widening of risk spreads if they had not shown commitment to fiscal correction. He also assesses the bank-sovereign debt "doom loop," documenting the adverse influence of sovereigns on borrowing costs of banks in Greece and Italy and vice versa in Ireland and Spain. He concludes that interest rate shocks from sovereigns to banks were not fully passed on to private sector borrowers, but instead financial fragmentation arose partly in the form of severe credit rationing. Cline further assesses the effectiveness of some potential European institutional innovations to deal with the crisis and analyzes the possibility of introducing eurobonds in the future.

We at the Peterson Institute are proud to have made important ongoing contributions to the policy debate on how to resolve the euro area debt crisis. In June 2009, Nicolas Véron and I published "A Solution for Europe's Banking Problem," a Policy Brief that set out a vision for unified bank supervision and regulation in Europe, one now coming to fruition in the Single Supervisory Mechanism. From 2010 through early 2014, PIIE published two dozen Policy Briefs and Working Papers on the crisis as well as a conference volume on policy options in March 2012 (*Resolving the European Debt Crisis*, Special Report 21, ed. Cline and Guntram Wolff). The Institute has been the leading US forum for serious discussion of euro issues. We hosted speeches and discussions on the issues by euro area finance ministers, central bank board governors and members, EU commissioners, two ECB presidents, and three heads of state. Several senior members of the Institute staff—notably Anders Åslund, C. Fred Bergsten, Jacob Kirkegaard, Angel Ubide, and Nicolas Véron in addition to Cline—have provided widely followed commentary on the crisis as it has evolved. In tandem with this book, PIIE is publishing an analytical insider's account of the crisis by Simeon Djankov, finance minister of Bulgaria from 2009 to 2013, titled *Inside the Euro Crisis: An Eyewitness Account*.

The Peterson Institute for International Economics is a private, nonprofit institution for rigorous, intellectually open, and honest study and discussion of international economic policy. Its purpose is to identify and analyze important issues to making globalization beneficial and sustainable for the people of the United States and the world and then to develop and communicate practical new approaches for dealing with them. The Institute is completely nonpartisan.

The Institute's work is funded by a highly diverse group of philanthropic foundations, private corporations, and interested individuals, as well as income on its capital fund. About 35 percent of the Institute's resources in our latest fiscal year were provided by contributors from outside the United States. Interested readers may access the data underlying Institute books by searching titles at http://bookstore.piie.com.

The Executive Committee of the Institute's Board of Directors bears overall responsibility for the Institute's direction, gives general guidance and approval to its research program, and evaluates its performance in pursuit of its mission. The Institute's President is responsible for the identification of topics that are likely to become important over the medium term (one to three years) that should be addressed by Institute scholars. This rolling agenda is set in close consultation with the Institute's research staff, Board of Directors, and other stakeholders.

The President makes the final decision to publish any individual Institute study, following independent internal and external review of the work.

The Institute hopes that its research and other activities will contribute to building a stronger foundation for international economic policy around the world. We invite readers of these publications to let us know how they think we can best accomplish this objective.

ADAM S. POSEN
President
March 2014

Acknowledgments

For comments on earlier drafts, I thank without implicating peer reviewers Tamim Bayoumi, Daniel Gros, and Ángel Ubide, as well as Anders Åslund, Ajai Chopra, Stijn Claessens, Joseph Gagnon, Jacob Kirkegaard, Douglas Rediker, Edwin Truman, Nicolas Véron, and participants at a study group held on November 1, 2013. I thank Jared Nolan and Yimei Zou for excellent research assistance.

This book is dedicated to my younger grandchildren:
Geoffrey, Elisabeth, Emily, and Claire

1

Overview and Policy Implications

In the nearly four years since the first International Monetary Fund–European Union (IMF-EU) support program for Greece in May 2010, the sovereign debt crisis in the euro area has passed through three phases. The first involved the Greek crisis and its contagion to Ireland (late 2010) and then Portugal (early 2011). In the second phase contagion reached the far larger economies of Italy and Spain, where sovereign risk spreads reached 500 to 600 basis points in late 2011 and the second quarter of 2012, threatening to precipitate a self-fulfilling prophecy of insolvency. In this phase there were persistent market expectations that at least one country would exit from the euro. The third and present phase began in mid-2012, when European Central Bank (ECB) President Mario Draghi pledged to do "whatever it takes" to preserve the euro and announced the ECB's program of Outright Monetary Transactions (OMT) for purchasing government bonds in the secondary market for countries in adjustment programs. By the third quarter of 2013, even though no bond purchases in the OMT had yet been necessary, the results were impressive. Spreads had eased back to the range of 250 basis points for Italy and Spain and also fallen sharply for Ireland and Portugal. By February 2014, spreads had narrowed further.

The crisis has been multifaceted. High public debt and fiscal deficits drove the crisis in Greece. As domestic political instability aggravated the steep economic downturn, it became necessary not only to restructure Greek public debt with a major haircut for private creditors but also to mobilize official support from the euro area and IMF amounting to a remarkable 124 percent of GDP (table 7A.1 in chapter 7 for 2014), making Greece a special case in several dimensions. In Spain and Ireland, the collapse of housing bubbles contributed to recession and a downswing into fiscal deficits, and in Ireland the associated bank bailouts added about 40 percent of GDP to government debt. Italy's persistently high government debt even before the Great Recession, along with political uncertainty, heightened its vulnerability even though its fiscal and current account deficits were smaller than those of other periphery economies under stress. Portugal, like Greece and Spain, had been vulnerable to a sudden-stop financial squeeze given reliance on external financing of large current account deficits. A theme common to the five economies, however, is that they have suffered from the paradigm shift from the previous financial market view that industrial countries could not default, and that therefore there was no reason for differences among euro area government borrowing rates once the single currency eliminated currency risk. That paradigm has been shattered by the Greek restructuring, leaving a legacy of market perception that sovereign risk can indeed be severe within the euro area.

Figure 1.1 shows the basic fever chart of the euro area sovereign debt crisis: the size of sovereign spreads above the 10-year German bund for the debt-stressed periphery economies. Greece literally goes off the chart as its spreads soared before debt restructuring, but there has been clear improvement for Ireland, Portugal, Italy, and Spain since the height of the crisis. Moreover, Ireland successfully completed its IMF-EU support program in December 2013, and Portugal is on track to do so in May 2014 (albeit perhaps with the aid of a precautionary credit arrangement). Both countries encountered strong demand for bonds issued in early 2014 on relatively favorable terms. Even Greece was able to reenter the medium-term market in April 2014.[1]

As of early 2014, the chances thus seem reasonably favorable that the euro area debt crisis can be managed going forward in a fashion that avoids extreme shocks to the euro area and world economies. The seemingly decisive OMT initiative confirms the sense of a conference held in September 2011 by the Peterson Institute for International Economics and Bruegel: that the ECB was the only institution capable of providing the bridge between forceful action needed immediately and the new institutions that would be needed for the euro area but would require a long process of negotiation (Cline and Wolff 2012, 2).

Even so, it is premature to declare that the crisis is "over" (in the optimistic terminology of French President François Hollande already in mid-2013).[2] The historical lesson of sovereign debt crises is that they can experience misleading phases of apparent hopefulness only to be followed by deterioration, as occurred in the Latin American debt crisis of the 1980s. Whereas recovery by 1984 from the severe global recession of 1982 raised hopes that export growth

---

1. In January 2014 Ireland placed €3.75 billion in 10-year bonds at 3.54 percent. In February, Portugal placed €3 billion in 10-year bonds at a yield of 5.1 percent. In April, Greece placed €3 billion in five-year bonds at a yield of 4.95 percent. Ralph Atkins and Robin Wigglesworth, "Strong Demand for Ireland's Post Bailout Bond," *Financial Times*, January 7, 2014; Peter Wise, "Portugal Draws Strong Demand in Debt Sale," *Financial Times*, February 11, 2014; Robin Wigglesworth and Elaine Moore, "Greek €3 billion Bond Sale Snapped Up," *Financial Times*, April 10, 2014.

2. Rupert Neate, "François Hollande: The Eurozone Crisis Is Over," *Guardian*, June 9, 2013.

Figure 1.1   Sovereign risk spreads above 10-year German bunds, 2008–14

basis points

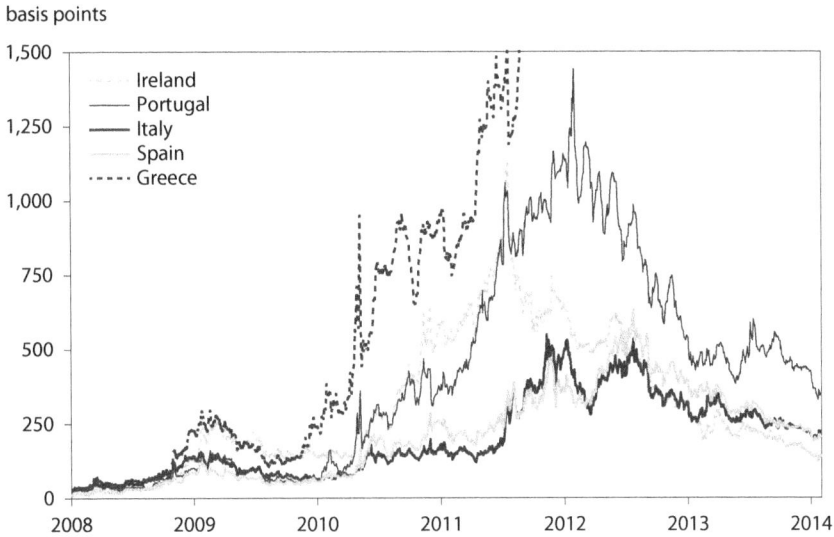

Source: Datastream.

would enable full debt servicing, by the end of the decade the main debtor nations of the region (except Chile and Colombia) needed substantial debt relief through the Brady Plan.

A fundamental requirement for sustained exit from a sovereign debt crisis is political will, and in particular the ongoing willingness of the public to generate primary (noninterest) fiscal surpluses on the order of 2 to 4 percent of GDP (or more in the case of Italy) to cover interest costs of the debt. In the euro area, only time will tell whether this political sustainability is present in all of the countries that have experienced debt stress.

Other obstacles may also need to be overcome. The effectiveness of the OMT could be undermined by a ruling of the German Constitutional Court, as discussed below. The new round of turmoil in emerging markets in early 2014 could prompt a rebound in sovereign risk spreads in the euro area periphery. A renewed flareup in the special case of Greece, where further relief may be needed and the main opposition party (Syriza) has rejected the IMF-EU adjustment program, could similarly play a destabilizing role.

Nevertheless, this study finds that the economic fundamentals should be broadly supportive of successful management of, and exit from, the crisis going forward. The first part of the book, chapters 2 through 5, sets the stage for the analysis in qualitative terms, by examining several leading functional issues that have dominated the policy debate. The core quantitative framework that provides the basis for the assessment of debt sustainability is a debt simulation model that applies a new methodology to identify the likely range of outcomes. Chapter 6 sets forth the model and applies it to Ireland, Portugal, Italy, and Spain; chapter 7 applies the model to Greece. The debt simulations explore whether sovereign debt is on track to spiral further out of control or instead revert back toward more sustainable levels. This overview chapter presents a synthesis of policy implications and then summarizes the qualitative analysis of functional issues and the quantitative method and findings.

The purpose of this book is to contribute to policy analysis of the evolution to date of the sovereign debt crisis in the euro area, and of the best strategy for resolving the crisis in the decisions that lie ahead. The analysis focuses on sovereign debt, and does not examine debt problems of the private sector except with respect to the role of bank losses in precipitating public debt problems (and vice versa). The approach is primarily macroeconomic, and does not attempt to provide a close examination of structural reforms achieved to date or those still needed. Nor does the study assess the political dynamics of domestic forces conducive or corrosive to orderly resolution of the crisis. Finally, although the analysis considers major aspects of the evolving institutional framework of the euro area insofar as it affects sovereign debt sustainability, including the development of firewalls, the debate on eurobonds, progress toward banking union, and the debate on a debt restructuring mechanism, the study does not attempt to provide an in-depth examination of the prospects for further institutional change.

The next section enumerates the principal findings and policy implications of this study. At their core is the finding that Ireland, Italy, Portugal, and Spain are solvent and should be able to continue their progress toward fiscal consolidation and a return to more normal financial market access. The corresponding policy implication is that maintaining the potential support of the OMT is crucial but that initiatives such as a debt restructuring mechanism would be counterproductive. As before in its restructuring, Greece could prove an exception in potentially needing more relief.

Policy Implications

The first, highest-level policy implication is that the euro area has made the right decision to do "whatever it takes" to keep the euro area from breaking apart, including avoiding an exit just by Greece. The stakes are too high to risk potentially massive financial crisis effects from a breakup.

The second, crucial policy implication is that the strategy of temporary official assistance to Portugal and Ireland, steady progress toward fiscal consolidation in all of the periphery economies, and the backstop of OMT to deal with adverse swings in financial markets has been working and should be continued as Ireland and Portugal now complete their programs and the periphery economies more generally return toward more normal conditions for market access. Debt ratios in the four peripheral economies excluding Greece can reasonably be expected to trend to the 100 to 120 percent range by 2020. The proper diagnosis for the four economies is that their sovereigns are solvent, so it would be counterproductive to restructure their debt (thereby imposing credit reputation damage). The OMT in particular is the most important official underpinning of this process, because by preventing a self-fulfilling prophecy of insolvency from a surge in market interest rates, it provides time for the economies to carry out fiscal and structural reform.

A third implication is that Greece may need some further debt relief, this time from the official sector because it is the creditor for most of the debt. Such relief should be contingent on continued progress on fiscal and structural reform.

A fourth implication is that despite critiques of excessive austerity in the euro area crisis, there has been little alternative to fiscal consolidation, and it would be a serious mistake to allow fiscal deficits to widen again (even if the pace of adjustment is eased). The simple arithmetic of debt sustainability turns crucially on attaining a meaningful primary surplus, and the welfare losses that would arise from a collapse into debt default would make any growth costs from seemingly excessive near-term demand reduction from fiscal adjustment seem minimal in comparison.

A fifth implication is that the pursuit of financial integration in the sense of equality of private sector interest rates in the euro area has inherent limits. So long as the nations have separate fiscal authorities, they inevitably will have differences in sovereign default risk premiums, and there is an inevitable relationship of private borrowing rates within the economy to the sovereign borrowing rate. The corollary is that monetary policy can do more to address the euro area debt crisis by offering country-specific OMT to curb excessive country spreads than it can accomplish by general across-the-board monetary ease (through a lower policy rate or quantitative easing with asset purchases proportionate to GDPs).

A sixth implication is that although full-fledged debt mutualization through eurobonds does not seem to be in the cards politically in the absence of further fiscal and political integration, euro area governments might usefully explore as a contingency a bond insurance sinking fund whereby there would be mutual guarantees to peripheral economy borrowing in exchange for a premium paid annually into the insurance fund.

A seventh implication of the findings is that a shift toward restructuring (as seemingly implied by a recent IMF staff study [2013i] favoring early preemptive restructurings) would likely be counterproductive. If going forward it were to develop that the IMF insisted on restructuring for Portugal (for example), the euro area would be well advised to go its own way and manage further adjustment plans for Portugal with its own resources and institutions, including the Enhanced Conditions Credit Line (EFSF 2011).

At a deeper level, the outcome of the euro area sovereign debt crisis will ultimately be determined by the political will of the governments facing debt stress, progress toward structural reform that improves medium-term growth, and progress in reshaping the institutional architecture of the euro area. The central projections of this study should thus be viewed as broadly indicating that the necessary economic conditions for resolving the crisis are on track, without implying that these conditions will be sufficient, especially if unaccompanied by sustained political will.

Leading Policy Issues

Fiscal Adjustment and Monetary Policy

Chapter 2 examines one of the most acrimoniously debated issues in the euro area crisis: whether the agenda of fiscal adjustment has been necessary and has contributed to resolution of the crisis, or whether instead it has been misguided and counterproductive. The basic critique is the Keynesian argument that attempts to reduce the fiscal deficit will instead merely cause a reduction in output because of deficient demand.

The fundamental answer to the critics of fiscal adjustment is that there was little alternative because financing was not available for larger deficits. Greece, Ireland, and Portugal became cut off from financial markets, and larger new borrowing from markets was not an option. The magnitudes of official support from the IMF and euro area governments were already large, and political leaders in Germany and other core economies were under pressure from publics to limit such support. Significantly, the path of spreads lends support to the notion that breakdowns in fiscal adjustment prompted new surges in sovereign risk spreads (as discussed for Italy and Spain; see figure 2.2), so a move toward greater fiscal stimulus could have prompted even larger increases in their risk spreads.

The IMF did find that its early adjustment program projections had understated the growth tradeoff from fiscal adjustment because macroeconomic multipliers are larger than usual when unemployment is high and interest rates are already close to zero so the usual monetary stimulus policy of reducing interest rates is no longer available. Output reduction from fiscal tightening is therefore greater than usual. There has accordingly been some pattern of easing the ambitions of the timing of fiscal adjustment in successive program reviews. Nonetheless, a model developed in appendix 2C shows that if the stakes involve the risk of a collapse in confidence in the country's ability to honor its sovereign debt, the multiplier can turn negative, such that attempts to stimulate the economy through further fiscal expansion can reduce economic welfare by increasing the probability of a catastrophic default.

Other IMF research finds that even though a high multiplier when unemployment is high could imply a perverse increase in the ratio of debt to GDP as a consequence of fiscal tightening (because of the resulting decline in the denominator, GDP), such an effect would likely be only temporary.[3] The benefits of the fiscal adjustment in reducing the deficit and thus the cumulative

---

3. For most references pertaining to this overview, see the chapters in question.

debt would successfully reduce the debt ratio over time if not in the first year. A broadly similar model exercise in appendix 2B finds the same result.

It is important to recognize that some of the fiscal corrections have been large; Greece cut its cyclically adjusted primary deficit by 15 percent of GDP from 2009 to 2012. The massive destabilization in expectations from successive political collapses and threats of exit from the euro almost certainly caused output losses to exceed those that might have been expected just from fiscal compression, but again there was little alternative to the cutbacks in any event. Moreover, excluding Greece, there is no clear pattern among the four other peripheral economies relating more severe fiscal adjustment to more severe output contraction (figure 2.3).

The overall diagnosis is that fiscal adjustment and movement toward eventual sizable primary surpluses (fiscal surplus excluding interest payments), on the order of 3 percent of GDP or more, was integral to managing the debt crisis. Importantly, of the total fiscal adjustments needed from 2010–11 to 2017, about two-thirds (Ireland and Spain) to three-fourths (Greece, Italy, and Portugal) were already accomplished by 2012. Consequently, the pace of fiscal adjustment can be eased significantly going forward (from a range of about 2 to 4 percent of GDP per year in 2010–12 to 0.5 to 1.5 percent in 2013–15; figure 2.4), facilitating a recovery in growth.

Chapter 2 concludes with a brief examination of the role of monetary policy. With the benefit of hindsight, during the course of the euro area debt crisis the ECB arguably kept policy interest rates too high for too long, given disappointing growth for the euro area as a whole. However, by late 2013 the ECB had cut the policy rate to 0.25 percent, effectively the zero bound. The question arises whether a shift to aggressive quantitative easing could help spur growth. Although the ECB's balance sheet has actually risen more than that of the Federal Reserve (by 18 percent of GDP from mid-2007 to end-2012, compared with 13 percent), its acquired assets have mainly been repurchase obligations of banks and bonds of periphery governments, with maturities of three to four years or less. The key to quantitative easing is its influence in reducing long-term interest rates. Based on the US experience, the remaining scope for compressing long-term interest rates (e.g., 10-year maturities) in the euro area appears to be relatively limited, so the potential for quantitative easing to boost output may be limited also.

Banks and Sovereign Debt

A second salient issue in the debt crisis has been the "doom loop" between the sovereign and the banks in the country in question. Aside from the historical interest of which party inflicted greater damage on the other, the primary issue is whether looming bank recapitalizations in the future will impose crippling debts on sovereigns. Also at stake are the questions of financial fragmentation, whereby different sovereign strengths translate to differing private sector financial conditions despite the supposed single monetary area, and whether the emerging euro area institutions (banking union, European Stability Mechanism [ESM]) adequately address the problems.

Banks and sovereigns are joined at the hip. As the peripheral crisis worsened, foreign creditors (including foreign banks) reduced holdings of government obligations while domestic banks increased holdings. Zero risk weighting under Basel standards, plus the greater internalization of an external benefit from shoring up the government to in-country banks, contributed to this dynamic.

Ireland is the clearest case in which collapse in the banking sector imposed severe new debt responsibilities on the sovereign. Run-ups in bank deposits and assets associated with the real estate booms were unsustainable in both Ireland and Spain. In Ireland, government support to the banking system added some 40 percent of GDP to public debt. The absence of any bail-in requirement for creditors (except for the wiping out of stockholders and subordinate creditors) was understandable in the context of the post-Lehman environment of international crisis, but generous from a subsequent vantage point after imposition of massive losses on creditors and even uninsured depositors in Cyprus in early 2013. The impact of the banking problem on sovereign debt was milder in Spain than in Ireland, amounting to about 6 percent of GDP (although more losses could lie ahead).

The Irish case has generated a particularly poignant irony. In the euro area, monetary finance of governments is in principle prohibited. And sovereign debt is considered more risky in the euro area because the single currency means no country can print money to pay its debt in the way most sovereigns can. Yet the burden of the bank-derived debt in Ireland has in fact been handled precisely by monetary finance. The Central Bank of Ireland provided some €40 billion in financing to the government to deal with the losses, and an early 2013 conversion of this debt from promissory notes to bonds paying lower interest will reduce the government's interest costs by about 1⅓ percent of GDP annually. So Ireland might be seen as the exception that proves the rule: no monetary finance, unless the causation comes from the banking sector itself rather than general fiscal excess.

Greece is the clearest case of damage imposed by sovereign default on public debt held by its banks. Greek banks held about €60 billion in government debt at the end of 2011, so the haircut of 53 percent in the restructuring of early 2012 eliminated about €30 billion, or 6 percent of their assets and hence almost the entirety of their capital. The resulting need to recapitalize the banks caused substantial leakage to the net reduction in sovereign debt from the restructuring, necessitating additional borrowing of €25 billion. The sovereign haircut in Greece spilled over to heavily exposed banks in Cyprus.

Regarding financial fragmentation, there is indeed a close correlation between sovereign spreads and credit default swap (CDS) rates of the banks in the country and, by implication, the interest rates banks must pay to borrow and must charge on loans. The corresponding implication is that as sovereign risk diverges, so will country lending conditions. The search for uniform monetary conditions is to some extent inherently chimerical as a result, so long as there is no fiscal union or mutualization of debt. The surprise is that the transmission of the sovereign differential to lending rates seems to be substantially muted and delayed. Thus, whereas quarterly average sovereign spreads above German bunds peaked in the third quarter of 2012 at 430 basis points in Italy and 500 basis points in Spain, in that quarter the spread of interest rates on new bank lending to the private sector in Italy and Spain was only 100 basis points above corresponding rates in Germany. Although these spreads continued to widen to 140 basis points by the first quarter of 2013, they remained lower than the sovereign spreads of 300 basis points in Italy and 350 basis points in Spain at that time (see figures 2.2 and 3.5). Nonetheless, a substantial tightening of borrowing conditions showed up in the reduction of availability of credit, reflecting the phenomenon of credit rationing whereby lenders curb volumes rather than raising rates to levels that only more risky firms might be willing to pay.

As for sovereign debt vulnerability to future bank losses, estimates by the Organization for Economic Cooperation and Development (OECD) and other experts imply that the scope of damages may be more limited than many fear. Using benchmarks of 5 percent of assets or more for the target leverage ratio, these various estimates indicate that capital shortfalls are likely to be on the order of 3.5 percent of GDP or less in Ireland and Portugal, and 2.5 percent of GDP or less in Italy and Spain. Appendix 3A in chapter 3 provides an alternative set of estimates by applying an earlier IMF model relating bank losses to unemployment and growth rates. When the estimated losses are compared with impairments already taken by the banks, it turns out that banks in all four economies have already accounted for losses comparable to or in excess of the predicted amounts, with banks in Spain having taken especially large writeoffs in 2012. Even using the higher end of the OECD and other estimates of capital shortfalls, considering that debt ratios are in the vicinity of 120 percent of GDP in Ireland and 100 percent of GDP in Spain, and considering that much of the needed capital would come from the private sector rather than governments, the extra shock from these ranges of bank recapitalization losses would seem modest.

Chapter 3 closes with a review of institutional evolution in the form of banking union, as well as the ESM's scope for direct bank recapitalization. There was a brief moment in mid-2012 when it appeared that direct ESM recapitalization of banks could alleviate a debt burden otherwise borne by the government in Spain (and even in Ireland retroactively), but Germany, Finland, and the Netherlands promptly rejected that possibility by ruling out ESM direct recapitalization for "legacy" assets. Subsequently the scope for ESM bank recapitalization was limited to €60 billion, so in any event the scope for its preventing meaningful additions to sovereign debt will be modest. More broadly, the hope that the doom loop will be severed by banking union, because unified supervision will set the stage for mutualized responsibility, seems somewhat detached from the underlying reality that debt mutualization is unlikely without fiscal and political union. There may be greater scope for ending the doom loop through a tougher stance on imposing losses on creditors and uninsured depositors (as in Cyprus) rather than increasing public debt to recapitalize banks, but realistically public sector support in a crisis cannot (and should not) be ruled out. Similarly, limits to progress on mutualized responsibility are evident in the area of depositor insurance, which seems to have lagged the most in banking union discussions.

External Adjustment and Breakup Costs

Chapter 4 considers the relationship of external current account imbalances to the sovereign debt crisis. It argues that those analysts who place external imbalances at the heart of the debt crisis have a good case with respect to sudden-stop causation but are less persuasive with regard to future sustainability of debt now that financing has been arranged and current account deficits sharply narrowed. Current account deficits certainly did reach excessive levels: as much as 15 percent of GDP in Greece, 13 percent in Portugal, and 10 percent in Spain in 2008. The large current account deficits in four of the five periphery economies (Italy being the exception) made them vulnerable to a sudden stop in capital inflows. There is a clear relationship between the size of current account deficits (as a percentage of GDP) in 2007–08 and the size of the sovereign risk spread at the height of the crisis in 2012 (figure 4.1a). But by 2013 there was no longer a relationship between the sovereign spread and the current account, as measured by the actual and expected path for 2012–16 (figure 4.9). Moving current accounts further into surplus is not needed for resolving the debt crisis even if large deficits played a role in causing it.

Although a sudden stop contributed to a liquidity squeeze, two structural features meant that it was not as severe as would have been the case for emerging-market economies. First, because the debt was in euros, so long as the country remained in the single currency there would be no balance sheet impact that has been so severe in emerging-market crises in which a sharp depreciation of the currency causes a much larger burden of debt owed in foreign currency relative to domestic tax revenue (for governments) or earnings (for firms). Second, the Target2 balances assured automatic financing of current account deficits, if not of governments suddenly facing unfavorable credit markets.

Real effective exchange rates did become overvalued, although the focus has been too much on relative unit labor costs against Germany and too little on overall real effective exchange rates against the world as a whole. On the latter measure the periphery has made major corrections. As a group, the four peripheral economies excluding Italy (where current account deficits were smaller) depreciated by 11 percent in real effective terms (averaging the Bank for International Settlements [BIS] index deflated by consumer price indices [CPIs] and the IMF index deflated by unit labor costs) from 2008 to 2012 (figure 4.8). In part this outcome reflects some success in internal devaluation, especially in Ireland where unit labor costs have fallen sharply as public sector wages were cut by 14 percent (or more for high-end wages). In any event, the current account deficits have disappeared: for the same four economies, the current account has swung from a GDP-weighted 10 percent of GDP deficit in 2008 to a surplus of 1 percent in 2013.

Nor has the elimination of the current account deficit been solely from demand compression and hence just a symptom of recession. For the five periphery economies (this time including Italy), real exports of goods and services rose by 8.4 percent from 2006–08 (before the Great Recession) to 2010–13 (in the midst of the euro area debt crisis). Export gains were especially large in Ireland (24 percent), Spain (17 percent), and Portugal (15 percent). However, real imports did fall, by 6.5 percent for the same grouping over the same period—almost the same proportionate decline as real GDP (which fell 5.8 percent). So the external adjustment was about half on the side of real export expansion and half on the side of import compression. Recessionary contraction of imports was especially pronounced in Greece, where real imports fell by 30 percent from 2006–08 to 2010–13 as real GDP fell by 18 percent (and real exports declined by 7 percent rather than rising as elsewhere in the periphery).

Some seem to think that the net international investment position (NIIP) carries the same weight as the public-debt-to-GDP ratio in driving country risk borrowing spreads. It is true that Spain, Portugal, and Ireland have large net international liabilities, on the order of 150 percent of GDP, and faced relatively high interest rates, in the range of 4 to 6 percent in the first quarter of 2013, whereas the Netherlands and Germany have sizable net international assets of about 50 percent of GDP and enjoyed low interest rates of 1.5 to 2 percent (figure 4.10). But although a cross-country test for 18 industrial countries does confirm a significant negative relationship between the NIIP and the sovereign CDS rate (a proxy for sovereign risk spread), the size of this relationship is relatively small. Reducing the net liability position by 100 percent of GDP would reduce the risk spread by only 70 basis points. So it is not fruitful to conceptualize the challenge facing the peripheral countries as one requiring a major shift to current account surplus so that NIIP positions can be improved substantially, because the NIIPs are not the key to the sovereign risk spread.

Those who emphasize current account imbalances going forward and effective exchange rate overvaluation have a somewhat stronger case working through the relationship of the exchange rate to growth, and thereby to the key growth component of future debt sustainability. There is a long tradition in the international economics literature holding that for a country needing to tighten fiscal policy but already in a position of excessive unemployment and also in a position of excessive external deficit, the proper policy mix is fiscal tightening combined with exchange rate depreciation. Increased export activity will then tend to offset reduced activity from the reduction in domestic demand while also contributing to improvement in external imbalance. The single currency prevents depreciation, but some advocate major expansion of activity and higher inflation in the core northern economies as the means by which the periphery can carry out an effective depreciation. But even if Germany and the rest of the north accepted inflation of 3 percent over a five-year period while inflation remained at 2 percent in the periphery, the resulting boost to growth in the periphery applying plausible parameters would be too small to boost the output level at the end of the period by more than about 1 percent, too small to meaningfully alter the path of the debt-to-GDP ratio.

A related argument is that there must be this type of reflation in the core to permit rebalancing in the periphery or else the euro area as a whole will enter into a current account surplus position that is intolerable to the rest of the world economy. As it turns out, however, the elimination of the current account deficit of the periphery has coincided with an almost equal reduction in the surpluses of the super-surplus economies of China and Japan alone. From 2008 to 2013, the current account of the five periphery economies swung from a deficit of $320 billion to a surplus of $30 billion. In the same period, the combined surpluses of China and Japan fell from $420 billion to $160 billion. There is no compelling case that the resulting surplus of the euro area as a whole is inconsistent with global balance.[4]

As for a breakup of the euro, a few leading economists have called for an exit from the euro by Greece or other peripheral economies (or at least a temporary "holiday") because of their view that growth cannot return without real depreciation and that internal devaluation would be too slow and sacrifice too much output. The majority view, however, is that exit from the euro would be damaging to the country leaving and impose major contagion effects on the other euro members. Public debt would have to be redenominated in a new (or pre-euro) currency, imposing de facto default losses on creditors. In a democracy the decisions would require public discussion, which would trigger preemptive bank runs. Banking crisis and capital flight would prompt contagion to other peripheral economies. The preponderance of this view seems to have brought Germany and some other northern countries back on script, to preserving the euro from a period of flirtation (in late 2011 and early 2012) with the notion that perhaps Greece ought to be forced out of the euro.

Four studies have made prominent estimates of the costs of breakup. One, the winner of a prize formulated in search of the best way to breakup the euro, argues that because the costs of remaining in the straitjacket of being unable to depreciate and grow are extremely high, Greece and some other peripheral economies would be better off exiting (Bootle 2012). Even this study recognizes contagion costs to partners, estimating that exit by all five peripheral economies would cause a loss of about 2 percent of GDP for other members. The other three studies instead find potentially large costs. A study by UBS

---

4. The most recent IMF (2013n) projection places the euro area's current account balance for 2013 at 2.3 percent of GDP, significantly higher than the 0.7 percent of GDP deficit in 2008 but still within the ±3 percent of GDP band considered consistent with fundamental equilibrium of the exchange rate in the series of estimates begun in Cline and Williamson (2008) and updated semiannually thereafter.

suggests that an exiting country could have a loss of 40 to 50 percent of GDP in the first year alone, but this study assumes the country would be expelled from the European Union and face retaliatory tariffs equal to the depreciation (Deo, Donovan, and Hatheway 2011). A study by ING identifies more moderate costs, with output loss of 9 percent over three years for Greece if it were to exit and spillover losses of 2 percent of GDP for other periphery countries and 1.2 percent for core countries (Cliffe and Leen 2010). The study estimates that core economies have exposure of more than one-third of their GDP to peripheral economies (counting both government loans and claims of their banks). The fourth study, a short box in an IMF report in January 2013 (IMF 2013c), focused on financial risk contagion and concluded that although other peripheral country risk spreads have become less correlated with spikes in Greek spreads, and despite reductions of exposure to Greece, the euro area could lose a cumulative 12 percent of GDP over three years if the financial shock of a Greek exit proved to be comparable to that of the Lehman collapse. The broad implication is that there are potentially extremely high tail-risk costs from a breakup, and it behooves the euro area member countries to pay at least a moderate ongoing premium to maintain catastrophe insurance against this risk.

Eurobonds, Firewalls, OMT, and Debt Restructuring

Chapter 5 concludes the survey of key policy issues with discussion of four other subjects. The first, the notion of creating eurobonds to mutualize debt in some fashion so that peripheral economies could avoid the high sovereign risk premiums that threaten debt sustainability, is arguably academic given German opposition in particular to mutualization without full fiscal union. The three most prominent proposals—"blue-red" bonds (with the first 60 percent of GDP in debt enjoying joint guarantee but the rest not), a Debt Redemption Fund (buying up the excess above 60 percent of GDP for redemption over 25 years with collateralized revenue streams), and "ESBies"—an exchange-traded-fund-like pool of government bonds to create a European Safe Bond asset—all fail to come to grips with the central problem of curbing sovereign spreads on new debt (hence debt at the margin) to avoid self-fulfilling market prophecies of default. The discussion includes my own proposal to create a bond insurance fund, in which the euro area would guarantee new periphery sovereign bonds in return for annual payments into a bond insurance fund by the governments in question, in amounts on the order of 250 basis points and hence consistent with manageable ceilings to effective borrowing rates. The bond insurance sinking fund would build up assets that would compensate euro member countries if they had to pay amounts guaranteed because another member defaulted. To be sure, if spreads were to remain as low as their levels in early 2014, on the order of 150 to 200 basis points for Ireland, Italy, and Spain, such an instrument would not be needed for them, although it could still be relevant for Portugal (where spreads remained well above 300 basis points). The mechanism could usefully be explored, however, as a contingent instrument to be deployed should less favorable market conditions return in the future.

For a time, it seemed that the alternative of building large financial firewalls to protect partner economies against contagion from Greece or other euro area economies facing heightened default risk, starting with the European Financial Stability Facility (EFSF), might provide a strong basis for dealing with the crisis. However, with the decision to limit the successor European Stability Mechanism to €500 billion, the euro area has in effect limited this firewall to a scale capable of cleaning up the debt problems of the smaller peripheral economies but completely inadequate to address the much larger magnitudes that would be involved if Italy and Spain were to lose capital market access. The hope for substantial use of the ESM to deal with the banking problem has also been significantly curtailed by a specific limit of €60 billion that may be used for this purpose and only under strict conditions (including prior bail-ins).

The OMT, by contrast, has turned out to be the "mother of all firewalls." In effect, it provides a vehicle for reinstating the availability of the central bank to backstop public debt for euro area members even though they do not possess their own individual currencies that can be printed by their national central banks. The OMT deserves much of the credit for the major reduction in peripheral country sovereign risk spreads from high levels in the second quarter of 2012 to much more manageable levels a year later, even though no actual market purchases had taken place. As such, it has proven to be an especially effective "financial bazooka," designed to prevent market runs by intimidating market participants otherwise keen to speculate against an economy.

In early 2014, the German Constitutional Court issued a preliminary ruling that challenged the OMT as "incompatible with primary law" (of the European Union) because it "exceeds the European Central Bank's monetary policy mandate and ... violates the prohibition of monetary financing of the budget" (Federal Constitutional Court 2014). The court noted that the OMT might be legal if applied without subjecting the ECB to cuts in debt, but that restriction would eliminate the pari passu commitment that has given the OMT credibility in financial markets (which would otherwise fear subordination in the event of OMT purchases). But the court referred the issue to the European Court of Justice, widely regarded as likely to have a much more supportive view of the OMT, with the consequence that financial markets tended to view the ruling as a victory for the OMT accompanied by a principled but not binding objection by the German court.[5]

Even under the mainstream assumption that the German court challenge will not derail the OMT, the discussion in chapter 5 raises the question as to whether this financial bazooka might backfire if actually deployed. A reason is that it requires that a country be in an adjustment program to be eligible. Yet if the adjustment program were to be supported by the IMF, and if the IMF

---

5. Gideon Rachman, "Courts, Voters and the Threat of Another Euro Crisis," *Financial Times*, February 10, 2014.

were to insist that there be debt restructuring because of doubts about debt sustainability, there could be a counterproductive effect of scaring off private investors concerned about being caught up in private sector involvement (PSI). Indeed, a key feature of the OMT is that the ECB accepts pari passu treatment with private creditors, so this instrument does not raise the specter of subordination that deepens PSI haircuts, thereby avoiding counterproductive flight by private holders. But IMF lending would be senior. One solution would be to have any IMF involvement be strictly to assist in technical design rather than lend its own funds. Another solution could be to have the adjustment program in question be a euro-area-based one such as an Enhanced Conditions Credit Line, without IMF involvement.

Some prominent critics of the ECB argue just the opposite of the German court challenge: that the ECB's failure was to wait too long to launch OMT. Thus, in mid-2013, UK economist and columnist Martin Wolf judged that "The European Central Bank could have offered two years earlier the kind of open-ended support for debt of hard-pressed countries that it made available in the summer of 2012."[6] However, the assumptions of political economy implicit in this critique strain credulity. As shown in figure 1.1, spreads were still low in mid-2010 except in Greece. The ECB was loath to write a blank check without policy reforms.[7] German opposition to monetary financing by the ECB was so intense that it led to the resignation of the German member of the ECB board in September 2011 over even the limited purchases of Italian and Spanish government bonds in the Securities Markets Programme.[8] In mid-2010 the EFSF had just been created and the ESM did not yet exist, so the infrastructure for adjustment programs that are required for OMT might have been less credible. More fundamentally, it seems to have taken the specter of an exit of Greece from the euro (in late 2011 and through much of 2012), with unknown but likely costly spillover to the rest of the euro area, to set the stage for the ECB's decision to mount the OMT in mid-2012, with support even from Germany's chancellor.[9]

Chapter 5 next reviews the issue of debt restructuring, notably the IMF's recent self-critique of having waited too long to restructure Greek public debt, as well as the Fund's apparent broader conclusion that earlier, preemptive restructurings could be desirable. Although the Fund cites as an argument the greater cost to the public sector resulting from financing exit of private creditors, a close look at the maturities involved in the Greek case suggests that

---

6. Martin Wolf, "How Austerity Has Failed," *New York Review of Books*, July 11, 2013.

7. See, for example, Guy Dinmore, "ECB letter shows pressure on Berlusconi," *Financial Times*, September 29, 2011.

8. Andreas Framke and Alexander Hübner, "Top German quits ECB over bond-buying row," Reuters, September 9, 2011.

9. Graeme Wearden, "Merkel backs ECB rescue plan as markets remain cheerful," *Guardian*, September 7, 2012.

the amounts coming due prior to the first PSI stretchout (without a haircut) amounted to only about one-fourth of the public funding. The central question is whether damage from unnecessary haircuts exceeds or is less than the cost to the public of funding rather than requiring earlier PSI haircuts. The chapter's discussion also takes note of the euro area decision that all new public borrowing should have collective action clauses (CACs). It notes the irony that prior G-10 standards (adopted in 2003) had urged CACs for public debt *in foreign currency*, with the revealing implication that once again euro member countries do not really have their own currency.

The recent experience of restructuring in Greece and court decisions regarding payments to holdouts in Argentina's 2005 debt restructuring have revived interest in the Sovereign Debt Restructuring Mechanism (SDRM) considered in 2002 as a possible reform of international financial architecture. One recent proposal calls for a European Sovereign Debt Restructuring Regime that would require countries seeking support from the ESM to restructure debt if it exceeded 90 percent of GDP, and that assets of such countries be immune to legal action from holdouts (Buchheit et al. 2013). However, as argued in chapter 5, this approach would undermine the OMT, which takes just the opposite approach (pari passu treatment with private creditors instead of preemptive restructuring, so long as the country enters an adjustment program). Calls for SDRM-type arrangements in the euro area imply that sovereign insolvency is likely to be relatively common. Instead, the Greek insolvency is much more likely to have been unique, and any other episodes would seem more appropriately addressed on a case-by-case basis. The alternative of a major institutional change toward an SDRM structure would instead likely cause increases in spreads for Italy and Spain in particular, both of which are likely for the next several years to have debt ratios exceeding the 90 percent threshold featured in one prominent proposal, risking the unleashing of a self-fulfilling prophecy of default.[10]

Chapter 5 closes with an initial summary profile of the central question of the second part of the book: evaluation of the sustainability of debt based on prospective paths of debt relative to GDP. A broad-brush diagnosis suggests that there are two polar cases in the euro area crisis, with Greece being one of the poles (with what has turned out to be unsustainable debt) but the four other peripheral economies at the other pole (with sustainable debt). The ratio of debt to GDP reached far higher levels in Greece, and the decline of GDP from its 2007 peak has been far steeper in Greece, than in the other economies (figure 5.2). Differences among the other four countries tend to have offsetting influences, such as the high level of the primary surplus in Italy as an offset to its high debt level, or the larger primary deficit in Spain being an offset to its lower starting point for the ratio of debt to GDP.

---

10. As for the Argentine court cases, chapter 5 suggests that their precedential impact is likely to be limited because of the special circumstances of the Argentine restructurings.

Model Projections

Chapter 6 sets forth the European debt simulation model (EDSM) and applies it to make probabilistic projections of the ratio of debt to GDP (and other sustainability metrics) for Ireland, Portugal, Italy, and Spain. The economic framework for the analysis is the proposition that if debt is on track to spiral upward relative to GDP, from already high levels and with no stabilization in sight, it is or will become unsustainable, and some form of restructuring with a haircut is likely to be needed. Conversely, if the debt-to-GDP ratio is likely to stabilize or decline, given the likely terms of market access, then the debt is sustainable. The well-established condition for debt sustainability is that, in order to avoid further increase in the ratio of debt to GDP, the primary fiscal surplus (i.e., excluding interest payments) as a share of GDP must equal or exceed the product of the initial debt-to-GDP ratio times the difference between the interest rate and the growth rate.

In the euro area debt crisis, a benchmark for debt sustainability is that the debt should not exceed 120 percent of GDP. Considering that the traditional Maastricht target for the debt ratio is only 60 percent of GDP, it is not fully evident where this benchmark originated. In pragmatic terms it seems likely that it would have been awkward to be seeking a much lower debt ratio in program design for Greece than already existed in Italy, one of the donors. However, it also turns out that under normal euro area conditions, a level of 120 percent would be compatible with sustainability at plausible growth and interest conditions. Namely, if inflation is 2 percent, real growth is 1 percent, and the real interest rate is 3 percent, it requires a primary surplus of 2.4 percent of GDP to keep the debt ratio from rising above 120 percent.[11] Fiscal performance at this level should be achievable under more normal conditions of growth, so the 120 percent threshold has a meaningful analytical underpinning and is used as a benchmark in this study. The key challenge is to ensure that the default risk component of the interest rate is largely absent (as it was when the dominant paradigm was that industrial countries do not default).

The EDSM applies a new methodology to make probabilistic debt projections. It identifies five key variables that affect the path of the debt ratio: the growth rate, the interest rate on new debt, the level of the primary surplus, the prospective amount of "discovered debt" including public debt incurred to recapitalize banks, and prospective receipts from privatization. A simple scenario approach identifies a baseline, unfavorable scenario, and then a favorable scenario for each of these variables. With three scenarios, there are 243 (= 3^5) possible outcomes. The method then identifies whether the favorable or unfavorable scenarios for one variable are likely to be positively or negatively correlated with the favorable and unfavorable scenarios for each of the other

---

11. The nominal interest rate is the real rate plus 2 percent inflation. The debt sustainability equation under these conditions would be: $0.024 = 1.2 \times (0.05 - 0.03)$.

variables. For example, privatization efforts seem likely to be a substitute for a higher primary surplus, so the probability of the favorable scenario for privatization is set higher when the primary surplus is low than when the primary surplus is high. The overall effect is to permit the building up of a cumulative probability for the sequence of alternative combinations of scenarios. These probabilities are used to report the projections not only for the baseline but also for the most favorable 25th percentile of cases and the less favorable cumulative 75th percentile of cases, as well as an overall probability-weighted path for the projections. Appendices 6A and 6B set forth the model equations and contingent correlation methodology suggested here.

The baseline macroeconomic assumptions for the projections of chapter 6 are based primarily on the most recent IMF report for each country. The IMF's large staff and extensive experience make its projections the logical point of departure for the analysis. The probabilistic method of the EDSM then provides a meaningful basis for examining the robustness of the outlook even when the baseline is assumed broadly to track that of the IMF. In addition, application of the EDSM allows for significant departures from the IMF's assumed baseline, as is done in the incorporation of substantial privatization receipts planned by the government of Italy but omitted in the Fund's projections.

The favorable and unfavorable scenarios for the variables are chosen with special attention to characteristics, plans, and revealed past performance of the country in question. For the favorable growth scenario, the potential for snap-back growth from severe recession is the basis for placing the growth rate in 2014–20 at the 60th percentile of actual annual growth in 1990–2012 in some of the economies. Scope for privatization is important for Italy, where official plans call for 1 percent of GDP per year in privatization receipts. The unfavorable scenarios include an additional €40 billion in bank recapitalization costs in Spain (in contrast to zero additional amounts in the IMF baseline). In all four countries, the baseline for sovereign risk spreads takes actual levels in late 2013 and early 2014 as the point of departure and involves convergence to 175 basis points by 2018 (or 150 basis points for Ireland, in light of levels already reached). On the other hand, the baseline projection of the German bund rate involves a significant rebound (to 3.8 percent by 2017).[12]

Figure 6.6 provides a summary of the findings of the model projections. It shows the probability-weighted path of the ratio of debt to GDP for each of the four peripheral economies excluding Greece. It turns out that there is a convergence of debt ratios to a range of 98 to 119 percent of GDP by 2020, with Ireland, Italy, and Portugal all converging downward from initially higher levels and Spain converging upward from an initially lower level. If the 120 percent sustainability benchmark is considered meaningful, then, the principal finding is that debt should be on a sustainable path for the four peripheral economies

---

12. The bund rate is based on the IMF (2013g) projection of average real G-7 government bond rates plus the IMF projection of the German inflation rate.

excluding Greece. If so, then the current strategy of treating the problem as one of liquidity and providing lender of last resort financing (overtly in the program countries Ireland and Portugal, and on a contingent basis through OMT in the cases of Italy and Spain) is the right approach, and the alternative of a debt restructuring with substantial haircuts would be counterproductive. The diagnosis of solvency for these four periphery economies is the central quantitative finding of this study, and the contingent correlation method of probabilistic projection used to arrive at this finding is the principal methodological contribution.[13]

The book concludes with application of the EDSM to the case of Greece. There is first a review of my mid-2011 projections that suggested Greece might be able to manage debt without forgiveness if it achieved an ambitious primary surplus. It turned out subsequently that the decline in GDP was much greater than anticipated, and outcome on primary balance considerably lower. An environment of political chaos, with the collapse of successive governments and widespread fears of exit from the euro, contributed to this outcome. The debt ratio remains surprisingly high considering the 53 percent haircut on private creditors. The baseline debt ratio declines from 175 percent of GDP in 2013 to 127 percent by 2020. Return to private market access in major volumes and for long-term debt may require a lower debt ratio than the regional benchmark of 120 percent because of a damaged credit reputation from deep debt forgiveness in the restructuring. The implication is that some form of official debt forgiveness may be needed in the future. Invisible relief in the form of concessional interest rates and lengthy maturities is more likely to be politically acceptable to euro area partners in the near term than outright principal reduction. Complete elimination of interest on all debt to euro area partners would reduce the 2020 debt-to-GDP ratio from a baseline of 127 to 112 percent, still likely on the high side for a return to capital markets. On the other hand, the low interest rates on the now largely public sector lending to Greece mean that its debt burden as measured by the ratio of interest payments to GDP is considerably lower than otherwise implied by the ratio of debt to GDP. Markets could recognize this fact, especially if Greece builds a track record of meeting its fiscal targets. Indeed, in early April 2014 Greece successfully issued €3 billion in five-year bonds at a yield of 4.95 percent. In

13. As discussed in chapter 6, for Ireland, Portugal, and Spain this diagnosis is robust to a more pessimistic baseline in which political constraints limit the primary surplus to a relatively unambitious 2.5 percent of GDP (see table 6.6). Spain would be unaffected (its average baseline primary surplus in 2014–20 is only 0.2 percent of GDP). In Ireland and Portugal, debt ratios would still decline substantially but not by quite as much as in the baseline (average baseline primary surpluses in 2014–20 are 2.7 and 2.4 percent of GDP for the two economies, respectively). For Italy, however, such a ceiling would be farther below the baseline primary surplus (which averages 4.5 percent of GDP in 2014–20) and would essentially cause the debt ratio to plateau rather than decline substantially. Arguably even that outcome would constitute solvency given present financial market access (and the decline of spreads by early 2014), but it would imply greater vulnerability to a future adverse swing in market sentiment.

any event Greek debt should now be largely manageable through 2020. The question of whether additional relief will be necessary will only become salient thereafter, especially in the 2030s when large principal payments to the euro area official sector begin to come due.

2

Fiscal Adjustment, Growth, and Default Risk

One of the most important policy dilemmas facing the euro area in dealing with the sovereign debt crisis in the periphery (Greece, Ireland, Portugal, Italy, and Spain) has been whether attempting to solve the problem by reducing fiscal deficits would actually make it worse by aggravating recession. If the proximate metric of debt sustainability is the ratio of public debt to GDP, then with a high fiscal multiplier the debt problem might look even worse after a severe dose of fiscal austerity, because of a sizable reduction in the GDP denominator and a debt numerator that remains unchanged in the case of full success in arriving at a zero fiscal deficit.

Countries in the throes of being near sovereign default are nonetheless likely to be better advised to proceed with a credible program of fiscal adjustment, even if there is some short-term contractionary impact. The reason is that once markets shift to expectation of default, their risk spreads for new lending reach extremely high levels and ensure an outcome of insolvency and default, switching from a good equilibrium to a bad one.[1]

Debt Sustainability Dynamics

It is useful to begin with a recapitulation of the relationship of debt dynamics to the fiscal deficit, and in particular the influence of the primary surplus on the evolution of the ratio of debt to GDP. As demonstrated in appendix 2A,

---

1. Reviewing the growth versus austerity debate in the context of the European debt crisis, Giancarlo Corsetti (2012) similarly concludes that "weak growth in countries facing precarious fiscal positions is not sufficient evidence against fiscal austerity. Where sovereign risk is high, fiscal tightening remains an important avenue to bring down deficits at a limited cost to economic activity, as risk premiums recede over time."

the debt sustainability equation states that the primary surplus (as a percent of GDP) necessary to keep the debt-to-GDP ratio from rising equals the beginning level of that ratio multiplied by the difference between the (nominal) interest rate and the (nominal) growth rate:

$$\pi^* = \lambda_0 (r - g) \tag{2.1}$$

In equation (2.1), π^* is the critical primary (i.e., noninterest) fiscal surplus (as a fraction of GDP) needed to keep the ratio of debt to GDP constant. The debt-to-GDP ratio is λ, with subscript 0 indicating its base-year level. The average interest rate on public debt is r, and the growth rate is g.[2] Correspondingly, the proportionate change in the debt-to-GDP ratio is:

$$\dot{\lambda} = r - g - \frac{\pi}{\lambda_0} \tag{2.2}$$

The proportionate change in the debt-to-GDP ratio equals the interest rate minus the growth rate minus the primary surplus ratio as adjusted for the initial debt ratio. If debt starts out at 100 percent of GDP, the primary surplus ratio is subtracted directly, but if the ratio starts out higher, it takes a larger primary surplus to achieve the same proportionate reduction in the debt ratio.

There is no dispute about the direct effect of fiscal consolidation. By turning the primary balance from a sizable deficit into a sizable surplus, it swings fiscal policy from aggravating the debt problem to reducing it. That is, the change in the debt equals the interest paid plus the primary deficit (or minus the primary surplus).[3] The dispute arises with respect to the indirect effect of fiscal consolidation, working through an induced impact on the growth rate. The final two right-hand terms in equation (2.2) will cancel each other out or even cause the debt ratio to rise if there is a sufficiently large reduction in the growth rate induced by the fiscal austerity. The change in the rate at which the debt ratio changes will be the derivative of equation (2.2). With a one-year horizon, in which the effective interest rate is essentially unchanged because most of the debt is long-term, this derivative will be equal to the derivative of the last two right-hand terms of the equation with respect to the primary surplus. In turn, the derivative of the growth rate with respect to the primary surplus will simply be the negative of the Keynesian multiplier, μ. That is, a reduction in the primary deficit by $\Delta\pi$ will cause a reduction from the growth rate that otherwise would have occurred by $\mu \times \Delta\pi$. Thus:

$$\frac{d\dot{\lambda}}{d\pi} = -\frac{dg}{d\pi} - \frac{1}{\lambda_0} = \mu - \frac{1}{\lambda_0} \tag{2.3}$$

---

2. All of these are expressed as pure numbers; for example, a 3 percent primary surplus means $\pi = 0.03$, and a debt-to-GDP ratio of 120 percent means $\lambda = 1.2$.

3. See equation (2A.1) in appendix 2A.

Under conditions of full employment and scope for monetary policy to reduce the interest rate, the multiplier would be expected to be low, even zero in real terms, as discussed in appendix 2C. However, when unemployment is high and there is no scope for offsetting fiscal tightening through monetary ease, and in particular because monetary policy already faces the "liquidity trap" of a "zero bound" on interest rates that are already at zero, the multiplier can be substantially higher. If it is high enough, the final right-hand side of equation (2.3) can be positive, meaning that the derivative of the debt ratio with respect to the primary surplus is positive. Lower growth induced by fiscal tightening swamps the direct effect of a smaller primary deficit. The discussion below returns to the question of whether these conditions have been met in the European debt crisis.

Euro Area Fiscal Controls

The European debt crisis has been managed under the dominant policy presumption that fiscal consolidation is essential to long-term debt sustainability even if there are risks of near-term recessionary consequences from tightening. Although the Stability and Growth Pact (SGP) of 1997 provided for penalties if countries failed to meet the EU limit on deficits (3 percent of GDP) and debt (60 percent), waivers for larger French and German deficits in 2003 had undermined its effectiveness. Successive moves to tighten euro area rules on fiscal balance have featured prominently in the response to the debt crisis. In June 2010 the European Union adopted the "European semester" process whereby governments submit early drafts of annual budgets for coordination with the European Commission. In September 2010 the European Commission proposed a six pack of rules, adopted by the European Parliament a year later, providing for tighter enforcement of penalties for failure to adhere to programs for adjustment toward the SGP targets. The press for tighter fiscal rules culminated in the December 2011 European Council adoption of a Fiscal Compact treaty for euro members and all other EU members except the United Kingdom and Czech Republic.[4] The agreement paved the way for more aggressive European Central Bank (ECB) action, first in its long-term refinancing operation (LTRO) lending in early 2012 amounting to approximately €1 trillion and then more decisively in its pledge in July 2012 to purchase government bonds in Outright Monetary Transactions (OMT) to curb excessive

---

4. Formally the Treaty on Stability, Coordination and Governance, the fiscal pact establishes a balanced budget rule and requires signatories to implement domestic legislation to recognize it. A balanced budget is defined as being achieved if the structural deficit does not exceed 0.5 percent of GDP. The structural balance is cyclically adjusted and net of one-off or temporary measures. The pact also requires countries with debt exceeding 60 percent of GDP to reduce the excessive debt by one-twentieth annually. If a country not meeting the rule does not secure European Commission approval of its fiscal adjustment program, the EU Court of Justice may impose a penalty payment of up to 0.1 percent of the country's GDP (European Council 2012).

interest rate increases for member countries in difficulty but with adjustment programs approved by euro area authorities.

Taken literally, the Fiscal Compact appears to provide little if any room for the use of fiscal stimulus to fight a recession. The cyclically adjusted fiscal deficit cannot exceed 0.5 percent of GDP. In comparison, the cyclically adjusted fiscal deficit even in Germany in the Great Recession reached 3.5 percent of GDP in 2010 (IMF 2012b, 78). At most the Fiscal Compact seems to permit the operation of automatic stabilizers but little, if anything, else.

Fiscal Irresponsibility versus Great Recession

Despite the focus on tighter fiscal controls, the sovereign debt crisis of the periphery has arguably arisen more as a consequence of the Great Recession than because of chronic fiscal laxity. Figure 2.1 shows the fiscal balance as a percent of GDP for the past decade for the five periphery economies as well as Germany and France. In the period 2001–08 only one crisis economy is patently an outlier in terms of fiscal deficits: Greece. Moreover, two of the crisis economies, Ireland and Spain, managed to run fiscal surpluses or near-zero balances from 2001 through 2007. Even so, in both cases their surpluses were to some extent illusory because of unsustainable real estate booms, and the declines in their balances were especially large when the booms collapsed and the global financial crisis of 2008–09 arrived. Ireland then experienced a massive deficit in 2010 associated with socialization of bank losses.

Credit Market Access and Fiscal Space

As discussed below, much of the debate on the fiscal policy response to the euro area debt crisis has centered on whether there has been too much austerity too soon, with a counterproductive effect on growth and prospects for debt sustainability. An implicit assumption in raising this question, however, is that some source of financing is always available to cover the deficit, so the size of the deficit can be determined in some medium-term optimal fashion. Instead, three of the crisis economies—Greece, Ireland, and Portugal—lost access to private credit markets on any meaningful scale and for long-term debt. For them the official sector, primarily euro area governments and the European Financial Stability Facility (EFSF) but also the IMF, became the source of new lending needed to roll over debt coming due as well as finance current deficits. For the euro area governments, and especially Germany, there have been limits to the amount of lending domestic publics are prepared to extend. For its part, the IMF tends to focus on long-term debt sustainability, and the size of the deficit seems to have been a more direct driver of its calculations of debt sustainability than concern about adverse initial effects from a high multiplier (although the Fund has been recalibrating the multiplier upward, as discussed below).

Moreover, researchers at the IMF itself had done earlier work on "fiscal

Figure 2.1 Fiscal balances in euro area periphery economies, Germany, and France, 2001–13

percent of GDP

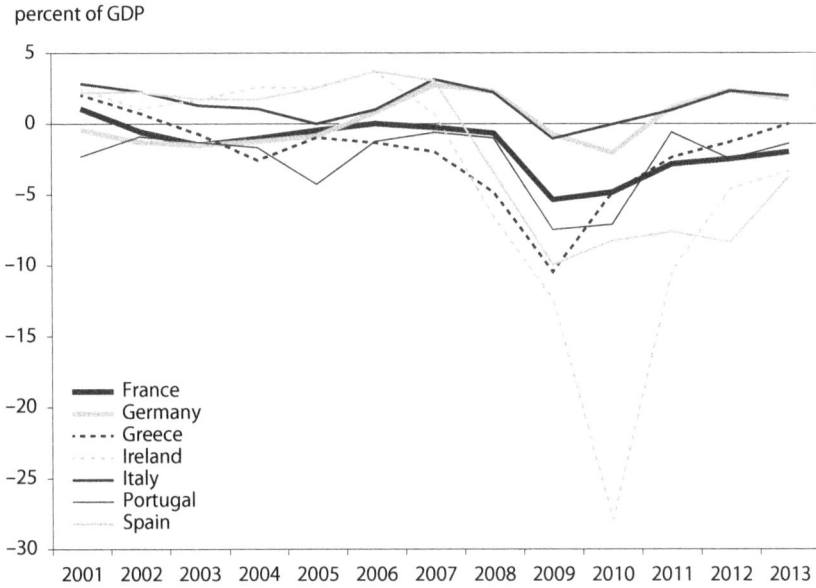

Source: IMF (2013n).

space," with the general finding that countries with already high debt have little room for maneuver in applying countercyclical fiscal stimulus (or avoiding fiscal consolidation because of high unemployment). Jonathan D. Ostry et al. (2010) examine a sample of 23 advanced economies during 1970–2007 and find that with debt ratios higher than 40 percent, the primary surplus responds positively to the lagged debt ratio. That is, when debt starts to reach high levels, countries adjust by increasing the primary surplus. They identify the "debt limit" as the debt ratio at which debt dynamics begin to show continued increase in debt relative to GDP even if the country responds as in its past performance in raising the primary surplus to address rising debt. The premise is that once markets recognize a prospective upward spiral in the debt ratio because of this inadequacy of the primary surplus reaction function, markets will quickly boost the interest rates to prohibitive, insolvency, levels. They then calculate "fiscal space" as the amount by which each country's calculated debt limit exceeds its baseline 2015 projection for the debt ratio. Already in 2010 the authors identified Greece, Italy, and Portugal (along with Japan) as having only a low probability of any remaining fiscal space; Iceland, Ireland, and Spain as having about 50 to 70 percent probability of some further fiscal space; the United States and United Kingdom as having a 70 to 80 percent probability of additional fiscal space; and Australia, Denmark, Israel, Korea, New Zealand, and Norway as having even higher probabilities of additional fiscal space. With analytical frameworks such as this, it is no surprise that the IMF's adjustment programs for Greece, Ireland, and Portugal called for substantial reductions in primary deficits, rather than encouraging fiscal gradualism.[5]

Expansionary Fiscal Consolidation?

The German view in particular has long been that fiscal balance, and particularly structural reform leading to fiscal consolidation, are essential to growth, and German Chancellor Angela Merkel has taken the lead in calling for fiscal union with tight budget controls.[6] The central notion was that improvement in private market expectations from consolidation, especially through expenditure reduction that makes room for private spending in the economy, would outweigh Keynesian demand effects.[7] A prominent study by Francesco Giavazzi and Marco Pagano (1990) lent empirical support to the notion of expansionary consolidation based on the cases of Denmark and Ireland in the 1980s. In the United States in the 1990s, "Rubinomics" similarly was premised on the idea that fiscal adjustment would be rewarded by the capital markets as the "bond vigilantes" would accept lower interest rates on public debt as a consequence. The long period of seeming irrelevance of Keynesian demand management during the "Great Moderation" of lesser macroeconomic volatility from the mid-1980s through the early 2000s further contributed to a policy environment in which necessary fiscal policy changes were more frequently perceived to be in the direction of restraint rather than stimulus.

The Great Recession sharply changed this policy environment and revived the prominence of Keynesian demand stimulus as a policy instrument for reducing high unemployment. Perhaps the most dramatic instance of this policy sea change was the London summit of the G-20 in April 2009, where leaders announced that they were "undertaking an unprecedented and concerted fiscal expansion, which will save or create millions of jobs which would otherwise have been destroyed, and that will, by the end of next year, amount to $5 trillion...."[8]

---

5. The first adjustment program for Greece called for the primary balance to swing from –8.6 percent of GDP in 2009 to +3 percent by 2013 and +5.9 percent by 2015. The corresponding program goals were an increase from –9.7 percent (excluding bank support) to –1.4 percent and then +1.8 percent, in Ireland; and from –7.2 to +2.1 percent and then +3.2 percent for Portugal (IMF 2010c, 26; 2011d, 39; 2011b).

6. See, for example, "Merkel Urges Euro Fiscal Union to Tackle Debt Crisis," BBC News, December 2, 2011.

7. Giavazzi and Pagano (1990, 1). Thus, in 1981 the German Council of Economic Experts wrote: "As in 1975, a situation has arisen in which the government must fear that an unchanged expansive fiscal policy will lead to a further worsening of expectations, thereby working against itself and in the end be counterproductive" (German Council of Economic Experts 1981, 209).

8. London Summit—Leaders' Statement, April 2, 2009, www.g20.utoronto.ca/2009/2009communique0402.pdf.

It did not take long, however, for concerns about longer-term fiscal balance to temper the enthusiasm of international policymakers for the use of fiscal stimulus. Just one year after the London summit, the IMF warned: "In most advanced economies, fiscal and monetary policies should maintain a supportive thrust in 2010 to sustain growth and employment. But many of these economies also need to urgently adopt credible medium-term strategies to contain public debt and later bring it down to more prudent levels" (IMF 2010h, xiv).

The IMF recognized that curbing deficits would have some negative demand impact, and in its fall *World Economic Outlook* (WEO) specifically rejected the view of expansionary fiscal consolidation, emphasizing instead that "fiscal consolidation typically reduces output and raises unemployment in the short-term" (IMF 2010g, 93). It argued that influential studies finding expansionary austerity, such as those by Giavazzi and Pagano (1990) and Alberto Alesina and Roberto Perotti (1995), had used the wrong measure of fiscal adjustment. Such studies had applied the change in the cyclically adjusted primary balance (CAPB). The Fund argued that this measure is biased by correlation with such exogenous economic influences as asset shocks (with asset booms boosting the measured adjustment by raising revenue and hence the CAPB whereas asset busts would reduce the CAPB and identify absence of adjustment despite policy measures undertaken). Instead the IMF researchers, following the example of Christina Romer and David Romer (2010) for the United States, adopted a policy-episode approach examining specific instances of tax increases and spending cuts. Their result was that a fiscal consolidation of 1 percent of GDP "typically reduces GDP by about 0.5 percent within two years and raises the unemployment rate by about 0.3 percentage point" (IMF 2010e, 94).[9]

The IMF researchers did find that the size of the multiplier, and thus the loss of output for a given fiscal contraction, is smaller if the country has high perceived sovereign risk. Dividing their sample evenly between countries with above- and below-median country risk on a leading ratings agency index yields a multiplier of 0.4 (instead of 0.5) for the higher-risk group but 0.9 for the lower-risk group (reduction in GDP after two years for 1 percent of GDP fiscal adjustment) (IMF 2010g, 107). High sovereign risk had characterized the cases of Denmark in 1983 and Ireland in 1987 studied by Giavazzi and Pagano (1990), and the Fund found mild support for expansionary austerity in these two cases but considers them unrepresentative.

In contrast to the IMF's finding of little scope for favorable effects of fiscal

---

9. A more complete report of the research is presented in Guajardo, Leigh, and Pescatori (2011). Note also that earlier research at the ECB applying a calibrated dynamic stochastic general equilibrium (DSGE) model had found that there would likely be short-term adjustment costs of fiscal adjustment, contrary to the expansionary fiscal consolidation literature. The model generated long-term gains, however, because of lower government interest burdens associated with lower debt and hence increased scope for reducing distortionary taxes. The authors did not arrive at a summary number for the short-term multiplier, however (Coenen, Mohr, and Straub 2008).

consolidation for countries facing high default risk, the model developed in appendix 2C suggests that after taking into account the reduction in the probability of default and the corresponding reduction in the probability-weighted loss of output from a default, the benefits from fiscal adjustment can more than offset the costs of a reduction in measured GDP. The discussion below returns to this framework.

Recalculating the Multiplier

An important recent development in the area of international fiscal policy analysis is that the same IMF researchers have now substantially increased the size of the multiplier, at least for a sample of 26 European economies and the period during and after the Great Recession. Olivier Blanchard and Daniel Leigh (2013) review the Fund's WEO growth projections for these countries and find that they systematically understated the amount by which fiscal consolidation would reduce growth.[10] Thus, a 1 percentage point of GDP increase in the fiscal consolidation forecast for 2010–11 (measured by change in structural fiscal balance) was associated with a GDP loss of about 1 percent in 2010–11, relative to the forecast.[11] The implication was that multipliers implicit in the forecasts were too low by unity (e.g., 0.5 instead of 1.5). This underestimation of the multiplier was higher in the early phase of the Great Recession, at 0.7 to 1 percentage point underestimate of growth reduction for 1 percent fiscal contraction in 2009–10 and 2010–11, than in the later phase, at 0.3 and 0.5 percentage point (and less statistical significance) in 2011–12 and 2012–13. The authors argue that the WEO forecasters had probably used multipliers that had been relevant for more normal past periods and therefore failed to take account of the larger multiplier under conditions of high unemployment and a zero-bound constraint on monetary easing (with interest rates already at zero). In earlier reporting of their results, they indicate that whereas the Fund forecasters had typically used a multiplier of 0.5, their results on forecast errors imply a range of 0.9 to 1.7 for the multiplier in the period and countries considered (IMF 2012a, 43)

Critics of fiscal austerity as a response to the European sovereign debt crisis were quick to seize on the new IMF multiplier estimates. Paul Krugman, perhaps the most prominent and trenchant critic of those who worry about fiscal deficits instead of excessive unemployment, wrote soon after the new

---

10. For evidence on excessively optimistic projections of growth in the extreme case of Greece, see chapter 7, and in particular figure 7.1.

11. Ironically, the authors' measure of fiscal tightening for purposes of their forecast-error study is the same one they reject as being misleading in assessing the evidence on expansionary austerity. In their behalf the argument can nonetheless be made that in this case the error would go in a direction that further strengthens their results: the bias of the CAPB is toward understating the adverse effects of fiscal tightening, so taking account of this bias would mean their result would be even stronger (the overoptimism was even more excessive).

IMF estimates: "... the unjustified assumption of small multipliers has helped make the crisis worse."[12] Paul de Grauwe and Yuemei Ji (2013) have suggested that there has been a "panic-driven austerity" in the euro area as countries tightened fiscal policy too much too soon for fear of otherwise being punished by capital markets. They argue that the markets were wrong in the signals they sent, and support this case with the fact that the spreads fell again once the ECB had made its mid-2012 pledge to "do whatever it takes" through the use of Outright Monetary Transactions buying government bonds. The main point, however, is precisely that extremely high risk spreads in the private markets set up a dynamic that can make insolvency a self-fulfilling prophecy, and a key role for fiscal adjustment is precisely to short-circuit this vicious circle by sending a strong signal that the country intends to manage its fiscal accounts without recourse to default and debt forgiveness.

Appendix 2B examines a popular argument of the high-multiplier-excessive-adjustment critique: that fiscal tightening can be counterproductive even for the debt burden because with a high multiplier it will reduce GDP and thus the denominator of the debt-to-GDP ratio. It turns out that under reasonable assumptions this "paradox of adjustment" is only transitory, and that except in the year of a fiscal stimulus the impact of a stimulus will be to raise the debt-to-GDP ratio from that in an adjustment-oriented baseline.

The exercise in appendix 2B obtains a result similar to that in recent work at the IMF. Luc Eyraud and Anke Weber (2013) conduct simulations that similarly find that when the multiplier is high (at unity), fiscal consolidation temporarily raises the debt-to-GDP ratio. In a high-debt country (such as Italy), with what the authors call "down-turn" multipliers that begin at unity but fall to zero by the fifth year (as also assumed in appendix 2B here), there is an increase in the debt-to-GDP ratio from fiscal consolidation in the first year but the debt ratio then begins to decline in the second year to levels below the baseline.[13] However, the authors warn that if the multiplier remains high rather than declining over time, and/or if the government engages in a succession of additional tightenings, the consequence can be a prolonged period of an increase in the debt ratio from the baseline. They apply their model to the euro area periphery economies and find that it does well in explaining the rise in the debt ratio from 2007 to 2011 for Greece, Portugal, and Spain (but not for Ireland, because of the additional factor of a large debt increase from bank recapitalization). They suggest that the slow response of the debt ratio to fiscal

---

12. Paul Krugman, "Deleveraging Shocks and the Multiplier," *New York Times*, October 9, 2012.

13. Note, however, that the mechanism is somewhat different from that in appendix 2B. Their model assumes that the negative effect on GDP from the first year's tightening disappears by the fifth year in the sense that output returns to its potential growth path and that the tightening in question is maintained on a permanent basis. The calculation in appendix 2B instead makes no allowance for a rebound in GDP, and reverses the fiscal shock after the first year. The reversal of the first-year paradox for the debt ratio is thus partly attributable to the reversal of the impact on GDP when the fiscal shock is eliminated in the second year.

adjustment "could raise concerns if financial markets react to its short-term behavior" (p. 2) and that country authorities should be careful not to overreact in adopting repeated rounds of tightening in a vain effort to set unachievable debt targets that do not take account of the slow response.

Fiscal Adjustment and Risk Spreads

The behavior of sovereign risk spreads for Italy and Spain provides some evidence for the influence of fiscal expectations on spreads. Figure 2.2 shows the 10-year government bond yield spreads above the German bund from mid-2011 through early 2013. A common influence affecting both was the adverse shock of contagion from Greece, first after the July 21, 2011, Greek package with its new emphasis on private sector involvement, and then again after the October 27, 2011 Greek package imposing a 50 percent haircut on private sector claims. Positive common influences, in contrast, came from initiatives by the ECB. The late December 2011 initiative of the ECB to provide nearly €500 billion in LTROs to banks, followed by a similar amount in early 2012, brought significant relief to spreads in the first quarter of 2012. The collapse of the Greek government and increased risk of a Greek exit from the euro contributed to a new round of rising spreads in both countries in the second quarter of 2012. But then the ECB's announcement of its intention to provide OMT purchases of government bonds if needed marked a new phase of lower spreads beginning in mid-2012, for both countries.

There is information about the impact of fiscal developments, however, in the differential performance of spreads for the two countries. The upswing of Italy's spread from being lower than that of Spain at the beginning of July 2011 to being considerably higher by the end of the year reflected fiscal uncertainty in the final phase of the Berlusconi government; the return of Italian spreads to below those of Spain by the second quarter of 2012 similarly reflected fiscal reforms of the Monti government on the one hand and fiscal disappointments in Spain on the other.[14] The news of large prospective fiscal losses in Spain from banking recapitalization contributed to a further widening between the two spreads by mid-year.[15]

---

14. At the end of February 2012, Spain announced that its budget outcome for 2011 had been considerably worse than expected (a deficit of 8.5 percent of GDP rather than the planned 6 percent). The prospect of large financing needs for bank recapitalization became evident in May 2012 and especially by June. Victor Mallet, "Spain's 2011 Budget Deficit Exceeds 8.5%," *Financial Times*, February 27, 2012; and Miles Johnson, "Spain Finalises Recapitalisation Plan," *Financial Times*, May 9, 2012.

15. In June 2012, euro area finance ministers agreed to back Spain in meeting needs for up to €100 billion for bank recapitalization. Soon thereafter, however, the finance ministers of Finland, Germany, and the Netherlands insisted that "legacy assets" originating prior to the proposed banking union's Single Supervisory Mechanism would "remain the responsibility of national authorities" rather than being assumed by the European Stability Mechanism. Thus, Spain could obtain euro area financing for the bank recapitalization but it could not avoid increasing its sover-

**Figure 2.2   Sovereign spreads for 10-year Italian and Spanish
government bonds above German bunds, 2011–13**

percent

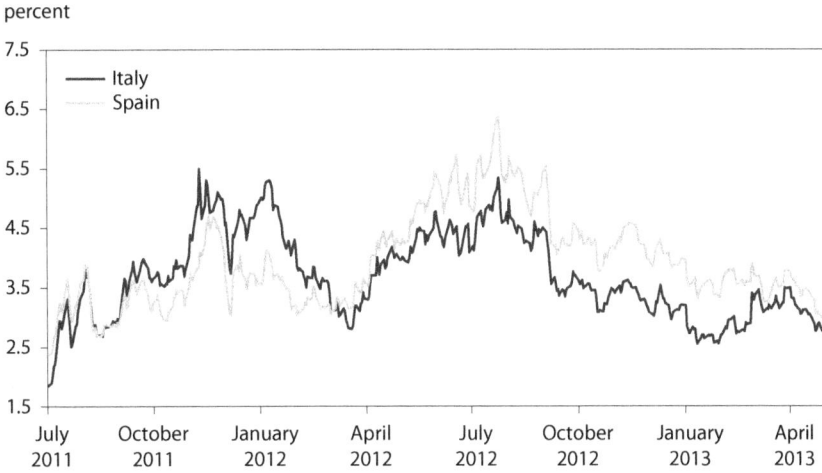

Source: Datastream.

Evidence on Growth Impacts

Figure 2.3 provides one basis for examining the critique of excessive austerity in management of the European debt crisis. The horizontal axis shows the change in the cyclically adjusted primary budget deficit as a percent of GDP from 2008 to 2012, in the series of plots marked "1," or from 2009 to 2012, in the series of plots marked "2." An observation further to the left on the graph indicates that the country made a larger fiscal adjustment, i.e., carried out greater fiscal austerity. The vertical axis shows the cumulative percent change in real GDP from the base period (2008 for "1" or 2009 for "2") to 2012. A strong case for excessive fiscal austerity would require a tight fit showing an upward slope, namely, showing that smaller fiscal adjustment permitted lesser reduction in output (or greater increase in output).

It is evident in the chart that any such case would hinge entirely on the weight given to Greece. In Greece it is certainly true that the cyclically adjusted primary deficit adjustment was larger than in the other four debt-stressed economies: either about 9 percent of GDP adjustment, using 2008 as the base, or 14 percent, using 2009 as the base. And it is evident that the output decline was also the largest in Greece: about 18 percent (2008 base) to 16 percent (2009 base). However, among the four other economies there is no particular relationship between the severity of the fiscal adjustment and the severity of

eign debt correspondingly. David Jolly, "Markets Skeptical of Spain's Bank Bailout," *New York Times,* June 11, 2012; Karl Whelan, "Germany to Spain and Ireland: Drop Dead," *Forbes,* September 25, 2012.

Figure 2.3 Change in cyclically adjusted primary fiscal deficit and in real GDP in euro area periphery economies

change in real GDP (percent)

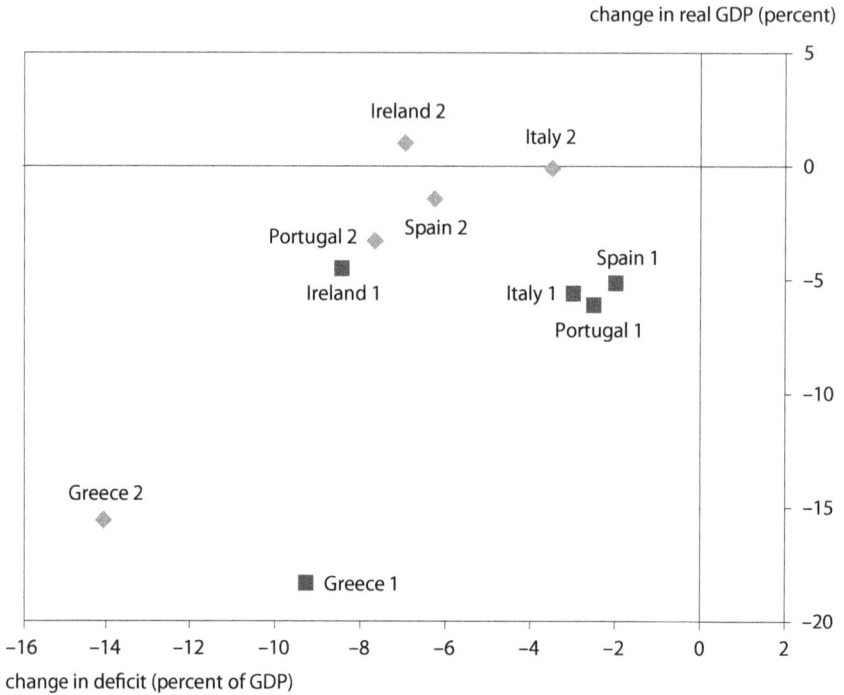

Note: The horizontal axis shows the change in the cyclically adjusted primary budget deficit as a percent of GDP from 2008 to 2012, in the series of plots marked "1," or from 2009 to 2012, in the series of plots marked "2." The vertical axis shows the cumulative percent change in real GDP from the base period (2008 for "1" or 2009 for "2") to 2012.

Source: IMF (2012b).

the output decline. Indeed, using 2008 as the base, the country showing the most severe fiscal adjustment as measured by the cyclically adjusted primary deficit was Ireland; yet Ireland experienced a smaller output decline than Italy and Portugal and about the same output decline as Spain, even though Spain showed much less fiscal adjustment by this measure using the 2008 base. If 2009 is used as the base, the four countries cluster more closely together, but again show no clear pattern of more severe output loss associated with a more aggressive fiscal adjustment.[16] To a considerable degree Greece should be seen as *sui generis*. It was in the grips of profound risk and uncertainty, including the

---

16. In a similar chart for growth and austerity in 2011–12, de Grauwe and Ji (2013) seem to obtain a strong negative relationship, but again it turns on Greece. They include Germany, yet surely Germany does not belong in the test because it was not facing the profound economic uncertainty associated with a slide toward debt crisis. If Germany is eliminated there is once again no particular pattern relating growth to austerity among the four debt-stressed economies (excluding Greece).

real threat of leaving the euro and the actual outcome of carrying out a debt restructuring with a deep haircut. Any country in that situation would likely have had a major recession even if it had done no structural deficit reduction whatsoever. Setting Greece aside, however, leaves the message that for the four other periphery countries it is difficult to identify a pattern indicating excessive output loss caused by excessive fiscal austerity.[17]

Welfare-Equivalent Multiplier with Default Risk

The essence of the euro area periphery debt problem has been that even as the region has faced high unemployment in the wake of the Great Recession, it has been constrained in applying the usual response of fiscal stimulus because of the risk of further destabilizing capital market expectations and precipitating a self-fulfilling prophecy of insolvency because of soaring market interest rates. Appendix 2C seeks to formalize the tradeoffs between normal countercyclical stimulus and avoidance of default risk by incorporating the latter into a more broadly defined "multiplier."

The appendix emphasizes the recent view that the multiplier without default risk depends on the state of the cycle, and in light of recent research posits a maximum multiplier of 1.5 when unemployment is extremely high but a multiplier of zero when the economy is at full employment. The analysis incorporates a conventional negative side effect of stimulus by taking account of the increase in market interest rates when fiscal stimulus causes crowding out. The analysis then adds the new dimension of default risk, suggesting that whereas this risk is absent when the debt ratio is at the Maastricht target of 60 percent of GDP, the risk becomes major when the ratio reaches the 120 percent threshold that has become a benchmark in the euro area debt crisis. On the basis of past surveys of output losses from financial crises, the appendix calibrates loss in event of default at 10 percent of GDP. It also posits that when the debt ratio reaches 120 percent of GDP, an increase in the fiscal deficit by 1 percent of GDP will increase the probability of default by 10 percent, yielding an expected welfare loss of 1 percent of GDP.

Implementation of this system with reasonable parameters yields a perimeter curve on a graph of excess unemployment (horizontal axis) against excess debt (vertical axis). To the bottom right of this graph, the total welfare-equivalent multiplier is positive, because the direct multiplier is large (high excess unemployment) but the excess debt ratio and hence default risk is low. Conversely, to the upper left of the graph (low excess unemployment, high excess debt) the influence of default risk dominates and the total welfare-equivalent multiplier

---

17. Note further that if the 2008 base is used the average multiplier is indeed high, at about 2 (output loss of about 5 percent for structural adjustment of about 2.5 percent of GDP); but if the 2009 base is applied, the multiplier collapses to only 0.25 (average fiscal adjustment of 4 percent of GDP but output loss of only 1 percent, reflecting the lower base of GDP in the sharp recession of 2009).

is negative. Under these conditions, fiscal consolidation improves welfare, even if there is an observed reduction in output as a consequence (because the expected welfare loss from the increased probability of default is not directly observed). Based on 2011 data for the United States when unemployment was at a peak 9 percent, and when debt held by the public was 68 percent of GDP, the United States was clearly in the positive zone for the welfare-equivalent multiplier. In contrast, for Italy in 2012, even though unemployment at 10.6 percent was 3.3 percent above its 2003–08 average (when there was no shortfall of output from potential, according to the IMF), the high debt ratio of 120 percent placed the country to the left of the zero multiplier perimeter, indicating that the total welfare-equivalent multiplier was negative once default risk was taken into account. Fiscal consolidation thus made sense even if there was some direct negative output effect.

The parameters and calculations in the appendix are primarily illustrative. In particular, they do not take into account special circumstances that might enable an economy to maintain a much higher debt ratio than 120 percent without encountering transit to default (for example, Japan's heavy reliance on a financial market with a strong home bias in Japan). Such circumstances would dislocate the perimeter between the negative and positive multiplier in figure 2C.1. More generally, any country with its own currency and its own central bank might find that this perimeter lies further to the left on the graph than would be true for a euro member country. Nonetheless, the exercise in appendix 2C may help clarify the policy framework that has been relevant in managing the euro area debt crisis.

Progress and Targets

The euro area periphery economies have actually made considerable progress toward their medium-term fiscal adjustment goals. The extent of the total adjustment goal can be measured by the change in the CAPB in the worst year of the base period spanning 2008–10 to the target outcome by 2017 (IMF 2012b). Comparison of this total adjustment goal against the actual extent of improvement in CAPB achieved by 2012 provides a sense of the degree of progress to date. Table 2.1 reports these comparisons for the five main debt-stressed economies.

As indicated in table 2.1, in three of the five debt-stressed economies the amount of fiscal adjustment already accomplished by 2012 reached fully three-fourths of the total required by 2017 (Greece, Italy, and Portugal). In the other two, adjustment through 2012 had reached approximately 60 percent of the total required by 2017 (Ireland and Spain).

A corollary of the fact that well more than half of the target adjustment was completed by 2012 is the fact that the annual pace of additional fiscal adjustment during 2013–15 should be considerably smaller than over the previous three years. Figure 2.4 shows that in each country the required pace of additional fiscal adjustment (measured by the CAPB) should be considerably

Table 2.1 Progress in fiscal adjustment as measured by the cyclically adjusted primary balance in euro area periphery (percent of GDP)

	Base					Achieved by 2012	
Country	Year	Level	Target, 2017	Actual, 2012	Total target adjustment	Amount	Fraction of total target
Greece	2009	−13.1	5.6	0.9	18.7	14.0	0.75
Ireland	2008	−10.7	3.2	−2.3	13.9	8.4	0.60
Italy	2010	1.0	5.8	4.7	4.8	3.7	0.77
Portugal	2010	−6.9	3.6[a]	1.0	10.5	7.9	0.75
Spain	2009	−8.5	2.2	−2.2	10.7	6.3	0.59

a. 2015 (maximum year).

Source: IMF (2012b).

Figure 2.4 Annual pace of fiscal adjustment in euro area periphery, base year through 2012 and 2013–15

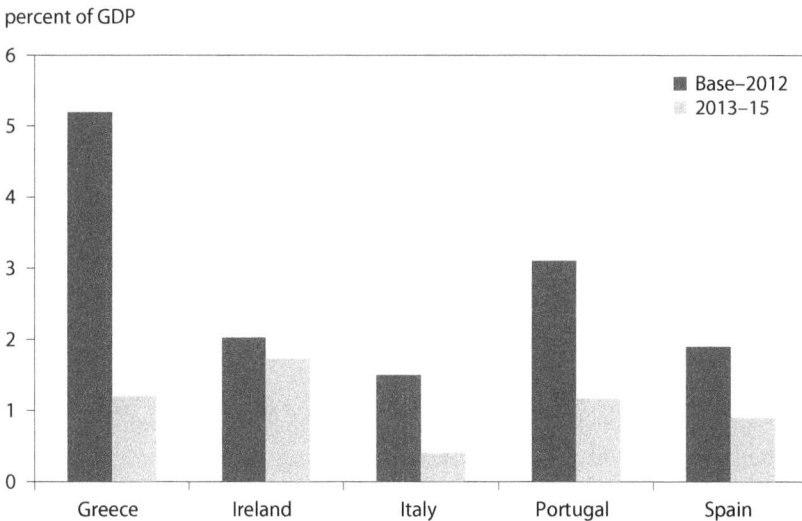

Source: IMF (2012b).

lower than that actually achieved in the initial adjustment period of two to four years.[18]

Both the fact that the majority of needed fiscal adjustment has already been accomplished and the fact that the required pace of further adjustment

---

18. The annual pace in the first period refers to the worst-year "base" date shown in table 2.1, so the pace of adjustment was sustained over a period ranging from two years (Italy, Portugal) to four years (Ireland).

should be substantially smaller going forward than in the past two to four years are supportive for the political feasibility of achieving the overall needed fiscal adjustment despite understandable debt fatigue in the euro area periphery.

Monetary Policy

In principle the constraints imposed by sovereign debt stress on fiscal stimulus that might otherwise be used to spur recovery could be overcome through either greater fiscal stimulus in the core economies of the north with greater fiscal space, by greater monetary stimulus for the euro area as a whole, or some combination of the two. As discussed in chapter 5, only limited scope seems likely for output gains in the periphery as a consequence of fiscal stimulus in the north. Euro area monetary policy, for its part, has lagged somewhat behind that in the United States and the United Kingdom in terms of stimulus from either reductions in short-term policy interest rates or adoption of unconventional large-scale asset purchases (quantitative easing). In the United States, the policy rate fell from about 5 percent in early 2007 to 2 percent by mid-2008 and then to close to zero by 2009 and after. In contrast, the ECB kept the short-term policy rate at about 4 percent through 2008, cut it to 1 percent during 2009–10, actually increased it to 1.5 percent in 2011, then reduced it again to 0.75 percent by late 2012 (Gagnon and Hinterschweiger 2013, 76). By November 2013 the ECB had cut the policy rate to 0.25 percent, in effect reaching the zero-bound interest rate adopted by the US Federal Reserve nearly four years earlier. A decline in inflation to less than half the target level of near 2 percent prompted the late-2013 cut.[19]

With rates near a zero bound, the question arises whether the ECB could usefully pursue further monetary expansion through quantitative easing. The ECB has actually increased its balance sheet by more than the Federal Reserve: an increase of 18 percent of GDP from July 2007 to December 2012, compared with 13 percent of GDP in the United States (Gagnon and Hinterschweiger 2013, 74). However, this increase has mainly represented lending to banks through LTROs and, to a lesser extent, purchases of periphery-economy government bonds in the Securities Markets Programme (SMP). The LTROs have maturities of three years or less, and the average of the remaining maturities in the SMP bonds is about four years.[20] In contrast, the essence of quantitative easing is the purchase of longer-term government bonds and other long-term assets (such as mortgage-backed assets) with the objective of driving down the long-term interest rate, which has a greater influence on investment and demand for consumer durables than the short-term interest rate. A comparison of the behavior of the term structure of euro area interest rates to

---

19. Jeff Black and Jana Randow, "ECB Cuts Key Rate to Record Low to Fight Deflation Threat," Bloomberg, November 7, 2013.

20. European Central Bank, "Details on securities holdings acquired under the Securities Markets Programme," press release, February 21, 2013.

Figure 2.5   Term spread for sovereign bonds, 10-year versus 6-month, 2008–13

percent

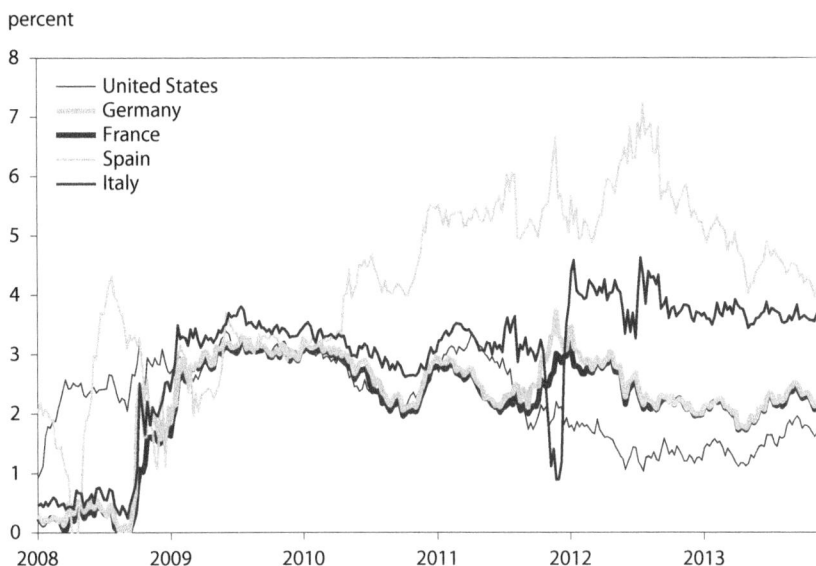

Source: Bloomberg.

those in the United States may thus shed light on whether there is much scope for unconventional monetary stimulus in the euro area. Figure 2.5 compares the spread between the 10-year government bond rate and the 6-month rate in the United States, Germany, France, Italy, and Spain during 2008–13.

It is evident that quantitative easing in the United States has reduced the term premium relative to that in Germany and France. During the second round of quantitative easing (QE2), which began in November of 2010, the term premium fell from a peak of 3.4 percent in April 2011 to a trough of 1.1 percent in July of 2012. During the third round (QE3), which began in September 2012, the term premium reversed a temporary increase and eased back from 1.6 percent to 1.2 percent by April 2013, prior to the announcement that the Federal Reserve might begin to "taper" purchases of long-term assets.

At the beginning of April 2013, the 10-year/6-month term premium for the United States stood at 1.2 percent; for Germany and France, it was at 1.7 percent. The implication is that the scope for reducing the term premium in the euro area through an aggressive program of quantitative easing comparable to that in the United States is on the order of 50 basis points. Although by the fourth quarter of 2013 the term premium was much higher for Spain (4.2 percent for Spain and 3.6 percent for Italy in late October 2013), these higher rates reflected a sovereign risk spread that is unlikely to be much affected by general quantitative easing that involves ECB purchases of long-term assets proportionate to euro area member country GDPs. Indeed, the term premiums are smaller than the 10-year sovereign risk differentials.[21]

Joseph Gagnon and Marc Hinterschweiger (2013, 88) combine several estimates from the literature to arrive at an estimate of a 1.5 percentage point reduction of US unemployment as the result of the cumulative impact of the three phases of quantitative easing. Applying the usual relationship (Okun's law), the corresponding increase in the level of GDP would have been 3 percent. As shown in figure 2.5, the total decline in the US term premium was on the order of 200 basis points. The broad relationship implied is that a 100 basis point reduction in the term premium causes a 150 basis point increase in the level of GDP. For the euro area, if the scope for reduction in the term premium is indeed about 50 basis points as suggested here, then, applying this relationship, the consequence of an aggressive program of general quantitative easing would be to boost the level of euro area GDP by about 0.75 percent. Although a one-time increase of this magnitude would be helpful, it would seem unlikely to provide much extra improvement in the debt sustainability prospects of the periphery economies. Yet it could be expected that aggressive quantitative easing would be vigorously opposed by the Germans, possibly increasing uncertainty.

---

21. In the period July–November 2013, 10-year sovereign spreads above the German bund were an average of 252 basis points for Italy and 262 basis points for Spain. In contrast, the corresponding differences between the 10-year to 6-month term premiums were 210 basis points for Spain and 140 basis points for Italy (Datastream). Under normal circumstances, the term premium moves relatively closely with the long-term sovereign risk spread, because short-term rates do not vary much with sovereign risk but long-term rates do. However, in periods of sharply escalating risk of default in the near term, the short-term sovereign risk spread can equal or exceed the long-term premium. Thus, in June 2011, the spread between three-month government obligations in Greece and those in Germany reached 1,600 basis points, whereas the corresponding 10-year spread was only 1,400 basis points (Datastream).

Appendix 2A
The Debt Sustainability Equation

Practitioners of fiscal stabilization frequently invoke the rule of thumb that to stabilize the ratio of debt to GDP, the primary surplus must be high enough to offset the excess of the interest rate over the growth rate.[22] The higher the initial level of debt relative to GDP, the greater the surplus must be. The summary rule of thumb is that the debt-to-GDP ratio will stabilize at the critical threshold primary surplus of $\pi^* = \lambda(r - g)$, where λ is the ratio of debt to GDP and g is the nominal growth rate. This appendix verifies this standard equation but notes that it is an approximation. In addition, it develops a more general equation for measuring the proportionate increase in the debt-to-GDP ratio when the primary surplus is above or below the stabilizing level.

Let D = public debt, Y = GDP, and the subscript indicate the period. Then:

$$D_1 = D_0 + rD_0 - \pi Y_1 = D_0(1 + r) - \pi Y_0(1 + g) \tag{2A.1}$$

That is, debt at the end of year 1 equals debt at the end of the previous year plus interest due during the year minus the primary surplus. Considering that $\lambda \equiv D/Y$,

$$D_1 = D_0(1 + r) - \pi \frac{D_0}{\lambda_0}(1 + g) = D_0(1 + r - \frac{\pi(1+g)}{\lambda_0}) \tag{2A.2}$$

The debt ratio in period 1 will then be this debt level divided by $Y_1 = Y_0(1+g)$, or:

$$\lambda_1 = \frac{D_0(1 + r - \frac{\pi(1 + g)}{\lambda_0})}{Y_0(1 + g)} = \lambda_0 \frac{1 + r - \frac{\pi(1 + g)}{\lambda_0}}{(1 + g)} \tag{2A.3}$$

As an approximation,

$$\lambda_1 = \lambda_0(1 - g)\left(1 + r - \frac{\pi(1 + g)}{\lambda_0}\right) \tag{2A.4}$$

Let all of the right-hand side of equation (2A.4) except the initial λ_0 be defined for convenience as Ω. Now consider the proportionate change in the debt ratio:

$$\dot{\lambda} = \frac{\lambda_1 - \lambda_0}{\lambda_0} = \frac{\lambda_0 \Omega - \lambda_0}{\lambda_0} = \Omega - 1 \tag{2A.5}$$

---

22. The analysis in this appendix was originally set forth in Cline (2010a) and in Cline (2003, annex A).

Thus:

$$\dot{\lambda} = (1-g)\left(1 + r - \frac{\pi(1+g)}{\lambda_0}\right) - 1 = r(1-g) - \frac{\pi(1+g)(1-g)}{\lambda_0} - g$$

(2A.6)

Considering that both g and r are small (on the order of 0.05), so that both rg and g^2 can be ignored, the right-hand side of equation (2A.6) simplifies to the approximation:

$$\dot{\lambda} = r - g - \frac{\pi}{\lambda_0}$$

(2A.7)

When the debt ratio is stabilized, $\dot{\lambda}=0$, so it must be the case at this critical primary surplus rate of π^* that:

$$\pi^* = \lambda_0(r - g)$$

(2A.8)

Equation (2A.7) thus gives the general equation for the proportionate change in the ratio of debt to GDP, and equation (2A.8) confirms the rule of thumb that the critical primary surplus rate needed to stabilize the debt-to-GDP ratio equals the debt ratio itself multiplied by the excess of the interest rate over the growth rate.

Appendix 2B
The Misleading Allure of Delaying Adjustment in the Euro Area Periphery

An ongoing policy debate on the euro area debt crisis has been whether austerity has gone too far too soon, causing excessive recessions in some countries and making them less creditworthy rather than more so.[23] The IMF has found that it had been underestimating the multiplier and therefore overstating projected output paths of countries involved in fiscal tightening (IMF 2012a, 41–43; Blanchard and Leigh 2013). De Grauwe and Ji (2013) have argued that undue panic stampeded countries into excessive fiscal tightening, but their implicit assumption is that the ECB should have announced Outright Monetary Transactions (its prospective program of purchases of sovereign debt of troubled countries taking adjustment measures) much earlier so financial markets would not have caused the panic in the first place. The European Commission has replied that the decline in spreads after OMT was linked to "concomitant consolidation efforts" (Buti and Carnot 2013). Krugman has riposted that the European Commission is laboring under "delusions" and should "be urging those countries not suffering from a debt crisis to be engaged in offsetting expansion" while acknowledging that those swept up in the crisis "have no choice about imposing at least some austerity."[24]

A crucial consideration in the debate concerns the high multiplier under conditions of high unemployment and ineffective monetary policy (zero bound on the interest rate). The argument is that fiscal contraction under these conditions raises rather than lowers the debt-to-GDP ratio, by depressing the denominator more than it increases the numerator. It turns out, however, that under reasonable assumptions this paradox is transitory, and over time the austerity *reduces* rather than increases the debt ratio (albeit at some loss of output from tightening under high-multiplier conditions, as the price of reducing the risk of eventual default crisis).

Consider the following set of accounting identities, where Y is nominal GDP, g is the trend (or potential) real growth rate, $\dot{p}$ is the GDP deflator inflation rate, FC is the fiscal consolidation in absolute terms, μ is the multiplier, τ is the ratio of revenue to GDP, ε is the ratio of primary (noninterest) expenditure to GDP, DEF is the fiscal deficit, INT is the interest bill, r is the interest rate on public debt, D is the debt stock at the end of the year, and λ is the ratio of debt to GDP.

---

23. An earlier version of this appendix appeared as a posting on the Peterson Institute's RealTime Economic Issues Watch blog (www.piie.com) on March 19, 2013 (Cline 2013b). For comments on an earlier draft, I thank without implicating Anders Åslund, Joseph Gagnon, and Angel Ubide.

24. Paul Krugman, "Delusions at the European Commission," *New York Times*, March 15, 2013, http://krugman.blogs.nytimes.com.

$$Y_t = Y_{t-1}(1+g)(1+\dot{p}) - FC_t \mu_t \tag{2B.1}$$

$$PS_t = Y_t(\tau_t - \varepsilon_t) \tag{2B.2}$$

$$FC_t = Y_{t-1}([\tau_t - \tau_{t-1}] - [\varepsilon_t - \varepsilon_{t-1}]) = Y_{t-1}(\varDelta\tau_t - \varDelta\varepsilon_t) \tag{2B.3}$$

$$DEF_t = INT_t - PS_t \tag{2B.4}$$

$$INT_t = rD_{t-1} \tag{2B.5}$$

$$D_t = D_{t-1} + DEF_t \tag{2B.6}$$

$$\lambda_t = \frac{D_t}{Y_t} \tag{2B.7}$$

If one calibrates this system to approximate the conditions of Italy in 2012 (as reflected in IMF 2012b), the baseline with intended fiscal adjustment can be compared against an alternative in which there would be a 1 percent of GDP fiscal stimulus in 2013 (i.e., a 1 percent of GDP reduction in fiscal consolidation from the baseline level).[25] One can then observe the path of output and debt to test the paradox that tightening worsens the debt ratio. The multiplier is set at an aggressive 1.2 in 2013, but declines linearly to 0 by 2017. The resulting projection of the debt-to-GDP ratio is shown in figure 2B.1.

In the baseline, the debt ratio peaks at 126.1 percent of GDP in 2013 and declines to 102.7 percent by 2022. If a fiscal stimulus shock of 1 percent of GDP is applied in 2013 by an increase in spending from the baseline (boosting ε from 0.452 to 0.462), there is indeed a debt-ratio paradox in the first year. The debt-to-GDP ratio declines from 126.0 percent of GDP in 2012 to 125.6 in 2013 instead of rising to 126.1, because the rise in output relative to the baseline (thanks to the high multiplier) outweighs the larger increase in debt.[26] However, already in the second year (2014), the debt ratio in the stimulus path is higher than in the baseline (at 125.4 percent instead of 124.8 percent). The stimulus path continues to have a higher debt ratio through the end of the decade (at 103.4 percent instead of 102.7 percent in the baseline). The additional debt from the first-year stimulus leaves a legacy of a higher stream of interest payments (even with no increase in the interest rate), whereas the boost to GDP was concentrated in just the first year.[27]

This exercise suggests that delaying adjustment can only briefly achieve the paradox of reducing rather than increasing the debt ratio. Moreover,

---

25. For the calibration for 2013–22, g = .011, λ_0 = 1.26, $\dot{p}$ =0.015, r =0.045, τ rises from 0.48 in 2012 to 0.49 by 2017, ε falls from 0.456 in 2012 to 0.439 by 2017.

26. With the stimulus, GDP rises 2.64 percent; in the baseline, it rises only 1.44 percent. With the stimulus, debt rises by 2.93 percent of GDP; in the baseline, it rises by only 1.94 percent of GDP.

27. By the second year and after, the stimulus GDP path is only 0.3 percent higher than the baseline path.

Figure 2B.1   Italy-type ratio of debt to GDP: Baseline and with 1 percent spending stimulus added in 2013

percent of GDP

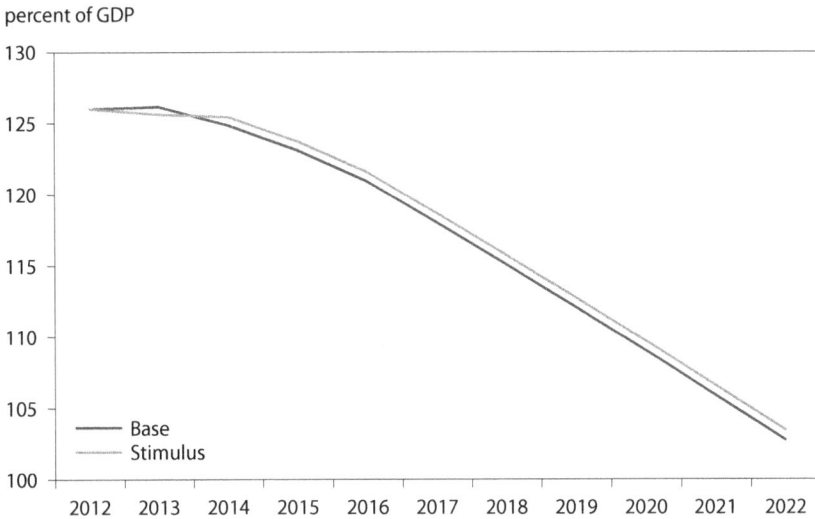

Source: Author's calculations.

the calculation makes no allowance for an adverse effect on market expectations regarding the interest rate facing the country. If markets respond to the announcement of a 1 percent of GDP stimulus by increasing the risk spread, the medium-term divergence between the two debt-ratio paths will be considerably larger than indicated in figure 2B.1 (as higher interest payments build up the debt more rapidly in the stimulus path). Indeed, if the country has lost capital market access, then it simply does not have the option of running a larger fiscal deficit unless official sources (euro area and IMF) are prepared to increase lending (as appears to have occurred in the recent relaxation of the Portugal adjustment program).

As noted, the path for the stimulus does place GDP about 0.3 percent higher in each year for 2014–22. If there were no risk of a severe debt crisis with collapse in capital market access, that gain (stemming from stimulus initially when the multiplier is high) would presumably be worth taking. But the euro area periphery economies have amply demonstrated that they have been on a knife-edge of credit risk. Even though the ECB's pledge of OMT has gone a long way since mid-2012 toward easing this risk for Italy and Spain in particular, the high level of Italy's debt and the upward trajectory of that of Spain suggest that accepting a slightly lower output path by eschewing stimulus could be a reasonable insurance premium to avoid risking a severe debt crisis, with its typical output losses amounting to double-digit percentages of GDP. A full welfare analysis of the merits of fiscal expansion, however, would require more complete evaluations of probabilities of such a debt crisis.

Appendix 2C
The Multiplier under Conditions of Default Risk

Recent international policy research has tended to reappraise the Keynesian output multiplier as having been relatively high for many industrial countries during the Great Recession, because of the combination of high unemployment and limits to the scope for offsetting fiscal tightening with monetary ease given the zero-bound constraint on interest rates.[28] This appendix considers not only the relationship of the multiplier to the degree of excess unemployment but also the influence of the risk of sovereign default in arriving at a "total welfare-equivalent multiplier." Illustrative calibrations suggest that whereas the United States has recently been in a range of a high positive multiplier, a country such as Italy may have faced a negative welfare-equivalent multiplier because of default risk.

Cyclically Dependent Multiplier

First principles of Keynesian economics suggest that the multiplier for fiscal stimulus should be higher when the economy is below full employment than when it is at full employment. Indeed, first principles would place the full-employment multiplier at zero: Any additional demand induced by public spending would simply divert productive resources away from the production of alternative goods.[29] Yet a survey of the empirical literature on the multiplier (Parker 2011, 703) finds that most estimates "almost entirely ignore the state of the economy." An important exception (Auerbach and Gorodnichenko 2010) places the cumulative multiplier over five years at 0 to 0.5 in times of expansion, in contrast to 1 to 1.5 in a recession. Another survey (Ramey 2011, 673) concludes that the multiplier is "probably between 0.8 and 1.5."

It has also been argued that the multiplier can be negative because of confidence effects, and that fiscal austerity can thus be expansionary. In the US context, "Rubinomics" in the 1990s was associated with this case, based on the premise that the decline in interest rates from improved investor confidence would spur investment sufficiently to more than offset reductions in demand from cuts in public spending or increases in taxes. However, that period was not one of high unemployment and already-low interest rates, the current situation. As discussed in the main text above, past international evidence for

---

28. This appendix is drawn from Cline (2012d), which incorporates welfare estimates for alternative budget paths for the United States. A summary version of that study was presented at the XXIV Villa Mondragone International Economic Seminar, Rome, June 26–28, 2012, and is available in Cline (2013c).

29. The zero multiplier would refer to real output effects; it could still be possible that an increase in public spending or reduction in taxes under conditions of full employment could boost nominal GDP if the central bank took no offsetting measures to prevent induced inflation.

"expansionary austerity" (i.e., a negative multiplier) has been called into question by recent studies applying actual historical episodes of fiscal tightening rather than the observed cyclically adjusted primary balance, which is subject to endogeneity from fiscal and growth surprises.

As a working hypothesis, this appendix thus assumes that the lower bound on the output multiplier is zero. Calibrated to the United States, it also assumes that at an unemployment rate as high as 9 percent (the US average in 2011) the multiplier is at its upper bound, set at 1.5.

Default Risk and Crowding Out

A higher ratio of net public debt to GDP should be expected to increase the risk of sovereign default. Episodes of sovereign default impose large welfare costs by causing financial crises and deep recessions. In principle, then, one can think of the expected economic cost of an increase in the public-debt-to-GDP ratio as the product of the increase in the probability of a sovereign default multiplied by the welfare cost of default.

The more conventional cost of excessive debt is associated instead with the increase in interest rates induced by crowding out, as public spending preempts resources otherwise available for private investment. The underlying assumption is that the monetary authority does not accommodate the extra spending, under conditions of full employment, given its commitment to price stability. Higher interest rates from crowding out eventually curb capital formation, causing a reduction in potential output from levels that would otherwise be achieved with a higher capital stock.

Optimal Fiscal Policy

In the context of persistent unemployment, optimal fiscal policy will then face the task of identifying the level of fiscal stimulus (if any) that represents the point at which, at the margin, output gains from additional stimulus begin to be fully offset by considerations of sovereign default risk and long-term crowding-out effects associated with the government's need to borrow more in order to pay interest on a higher stock of debt. Because of the perceived high risk of sovereign default in several countries in Europe's periphery, for these countries the choice of fiscal policy will presumably tilt more toward reducing fiscal deficits than toward seeking to stimulate the economy despite the presence of unemployed resources. For the United States, recent high unemployment on the one hand and the prospect of large long-term deficits from rising health costs on the other make it natural to consider policies of credible fiscal adjustment for the medium term combined with some fiscal stimulus in the short term.

Calibrating the Tradeoffs

The key determinant of the size of the multiplier is the amount by which the unemployment rate is in excess of the normal level associated with production at full potential of the economy (natural rate of unemployment). Defining this excess as v:

$$v_t = u_{t-1} - u^*$$
(2C.1)

For the case of the United States, $u^* = 5$ percent. At the 2011 average level of unemployment, 9 percent, the excess unemployment was $v = 4$ percent.
The multiplier is then:

$$\mu_t = \alpha v_t; s.r. 0 \leq \mu_t \leq 1.5$$
(2C.2)

Given the multiplier, the percent change in output attributable to a fiscal stimulus s (percent of GDP) will be:

$$z_t = \mu_t s_t$$
(2C.3)

The stimulus is an ex ante concept and equals the sum of the policy-imposed increase in expenditure plus policy-imposed direct reduction in tax revenue.[30] Assuming an upper bound of 1.5 for the multiplier when unemployment reaches 9 percent, and the lower bound of zero when unemployment reaches $u^* = 5$ percent, the constant α is 0.375.

The change in output resulting from the stimulus will have an induced effect on tax revenue. Expressing the base level of tax revenue as r percent of GDP, the increase in revenue from the growth impact of the fiscal stimulus (again as a percent of GDP) will be:

$$\Delta r_t = \rho z_t \theta$$
(2C.4)

where ρ is the tax revenue elasticity, and θ is the share of tax revenue in GDP.

For the United States, the Congressional Budget Office (CBO 2011, 22) places the tax revenue elasticity for personal income taxes (ρ) at about 1.5, meaning that a 1 percent increase in GDP from the baseline should boost tax revenue by 1.5 percent. Considering that federal revenue is usually about 18 percent of GDP, so that $\theta = 0.18$, an ex ante spending stimulus of 1 percent of GDP will have a maximum offset to the resulting increase in the deficit amounting to $1 \times 1.5 \times 0.18 \times 1.5 = 0.4$ percent of GDP when the multiplier is

---

30. For simplicity, it is assumed that the impact is the same for increased spending or reduced taxes.

at its upper bound. That is, the 1 percent stimulus boosts output 1.5 percent; this increase raises revenue by 1.5 × 1.5 = 2.25 percent; and 2.25 percent of 18 percent of GDP (revenue base) amounts to 0.4 percent of GDP.

Correspondingly, when the economy is in deep recession, stimulus is a bargain in terms of fiscal cost, at only 60 cents on the dollar in the example just considered. The symmetric implication is that when fiscal tightening is applied under conditions of high unemployment, there will be a secondary revenue loss caused by the induced output loss that erodes the initial reduction in the deficit.[31] This is the "debt trap" in which the effort to confront a debt crisis by fiscal tightening is made more difficult by induced output and revenue loss.

The net impact of fiscal stimulus on the fiscal balance will be smaller than the ex ante stimulus to the extent that there are induced growth and hence revenue effects. Thus:

$$\Delta d_t = s_t - \Delta r_t \qquad (2C.5)$$

where Δd_t is the change in the ex post fiscal deficit as a percent of GDP.

Against the gains from the demand multiplier effect, there are offsetting effects from the possible increase in the interest rate as a consequence of the fiscal stimulus. The standard concern is crowding out of private investment as the fiscal deficit raises the interest rate. For the United States, under normal economic conditions an extra 1 percent of GDP in the fiscal deficit is associated with a crowding-out increase in the interest rate by 4 basis points (see Gagnon and Hinterschweiger 2011, 10). Allowing the interest rate effect of stimulus to fall to zero as the economy approaches the high unemployment liquidity trap, and linearizing:

$$\Delta i_t = \Delta d_t (a - b v_t), s.r.\, 0 \leq \Delta i_t \leq a \qquad (2C.6)$$

Identifying the liquidity trap with 9 percent unemployment and normal conditions with 5 percent, then parameter a would be 4 basis points and parameter b would be 1 basis point.

Taking account of the welfare loss of crowding out requires translating the effect of the higher interest rate into an equivalent loss to be subtracted from the direct output gain from the stimulus applied to the multiplier. Setting this loss at k percent of GDP (absolute value):

$$k_t = \pi(\Delta i_t) \qquad (2C.7)$$

---

31. Thus, if 1 percent of GDP reduction in the fiscal deficit causes a 1.5 percent reduction in GDP, in turn causing a 1.5 × 1.5 = 2.25 percent reduction in revenue or 0.4 percent of GDP revenue loss (using the US revenue/GDP base), an ex ante reduction in the deficit by 1 percent of GDP turns out to provide a net reduction of the deficit by only 0.6 percent of GDP.

The welfare effect of the higher interest rate can be considered from the standpoint of the neoclassical production function. Suppose the opportunity cost of capital is 7 percent annually (including a risk factor that places the investment hurdle rate significantly above the long-term risk-free interest rate). Then a 1 percentage point increase in the interest rate would amount to a 14 percent increase in the cost of capital. If the elasticity of investment with respect to the interest rate is 0.5 (inelastic), investment would then fall by 7 percent. With gross private investment at about 15 percent of GDP, this decline would amount to 1.05 percent of GDP.

The elasticity of output with respect to capital equals the share of capital in income, about 30 percent. The elasticity equals the ratio of marginal product to average product. Average product is the inverse of the capital/output ratio (about 2.5), or 0.4. So the marginal product of capital is 0.12 (= 0.3 × 0.4), or 12 percent. Reducing investment by 1.05 percent of GDP would thus reduce output by 0.12 × 1.05 = 0.126 percent of GDP. With a capital life of 10 years, this loss would recur annually over the coming decade. Translated to the cumulative effect from the single year's decline in output, the loss associated with a full percentage point increase in the interest rate would be π = 1.26 percent of GDP.

Finally, policy should take account of the risk of financial crisis posed by a rising debt burden. Michael Hutchison and Ilan Noy (2005) place the typical loss of output from a banking crisis at 10 percent of one year's GDP (as discussed in Cline 2010b, 100). A banking crisis provides a rough guide to what could be expected from a sovereign debt crisis.

The likelihood that markets will force a debt crisis will rise with the ratio of public debt to GDP. Suppose that at the Maastricht target of 60 percent for the debt-to-GDP ratio, there is zero expectation of sovereign default. Suppose that if the debt ratio is 120 percent of GDP, as in the case of Italy, then a fiscal stimulus of 1 percent of GDP will be seen by markets as increasing the probability of default by 20 percent because of concern about fiscal unsustainability. Then the expected welfare cost of an increase in the fiscal deficit by 1 percent of GDP, from the standpoint of expected default cost, would be zero at the lower debt ratio and 2 percent of GDP (20 percent increase in probability times 10 percent welfare cost given default) at the higher ratio.

Identifying ψ as the maximum expected sovereign default loss attributable to a 1 percent of GDP increase in the (ex post) fiscal deficit, or ψ = 2 percent of GDP, and designating H as the extent by which the public-debt-to-GDP ratio exceeds 0.6, then:

$$L_t = \psi(\Delta d_t)\frac{H_t}{0.6}, s.r. 0 \leq \frac{L_t}{\Delta d_t} \leq 2 \qquad (2C.8)$$

Thus, if the debt-to-GDP ratio is 60 percent, there is zero expected default cost. If debt-to-GDP ratio is 120 percent, then H = 0.6, the final term is unity, and if the increase in the realized fiscal deficit is 1 percent of GDP, then the expected default cost is 2 percent of GDP. For debt ratios in between, the expected default cost of the increase in the fiscal deficit is interpolated between these extremes.

The overall net gain from applying the fiscal stimulus of s percent of GDP is then the direct growth impact (z), minus the crowding-out loss (k), minus the expected default cost (L), or:

$$w_t = z_t - k_t - L_t = s_t \mu_t - \pi(\Delta i_t) - \psi^* H_t(\Delta d_t) \tag{2C.9}$$

where w is the welfare-equivalent effect of the stimulus as a percent of GDP, and for convenience the default loss parameter and the denominator in the final term of equation (2C.8) are consolidated to $\psi^* = \psi/0.6$.

Substituting,

$$w_t = s_t \mu_t - \pi(\Delta d_t)(a - b v_t) - \psi^* H_t(\Delta d_t) \tag{2C.10}$$

After further substitution, equation (2C.10) can be expressed as a function of the size of the stimulus (s), the magnitude of excess unemployment (v), and the amount of what can be called excess debt (H), and for simplicity omitting the time subscript:

$$w = s(\beta + \gamma H + \lambda v + \delta v^2 + \Gamma H v);$$
$$\beta \equiv -\pi a$$
$$\gamma \equiv -\psi^*$$
$$\lambda \equiv a + \pi a \rho \theta a + \pi b$$
$$\delta \equiv -\pi b a \rho \theta$$
$$\Gamma \equiv \psi^* a \rho \theta \tag{2C.11}$$

The bracketed expression in the right-hand side of equation (2C.11) can be thought of as the total welfare-equivalent multiplier taking account of the extent of unemployment and existing public debt. It can be either positive or negative. Table 2C.1 summarizes the variables and parameters involved in arriving at the total welfare-equivalent multiplier, along with the parameter values suggested in the discussion above.

Multiplier under Alternative Conditions

Equation (2C.11) provides the basis for identifying a table of contingent welfare effects of stimulus as a function on the level of unemployment on the one hand and the ratio of government debt to GDP on the other. Table 2C.2 illustrates this "total welfare-equivalent multiplier" at alternative combinations of excess unemployment and excess debt.

As indicated in table 2C.2, the full potential welfare gain from fiscal

Table 2C.1   Variables and parameter values

Symbol	Unit	Value	Concept
v	Percent	0 to 4	Unemployment rate minus 5 percent natural rate; "excess unemployment"
H	Number	—	Excess of public debt/GDP ratio above 0.6 (Maastricht target)
μ	Number	0 to 1.5	Multiplier
s	Percent of GDP	—	Ex ante stimulus (increased spending plus reduced taxes)
z	Percent of GDP	—	Increase in GDP as consequence of stimulus
α	Number	0.375	Increase in multiplier per percentage point additional unemployment
Δr	Percent of GDP	—	Induced tax revenue increase
θ	Number	0.18	Base tax revenue share in GDP
ρ	Number	1.5	Tax revenue elasticity with respect to growth
Δd	Percent of GDP	—	Change in ex post fiscal deficit
Δi	Percent	—	Increase in interest rate from crowding out
a	Percent	0.04	Change in interest rate from 1 percent of GDP additional fiscal deficit at full employment
b	Percent	0.01	Reduction in interest rate impact for 1 percent additional unemployment
k	Percent of GDP	—	Welfare-equivalent loss from crowding out
π	Number	1.26	Welfare-equivalent loss for 1 percent rise in interest rate
L	Percent of GDP	—	Welfare-equivalent loss from increase in default risk
ψ	Number	2	Percent GDP welfare-equivalent loss from increased default risk when fiscal deficit rises by 1 percent of GDP and debt/GDP $\geq$ 1.2
ψ^*	Number	3.33	= ψ /0.6
w	Percent of GDP	—	Welfare-equivalent total multiplier effect of fiscal stimulus of s percent of GDP
$\beta, \gamma, \lambda, \delta, \Gamma$	Coefficient	—	Simplifying summations of parameters for particular variable

stimulus occurs when unemployment is high and the debt ratio is low. In the lower-left corner, 1 percent of GDP fiscal stimulus boosts welfare by 1.5 percent of GDP.[32] As unemployment falls, however, so does the welfare gain. Even if there is low public debt (column 1), the impact of fiscal stimulus turns negative when the unemployment rate falls to 5 percent. At that point there

---

32. More technically "welfare" measurement would require specification of a welfare function. The usage here is heuristic and can best be thought of as potential consumption measured in the same units as GDP.

Table 2C.2   Total welfare-equivalent multiplier including default risk

	Debt/GDP (percent)			
	60	**80**	**100**	**120**
H	0	0.20	0.40	0.60
v				
0	−0.05	−0.72	−1.38	−2.05
1	0.34	−0.26	−0.86	−1.45
2	0.73	0.20	−0.33	−0.86
3	1.12	0.65	0.19	−0.27
4	1.50	1.10	0.71	0.31

H = excess of debt/GDP ratio above 0.6
v = excess of unemployment rate above 5 percent

Source: Author's calculations.

is zero direct multiplier (full employment), but there is a crowding out effect. The net welfare effect is negative even at higher unemployment rates as the debt-to-GDP ratio rises, because the potential negative impact of a debt crisis becomes increasingly large. With the parameters used here, at the highest debt ratio the debt crisis risk turns the welfare effect of fiscal stimulus negative at all but the highest unemployment rate. This is the case that is being presumed in the fiscal policy measures adopted in some of the euro zone periphery economies affected by the debt crisis. That is, fiscal tightening has been pursued even though unemployment is high, because of the desire to reduce sovereign default risk. The worst impact of fiscal stimulus occurs when unemployment is low and public debt is high (upper right-hand corner of table 2C.2). Using the parameters of table 2C.1, in this case a fiscal stimulus of 1 percent of GDP causes a 2.05 percent of GDP welfare loss, because there is no rise in real output (resources are already fully employed), crowding out reduces future growth, and the risk of a sudden stop as capital markets fear default is high.

Figure 2C.1 shows alternative combinations of *H* and *v* that turn the total welfare-equivalent multiplier zero. Above and to the left of this perimeter the total multiplier is negative; below and to the right of the perimeter it is positive.[33]

For Italy, for example, in 2012 unemployment was 10.6 percent. During 2003–08, when Italy's output level was estimated by the IMF to have been consistently above rather than below potential (positive rather than negative output gap), unemployment was an average of 7.3 percent. A reasonable

---

33. Solving equation (2C.11) for the *H* that sets *w* to zero for a given value of *v* yields $H_{u=0} = -(\beta + \lambda v + \delta v^2)/(\gamma + \Gamma v)$. The perimeter in figure 2C.1 shows the combinations of *H* and *v* that satisfy this equation.

Figure 2C.1 Zero-value perimeter for total welfare-equivalent multiplier for alternative values of excess unemployment and excess debt

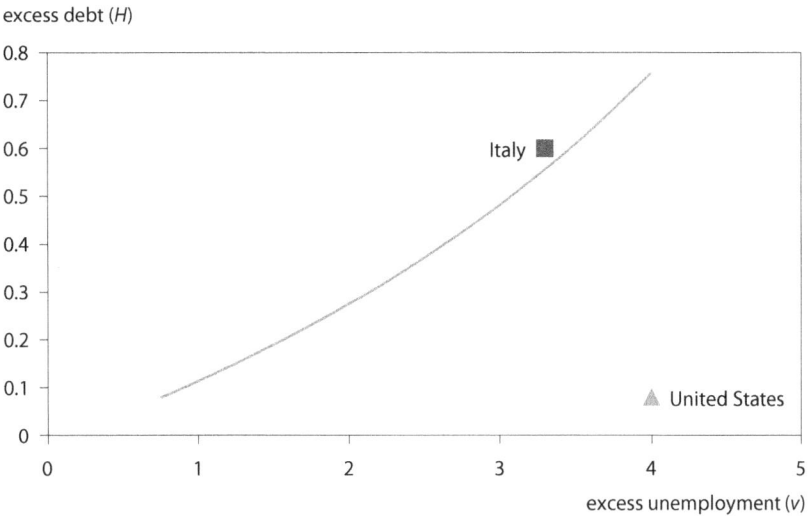

excess debt (*H*)

excess unemployment (*v*)

Italy ■

▲ United States

Source: Author's calculations.

estimate of excess unemployment in 2012 is the difference, or $v = 3.3$ percent. With a public-debt-to-GDP ratio of 1.2 and hence "excess" debt of $H = 0.6$, Italy was somewhat above and to the left of the zero perimeter line, so the welfare-equivalent multiplier was negative. In contrast, in the United States in 2011 federal debt held by the public was 68 percent of GDP, placing excess debt at $H = 0.08$, and unemployment was at 9 percent, placing v at 4 percent. At that time the United States was thus clearly to the right of and below the zero perimeter, so the total welfare-equivalent multiplier was positive.[34]

---

34. The comparison here uses gross general government debt for Italy but federal debt held by the public for the United States, the concepts that are the focus of market scrutiny and public policy in the euro area periphery and the United States, respectively. Detroit's current bankruptcy is testimony to the fact that the 19 percent of US GDP in state and local debt (Barnett and Vidal 2013) does not constitute contingent federal debt. Nor is the debt held intragovernmentally, notably by the Social Security Administration (16.7 percent of GDP in 2011; SSA 2014) and Federal Employees Retirement System (5.2 percent of GDP in 2011; Isaacs 2013) subject to destabilizing selloffs in the market, and therefore it differs from debt held by the public. In contrast, the 13.4 percent of GDP in federal debt held by the Federal Reserve (largely as a consequence of quantitative easing) is counted in debt held by the public, as it should be because in principle it will be sold off again to the market as monetary conditions permit. Moreover, an alternative measure of the burden of the debt—the ratio of net interest payments to GDP—shows even higher relative indebtedness of Italy to that of the United States (5.2 percent/2.2 percent = 2.37 in 2012; IMF 2013n) than does the ratio of gross general government debt as a percent of GDP (Italy) to federal debt held by the public as a percent of GDP (US): 120/72 = 1.67 in 2012. Finally, as stated in the main text, there are grounds

Even for a country such as Italy, fiscal adjustment—namely, negative fiscal stimulus (higher taxes, lower spending)—could produce a reduction in observed GDP even while providing a net positive welfare gain. The reason is that the actual GDP outcome would show up primarily for the direct output component of the multiplier (equation 2C.2 above). The negative component in equation (2C.9) from crowding out and reduced capital stock (equation 2C.7) would be realized only over a long period of time. So would the negative component in equation (2C.9) for default risk (equation 2C.8). Indeed, an actual default might not (and probably would not) ever actually occur; yet the social cost of the increased default risk would still be present. Consequently, a country such as Italy could benefit from fiscal tightening even though it would be observed in the subsequent year that output had declined as a result. The social value of reducing the default risk would outweigh the cost of the one-year loss to output from reduced demand.

for incorporating a country-specific shift in the sustainable debt, for example to address Japan's advantage of strong home bias of domestic investors, and doing so in the Italy-US comparison can easily accommodate formulation in terms of gross general government debt rather than federal debt held by the public for the United States.

3

The Bank–Sovereign Debt Nexus

This chapter examines another key functional issue in the euro area debt crisis: the relationship of sovereign debt stress to the nation's banks. The broad concern is that there has been a "doom loop" in which the weaknesses of sovereigns cause weaknesses in banks and vice versa. Bank losses spurred the sovereign crisis in Ireland, but the reverse occurred in Greece (spilling over into Cyprus). In Spain an increasing share of sovereign debt has been held by domestic banks as foreign holders have cut back. In June 2012 the euro area made important decisions in developing banking union, and by early 2014 the Single Supervisory Mechanism (SSM) was in place and key agreements had been reached regarding the bank resolution process. The European Central Bank (ECB) was on track to carry out an asset quality review and then assume supervisory responsibilities for some 130 large euro area banks by late 2014.

The analysis of this chapter finds that the sudden stop in foreign bank financing imposed a substantial liquidity squeeze on the peripheral economies and their governments. Bank deposits fell much more than could be explained by falling GDP. The discussion also examines the corresponding problem of financial fragmentation. Borrowing costs of the domestic banks showed a close correlation with those of their sovereigns. Banks seem to have passed along only a portion of the crisis-induced interest rate increase to customers, however. As would be predicted by credit-rationing theory, they curbed the volume of lending as another form of their adjustment, and perceived scarcity of finance was a much more severe problem in the periphery than in the core economies in 2012–13. A swing from rapid increases in bank lending to the private sector to net repayments was particularly sharp in Ireland and Spain.

To analyze the vulnerability of sovereign debt to future contingent debt imposed by the need to recapitalize banks, this chapter applies a simple model, previously estimated by the International Monetary Fund (IMF), relating bank losses to macroeconomic conditions. The estimates find surprisingly that the large writeoffs already taken, especially in Spain, should leave little in hidden losses that pose a threat to sovereign debt. Alternative estimates by the Organization for Economic Cooperation and Development (OECD) and by other experts also suggest such capitalization needs are modest in the periphery economies.

The chapter concludes with a review of progress toward banking union, and considers where the bail-in pendulum stands following its sharp swing from leniency but high cost to the sovereign in Ireland to severe treatment of creditors and uninsured depositors in Cyprus.

Banks Undermining Sovereigns: Ireland and Spain

Except for Cyprus, the clearest case of debt crisis causation running from the banks to the government has been that of Ireland.[1] Ireland did not have a sovereign debt problem in 2007, when its ratio of public debt to GDP was only 25 percent. Its banking system was large relative to the economy, however, with assets at five times GDP (compared with 46 percent in the United States and 170 percent if nonbank finance is included). Bank losses associated with the bursting of the real estate bubble came at a time of acute international financial uncertainty following the Lehman Brothers collapse, and at end-September 2008 the government announced it would provide €46 billion to recapitalize the banks, or 30 percent of GDP. Alan Ahearne (2012) places the total government recapitalization of the banks at 40 percent of GDP, which he estimates as higher than in any of the other major episodes of sovereign assumption of bank losses.[2]

Bank recapitalization was not the sole cause of Ireland's debt crisis. Large fiscal deficits during 2008–11 driven by recession boosted debt by about 40 percent of GDP. Considering that the banking crisis contributed to recession, however, one can interpret part of these deficits as an indirect cost of the banking crisis that added to the direct recapitalization costs. The overall effect was to raise Ireland's gross public debt to 117 percent of GDP at the end of 2012.[3]

---

1. This section draws on Cline (2012a, 203–204).

2. Ahearne (2012, 43) estimates gross recapitalization costs at 37 percent of GDP for Indonesia in 1997, 34 percent for Chile in 1981 (but only 6 percent on a net basis), 25 percent for Turkey in 2000, and 19 percent for both Korea and Thailand in 1997.

3. In principle there should have been some compensation in the form of bank assets acquired by the government. The OECD (2013) and IMF (2013g) show sharply different estimates of government assets, with the OECD estimate rising from 28.9 percent of GDP in 2007 to 43.8 percent in 2012, but the IMF estimate lower and rising much less, from 13.6 percent of GDP to 14.8 percent (difference between gross and net debt). The OECD estimates would seem more consistent with government acquisition of bank assets.

There are important issues regarding both the amount and the financing of the bank recapitalization in Ireland. In contrast to Cyprus (discussed below), neither senior bondholders nor uninsured depositors bore any part of the burden of the bank losses. However, shareholder equity in Irish banks, which had reached €25 billion in 2007, was wiped out; and subordinated bondholders lost €16 billion or 80 percent of their claims (Ahearne 2012, 44). With respect to financing, the government issued €25 billion (16 percent of GDP) in promissory notes for use as capital of the Irish Bank Resolution Corporation (IBRC), responsible for winding down two large failed banks. The IBRC in turn used the notes as collateral to borrow from the Central Bank of Ireland under Emergency Liquidity Assistance (ELA). In effect, then, Ireland constitutes an exception to the stylized rule that the European debt crisis has been aggravated by the fact that countries don't have their own central banks and so cannot provide full assurance to creditors that they will be paid (albeit at a risk of inflationary erosion from printing money). That is, Ireland did use financing by its central bank. But the Irish case might reasonably be seen as an exception that proves the rule, because this borrowing was exclusively used for the bank sector workout, rather than for general government spending.

In February 2013 Ireland's financing situation improved significantly with the liquidation of the IBRC and repayment of the ELA and replacement of the relevant debt on more favorable terms. The Central Bank of Ireland purchased €40 billion in bonds (€25 billion from the government, €15 billion from the National Asset Management Agency), or 24 percent of GDP. With average maturities of 34 years and interest at 260 basis points above Euribor, these bonds have much longer maturities as well as lower interest rates than the promissory notes they replace, and will reduce Ireland's financing needs over the next decade by about $1\frac{1}{3}$ percent of GDP annually (IMF 2013e, 5).[4]

Spain is the other major case of debt contagion from the banks to the sovereign. In June 2012, the Eurogroup heads of state agreed to provide Spain up to €100 billion in support from the European Stability Mechanism (ESM) for recapitalization of banks. A diagnostic exercise by the government identified a range of €51 billion to €60 billion in recapitalization needs, and the envelope of €100 billion was set to provide a safety margin. In December 2012 the ESM disbursed about €40 billion (in notes issued by the Fondo de Restructuración Ordenada Bancaria), and in February 2013 approximately €2 billion more.[5]

For a brief moment it appeared that the Eurogroup banking union initiative agreed in mid-2012 would make it possible for the ESM loans to

---

4. The promissory notes had average maturities of 7.5 years and average interest rates of 5.8 percent. Note that the Central Bank of Ireland must sell off €7.5 billion of the bonds into the market by no later than 2023. Karl Whelan, "Ireland's Promissory Note Deal," *Forbes*, February 11, 2013; NTMA (2013).

5. The first disbursement was to recapitalize four large banks, including BFA-Bankia; the second, an additional four banks (ESM 2013).

go directly to the Spanish banking sector rather than through the sovereign, thereby avoiding an increase in sovereign debt by an amount of up to about 10 percent of GDP (if the full €100 billion were used).[6] The Eurogroup leaders had stated at the June summit meeting that "We affirm that it is imperative to break the vicious circle between banks and sovereigns.... When an effective single supervisory mechanism is established, involving the ECB, for banks in the euro area the ESM could, following a regular decision, have the possibility to recapitalize banks directly."[7]

Soon, however, the finance ministers of Germany, Finland, and the Netherlands issued a statement indicating that "legacy assets" would be the responsibility of the sovereign even after establishment of the Single Supervisory Mechanism.[8] The immediate interpretation in financial circles was that both Spain and Ireland would be unable to shed the burden of debt associated with the recapitalizations in the recent banking crises onto the euro area more broadly through direct ESM support to their banks.[9]

For Spain, nonetheless, the magnitude of the bank recapitalizations envisioned so far is much smaller relative to GDP than was the case for Ireland. The estimate of €51 billion to €62 billion in prospective recapitalization costs identified in the mid-2012 diagnosis would represent no more than 6 percent of GDP, about one-sixth the size of the recapitalization burden for Ireland.[10]

Sovereigns Undermining Banks: Greece and Spillover to Cyprus

In Greece, the principal direction of debt stress contagion has been from the sovereign to the banks. The Greek banking system had not been particularly overdimensioned, with assets at the end of 2009 at 212 percent of GDP (less than half the ratio reached in Ireland). As the Greek government faced a deteriorating fiscal position, it increasingly borrowed from Greek banks. The banks in turn could lend to the government with zero risk weights for purposes of calculating regulatory capital (Basel rules). The mutual interest in lending was no doubt compelling but increasingly dangerous. Banks more than doubled

---

6. Stephen Fidler, Gabriele Steinhauser, and Marcus Walker, "Investors Cheer Europe Deal," *Wall Street Journal*, June 30 to July 1, 2012.

7. Euro Area Summit Statement, June 29, 2012, Brussels, www.european-council.europa.eu /home-page/highlights/euro-area-summit-statement?lang=ey.

8. Their September 2012 statement included, "the ESM can take direct responsibility of problems that occur under the new supervision, but legacy assets should be under the responsibility of national authorities" (Finnish Government 2012).

9. See, for example, Karl Whelan, "Germany to Spain and Ireland: Drop Dead," *Forbes*, September 25, 2012.

10. The estimates were by the firms Oliver Wyman and Roland Berger; see "Spain may need €62 billion to rescue banks," Reuters, June 21, 2012.

their claims on the government (loans and bonds), from €31.5 billion or 6.8 percent of their total assets at the end of 2008 to a peak of €63 billion (12.6 percent of their assets) in June of 2011 (IMF 2011e, 48; ECB 2013a).

When the private sector involvement (PSI) haircut of 53 cents on the euro, agreed in October 2011, took effect in April 2012, the result was a sharp drop in the value of Greek banks' claims on the government, which fell from €60.2 billion at the end of 2011 to €30.6 billion in April 2012 (ECB 2013a).[11] The decline in value represented about 6 percent of bank assets. Considering that their capital, broadly defined, amounted to only 5.8 percent of total assets at the end of 2011 (World Bank 2013), the direct impact of the October 2011 PSI agreement was to eliminate the capital of the banking sector. Consequently the financing program for Greece had to include €25 billion in new borrowing for bank recapitalization made necessary by the PSI (IMF 2012c, 28).

In Cyprus both contagion from the sovereign to the banks and vice versa were present, but the incoming contagion to the banks was from a neighboring sovereign, Greece. In Cyprus the banking sector constituted the main activity of the economy (along with tourism) and thus in some sense was inherently overdimensioned in comparison with most economies. At the end of 2012, bank assets amounted to about €130 billion, or about seven times GDP. Bank capital amounted to €15 billion, in principle a fairly robust 12 percent of assets. Unfortunately, some large banks had high exposure to Greek government bonds. The Cyprus Popular Bank (Laiki) held €3.4 billion in Greek government bonds, and the Bank of Cyprus, €2.4 billion.[12] The PSI haircut caused €1.9 billion in losses for the Bank of Cyprus alone.[13]

The Cyprus crisis broke new ground in the bank–sovereign debt nexus. For the first time, resolution of the banking crisis imposed losses on uninsured depositors (those with deposits exceeding €100,000) as well as senior creditors. Initially the program would have imposed a tax on all depositors, including the insured, but fortunately for the credibility of deposit insurance in the euro area, the Cypriot Parliament rejected the initial approach. Under the €10 billion financial rescue program of the Eurogroup and the IMF agreed in March 2013, Laiki Bank was closed and the Bank of Cyprus recapitalized.[14]

---

11. The exchange provided 15 cents on the euro in liquid assets (short-term notes from the European Financial Stability Facility) plus 31.5 cents on the euro in 30-year bonds with a coupon rising from 2 to 4.3 percent by 2021 (IMF 2012c, 45).

12. Jack Ewing, "Greek Crisis Leaves Cyprus Mired in Debt," *New York Times*, April 11, 2012.

13. The direct restructuring loss was €910 million, but there were additional losses of about €600 million on market-to-market treatment of the exchange bonds and €400 million on hedges related to the bonds (Alvarez and Marsal 2013, 6–7).

14. Gabriele Steinhauser, Marcus Walker, and Matina Stevis, "Bailout Strains European Ties," *Wall Street Journal*, March 26, 2013.

Bank of Cyprus creditors and uninsured depositors were required to convert their claims into equity in the bank, with an expected 60 percent loss of value.[15]

The Greek sovereign thus provoked losses to the Cypriot banks. These losses in turn imposed new debt on the Cypriot sovereign. Bank recapitalization needs will contribute €1.2 billion to new government debt, somewhat more than the €1 billion fiscal deficit in 2013. The bank recapitalization will contribute only about one-third of the total debt buildup from April 2013 to December 2014, given fiscal deficits of €2.3 billion over this period. So even in the case of Cyprus, the induced fiscal losses associated with severe recession will outweigh the direct costs of recapitalizing the banks (in considerable part because these costs were curbed by imposing losses on large depositors). The overall result for the public debt burden will be an increase from 86 percent at the end of 2012 to 123 percent by end-2014 (IMF 2013a, 33–34).

Trends in Bank Deposits and Sovereign Holdings

Declining Lending by Foreign Banks

The debt crisis in the euro area periphery has been marked by a major cutback in lending by international banks to euro area periphery economies. As indicated in table 3.1, Bank for International Settlements (BIS) data for international banks indicate that the total stock of their cross-border claims on the five peripheral economies fell from €4.0 trillion at the end of 2009 to €2.3 trillion at the end of 2012, or by 43 percent. Thereafter the cross-border claims stabilized, falling only an additional 1.1 percent by the third quarter of 2013. The declines from end-2009 to end-2012 were largest for Greece (by 76 percent) and smallest for Italy (by 33 percent).

The final column of table 3.1 shows the decline of cross-border bank claims from end-2009 to end-2012 as a percent of 2009 GDP. The most remarkable decline was in Ireland, by 242 percent of GDP. It is also striking that very little of the decline in Ireland was in holdings of government securities, underscoring again the banking rather than fiscal origins of the crisis there.

In contrast, in Greece the decline of foreign bank claims on the public sector amounted to 33 percent of GDP from end-2009 to end-2012, or more meaningfully, 21 percent of GDP from end-2009 to the third quarter of 2011 before the PSI haircut. Even the 21 percent measure (€49 billion) amounted to 62 percent of the short-term (€6 billion) and long-term (€73 billion) public sector amortizations coming due in 2010–11 (IMF 2010c, 28), so the sudden stop in foreign bank lending imposed a severe liquidity squeeze for Greek public debt. An almost identical squeeze occurred in Portugal (a cut of 19.9 percent of GDP in foreign bank holdings of public debt), whereas this effect

---

15. Michele Kambas, Stephen Grey, and Stelios Orphanides, "Why Did Cypriot Banks Keep Buying Greek Bonds?" Reuters, April 30, 2013.

Table 3.1 Cross-border claims of international banks on euro area periphery (billions of euros)

Country	2009Q4	2011Q3	2012Q4	2013Q3	Change, 2009–12 (percent of 2009 GDP)
Greece	235.9	134.2	57.6	71.7	−77.1
Banks	48.2	8.8	4.2	27.6	−19.1
Public sector	96.4	47.5	21.0	21.5	−32.6
Nonbank private sector[a]	91.2	77.9	32.4	22.6	−25.5
Ireland	875.7	596.4	483.7	453.5	−241.6
Banks	303.8	151.5	104.1	84.9	−123.1
Public sector	20.2	10.5	8.8	10.9	−7.0
Nonbank private sector[a]	551.7	434.4	370.7	357.7	−111.5
Italy	1,419.5	1,023.3	942.3	946.9	−31.4
Banks	391.3	270.6	206.2	204.0	−12.2
Public sector	394.5	210.5	222.3	230.3	−11.3
Nonbank private sector[a]	633.6	542.2	513.8	512.6	−7.9
Portugal	285.6	202.1	170.7	161.8	−68.2
Banks	85.1	38.7	28.3	23.0	−33.7
Public sector	54.2	23.0	20.8	19.4	−19.9
Nonbank private sector[a]	146.3	140.4	121.6	119.4	−14.6
Spain	1,145.2	777.9	616.4	611.9	−50.5
Banks	506.2	266.6	170.9	204.1	−32.0
Public sector	114.8	88.1	77.7	73.3	−3.5
Nonbank private sector[a]	524.2	423.3	367.9	334.5	−14.9
Periphery 5	3,880.0	2,626.2	2,127.6	2,090.8	−56.0
Banks	1,334.6	736.2	513.7	543.6	−26.2
Public sector	680.2	379.6	350.7	355.4	−10.5
Nonbank private sector[a]	1,865.2	1,510.4	1,263.3	1,191.8	−19.2

a. Includes local-currency claims on local residents.

Source: BIS (2014).

was milder in Italy (11 percent of GDP), Ireland (7 percent), and especially Spain (3.5 percent of GDP).

The sudden stop in international lending to the European periphery was even sharper for lending to their banks than overall. Thus, outstanding claims of international banks on domestic banks fell by 91 percent from end-2009 to end-2012 in Greece; by a nearly identical 66 percent in Ireland, Portugal, and Spain; and by 47 percent in Italy. For the five countries, the decline was 62 percent. In contrast, the decline in international bank lending to the public sector in the five countries was 48 percent; and the decline in claims on the nonbank private sector, only 28 percent. The decline of international bank claims on euro area periphery banks by almost two-thirds is a gauge of the banking sector fragmentation that has marked the euro area crisis.

Table 3.2 shows the corresponding claims for banks headquartered in the four largest "northern" euro area countries: Germany, France, the Netherlands, and Belgium. Their combined claims on the periphery five economies fell from €1.98 trillion at the end of 2009 to €1.03 trillion at the end of 2012, or by 48 percent, before stabilizing in 2013.[16] The implication is that rather than being a resilient source of financing for their euro partners, these "northern" banks fled the troubled periphery just as rapidly as (and actually a bit faster than) banks from the rest of the world.

The BIS data for banks in the large northern economies do not provide detail that would permit disaggregation into borrower sectors as shown in table 3.1. However, it seems likely that the greater concentration of the cutbacks in the sector of bank borrowers characterized claims of euro area partner lenders as well as international banks as a whole. If so, banking fragmentation was indeed a characteristic of the crisis as measured by claims of the euro area north banks on euro area periphery banks.

Declining Bank Deposits in the Crisis

A stylized fact of the euro area debt crisis has been that the periphery has experienced bank "jogs" of persistently declining deposits, raising the specter of bank crises. Pressure on banks aggravates the recessions, eroding revenue and aggravating government fiscal balances. Larger fiscal deficits and a decline in GDP boost the debt ratio.

Figure 3.1 shows the absolute nominal level of bank deposits for five periphery economies and Germany, with the right-hand vertical axis applying to the smaller economies (Greece, Ireland, Portugal) and the left-hand axis, the larger ones (Germany, Italy, Spain). The figure confirms the presence of falling bank deposits in the crisis in four of the five debt-stressed economies: Greece, Ireland, Portugal, and Spain. The decline in Greece has been the most severe: a fall of 36 percent from December 2009 to June 2012, with only a slight recovery in January–July 2013.[17] The corresponding maximum declines in subperiods through mid-2013 amounted to 13.5 percent for Ireland (August 2009 to January 2012), 10.2 percent in Portugal (October 2011 to January 2013), and 13.3 percent in Spain (December 2012 to July 2013). In contrast, in the United States the decline of deposits from its previous peak in the first quarter of 2009 to its trough in the second quarter of 2010 was only 5.4 percent. The

---

16. The corresponding decline for Austrian banks was from €50 billion to €21 billion.

17. The decline of deposits in Greece was more acute than that in the previously most prominent episode of sovereign default: Argentina at the end of 2001. Bank deposits had fallen by 20.8 percent over a period of 10 months (IMF 2013e).

Table 3.2   Claims of banks in euro area north on euro area periphery (billions of euros)

Country	2009Q4	2011Q3	2012Q4	2013Q3
Germany	703.8	473.9	378.5	374.6
Greece	45.0	36.8	25.3	30.6
Ireland	183.8	101.6	81.6	70.8
Italy	189.7	144.7	129.2	126.8
Portugal	47.4	30.0	21.7	22.4
Spain	238.0	160.9	120.7	124.1
France	911.3	617.2	501.7	508.6
Greece	75.2	43.2	2.7	2.1
Ireland	60.3	34.7	37.4	37.9
Italy	511.4	368.8	337.2	345.8
Portugal	44.7	25.8	17.0	15.7
Spain	219.6	144.6	107.3	107.0
Netherlands	243.6	136.2	108.5	105.1
Greece	11.9	3.8	2.4	1.2
Ireland	30.8	18.8	15.0	14.1
Italy	68.7	38.2	33.0	33.8
Portugal	12.4	5.0	4.5	4.2
Spain	119.7	70.5	53.5	51.8
Belgium	118.9	84.2	43.9	42.2
Greece	3.6	1.3	0.0	0.0
Ireland	60.8	38.4	23.9	19.6
Italy	29.9	23.0	10.2	10.0
Portugal	3.1	1.4	0.7	0.4
Spain	21.5	20.1	9.1	12.2
North 4	1,977.6	1,311.5	1,032.6	1,030.5
Greece	135.7	85.0	30.5	33.9
Ireland	335.7	193.5	157.8	142.4
Italy	799.7	574.8	509.6	516.3
Portugal	107.6	62.2	43.9	42.8
Spain	598.9	396.1	290.7	295.2

Source: BIS (2014).

Figure 3.1 Bank deposits in euro area periphery and Germany, 1999–2013

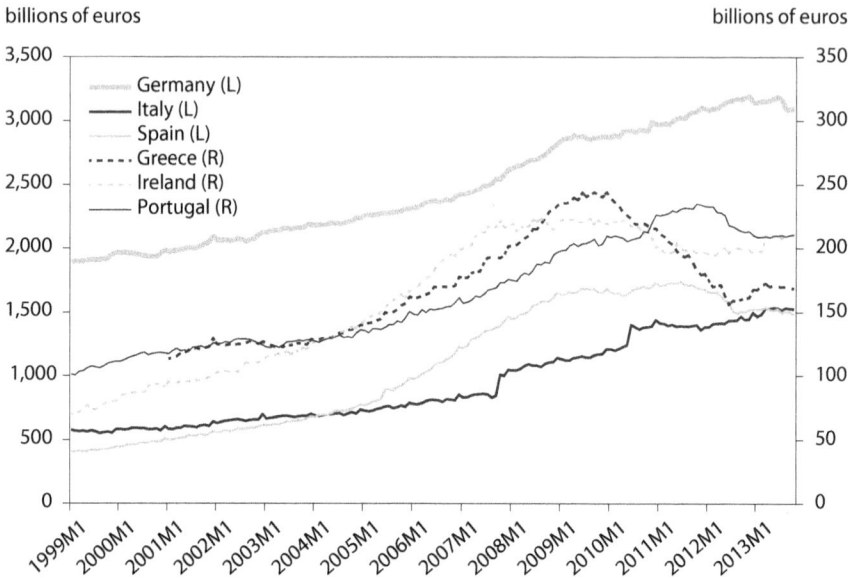

Note: Germany, Italy, and Spain on left axis (L); Greece, Ireland, and Portugal on right axis (R). Total deposits is the sum of demand deposits and other deposits.

Source: IMF (2014).

declines in deposits in the four euro area economies, excluding Italy, substantially exceeded any declines in GDP, suggesting downward pressure from eroding confidence rather than merely lesser demand associated with lower nominal GDP.[18]

As a stylized fact, then, bank deposits in three intermediate-stress economies fell about 12 percent (Ireland, Portugal, and Spain).[19] Deposits fell more than one third in the de facto sovereign default case of Greece, but did not fall at all in Italy. Italy is somewhat of an outlier, then, because whether judged by foreign claims on banks or by the level of domestic deposits, Italian banks have performed better than Spanish banks, yet the sovereign risk spreads of the two countries have moved closely in parallel (chapter 2, figure 2.2). Moreover, as discussed below, the credit default swap rates for the two largest banks have been very similar for Spain and Italy (see figure 3.4 below). The explanation

18. Nominal GDP changes from 2009 to 2012 were –9.8 percent for Greece, 0.2 percent for Ireland, 1.4 percent for Portugal, and –0.1 percent for Spain (IMF 2013n).

19. The declines were probably more severe for deposits of foreigners. Thus, in Ireland, private sector deposits in March 2011 were 10 percent below their level a year earlier for residents but 26 percent lower for nonresidents (Central Bank of Ireland 2013, 4).

of this seeming paradox would appear to be that there has been a greater incidence of a weak subsector of banks in Spain than in Italy. Difficulties in the Spanish "cajas" and the bankruptcy of Bankia, a large amalgamation of cajas, together with the revealed stress represented in the special borrowing program of Spain from the ESM for recapitalization of the banks, support this interpretation of the greater heterogeneity of the banking sector in Spain such that the overall sector has been weaker than in Italy despite comparable strength of leading banks. Moreover, when a third large bank is included in the comparisons, the weaker system in Spain begins to be apparent (figure 3.4).

Figure 3.1 also strongly suggests that for Greece, Ireland, Spain, and to a lesser extent Portugal, the rate of growth of deposits prior to the crisis was unsustainably high. In Greece, from the end of 2003 to the end of 2009 the nominal value of bank deposits grew at 10.7 percent annually. Deposits grew at a remarkable annual average of 16.7 percent in Spain in the five years ending September 2009; at 12.7 percent annually in Ireland during the five years ending in August 2008; and at a less frenetic but still high 7.9 percent in Portugal in the five years ending in May 2011. The property bubbles in Spain and Ireland paced this rapid expansion.

Bank Holdings of Sovereign Bonds

Another stylized fact of the euro area debt crisis is that as sovereigns came under market pressures, the share of sovereign debt held by domestic banks increased and the share held by nonresidents declined (Merler and Pisani-Ferry 2012c). One reason for this dynamic was that as a loss of confidence induced foreigners to cut back on holdings of periphery government obligations, domestic banks stepped in to fill the gap. Moral suasion may have induced them to do so, although it is difficult to document whether and to what extent governments pressured banks to buy government bonds that were otherwise losing investor demand. It also seems likely, however, that for at least the larger domestic banks, their own actions—especially if taken in tandem with peers—could positively influence the outcome for the sovereign and thereby likely positively influence economic conditions affecting their own profitability.[20] Also because Basel risk weightings for capital requirements treated sovereign debt as risk free and thus not requiring capital, a shift in assets toward the sovereign was a means of deleveraging at a time when banks needed to improve capital positions. In addition, the large program of long-term refinancing operations (LTROs) provided by the ECB at the end of 2011 and in early 2012 spurred bank purchases of sovereign bonds. This central bank lending to banks

---

20. In principle such a process can be seen as a benign form of internalization of externalities in an oligopolistic market structure, although resulting exposure to the sovereign yielded malign results for the banks in Greece. The five largest banks in each country hold the following shares of total bank assets: 80 percent in Greece, 70 percent in Portugal, 57 percent in Ireland, 51 percent in Spain, and 40 percent in Italy (Schoenmaker and Peek 2014, 29).

against collateral enabled them to purchase government bonds, earn interest far above the LTRO rate, and use the government bonds as the collateral (see, for example, van Rixtel and Gasperini 2013). Although in principle banks might have purchased bonds of other euro area governments (e.g., Germany) in response to both the risk weighting and LTRO funding influences, the much higher yields were an incentive to purchase bonds of their own sovereigns, and in effect they were doing so in an environment that had some attributes of gambling for redemption and thus encouraged pursuit of high yields.

Figure 3.2 shows the evolving composition of ownership of government bonds during 2010–13.[21] It is evident in the first panel that holdings by nonresidents were indeed declining in the countries under stress. From the first quarter of 2010 to the fourth quarter of 2012, nonresident holdings fell from 86 percent of the total to 72 percent in Ireland, from 51 percent to 40 percent in Italy, and from 46 percent to 33 percent in Spain.[22] Encouragingly, for Italy and Spain this decline stopped in the first quarter of 2012, and in Spain there was a modest rebound by the fourth quarter of 2012. There were also declines in Greece and (to a lesser extent) Portugal.

The second panel of figure 3.2 shows the rising share of domestic bank holdings of government obligations. This increase was from about 25 percent to a peak of 35 percent in Spain, from about 10 to 43 percent in Ireland, and from 15 to 24 percent in Italy. The bank share rose similarly but earlier from about 14 to 15 percent to 20 to 23 percent in Greece and Portugal (although data for the latter extend only through end-2012).

From the first quarter of 2010 to the second quarter of 2013 (or for Portugal, fourth quarter of 2012), the simple average share of nonresidents in holdings of government obligations of the five debt-stressed economies fell from 65.7 to 50.0 percent, whereas the average share held by resident banks rose from 16.0 to 27.8 percent. These data confirm the stylized fact of a flight of foreign investors from government bonds and their replacement by domestic banks.[23]

Finally, it is useful to consider the corresponding trend in holdings of nonbank residents, excluding the central bank and other public institutions. In the third panel of figure 3.2, it can be seen that this share held up well and even increased, especially in Spain and Italy. This category represents the general domestic public, and the steady or rising shares indicate that domestic confidence in public debt solvency appears to have been stronger than foreign investor confidence.

---

21. The data were specially compiled in a dataset developed by Silvia Merler and Jean Pisani-Ferry (2012c).

22. For Ireland there was a sharp further decline to 54.7 percent by the second quarter of 2013.

23. The rise in the share for banks, 11.8 percent simple average for the five countries, was approximately three-fourths the decline in the share of nonresidents.

Figure 3.2 Shares of government obligations by holder, euro area periphery and Germany, 2010–13

a. Nonresidents

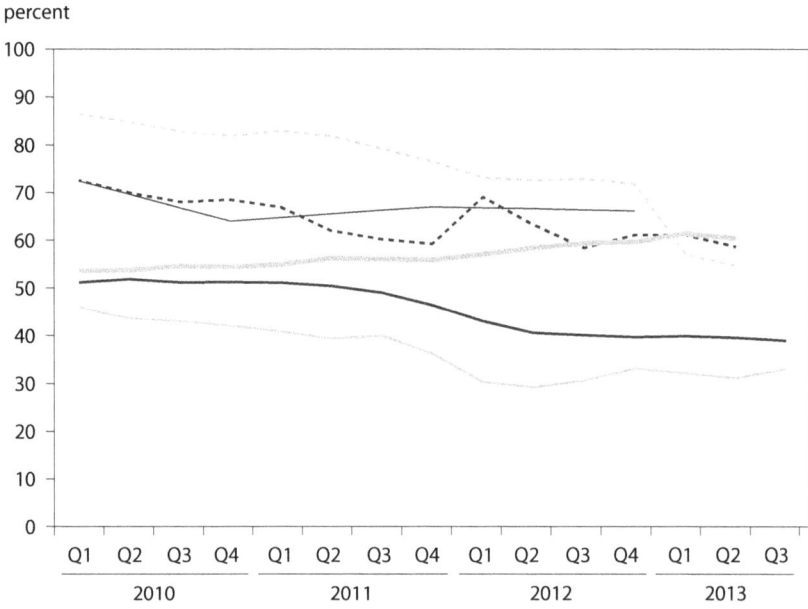

percent

b. Resident banks

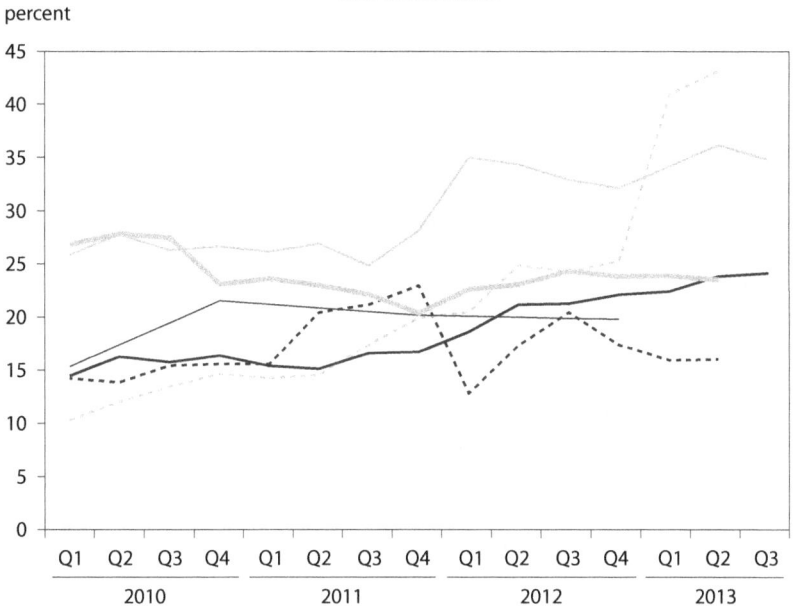

percent

····· Greece   ······ Ireland   —— Italy   ······ Spain   —— Portugal   ······ Germany

(continues on next page)

Figure 3.2 Shares of government obligations by holder, euro area periphery and Germany, 2010–13 *(continued)*

c. Resident nonbanks

percent

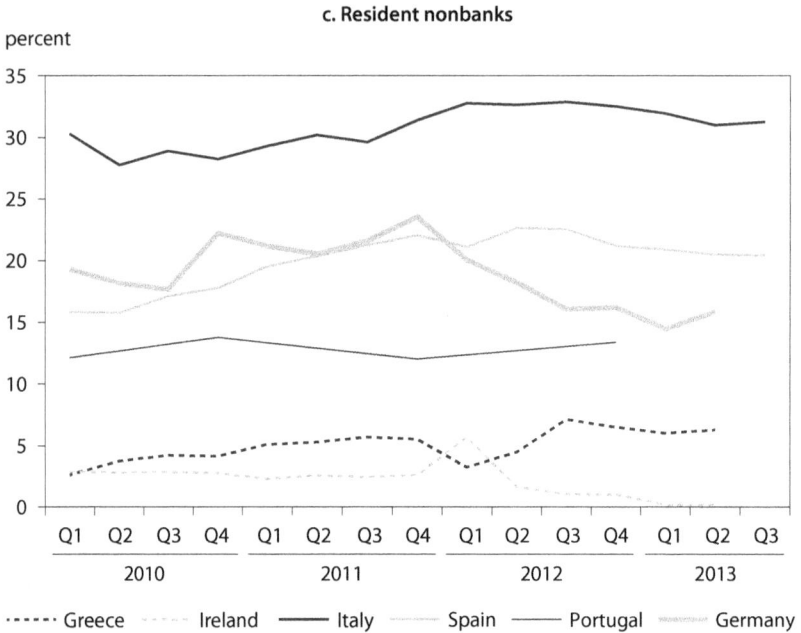

····· Greece   ···· Ireland   ── Italy   ── Spain   ── Portugal   ── Germany

Source: Merler and Pisani-Ferry (2012c).

Bank Vulnerability to Sovereigns

Despite the trend toward replacement of foreign holdings with domestic bank holdings of sovereign obligations, the share of these obligations in the domestic banks' assets has remained moderate. As shown in figure 3.3, the increase in this share during the euro area crisis has been largest in Spain and Portugal, rising by about 6 percentage points from 2008 to early 2013. Nonetheless, the level of this share in early 2013 was only about 8 percent in Portugal and 11 percent in Spain, smaller in both cases than the 16 percent share in Italy. (In Greece the share had peaked at 12 percent but then fell by more than half with the debt restructuring.)

The direct vulnerability of banks to the sovereigns would thus seem limited. In view of lower public debt in the other periphery economies than in Greece, and lower relative amounts of de facto senior debt owed to the official sector, plausible PSI haircuts imposed in a restructuring would be considerably lower than the 50 percent in Greece.[24] Suppose a still relatively high loss

24. At the end of 2012, Greek public debt owed to the IMF amounted to 11.4 percent of GDP, and that owed to the euro area official sector, 82.7 percent (IMF 2013c, 62). The total of 94.1 percent owed to the official sector was far higher than the corresponding amount for the two other

Figure 3.3   Share of home sovereign's obligations in assets of domestic banks, euro area periphery, 2007–13

percent

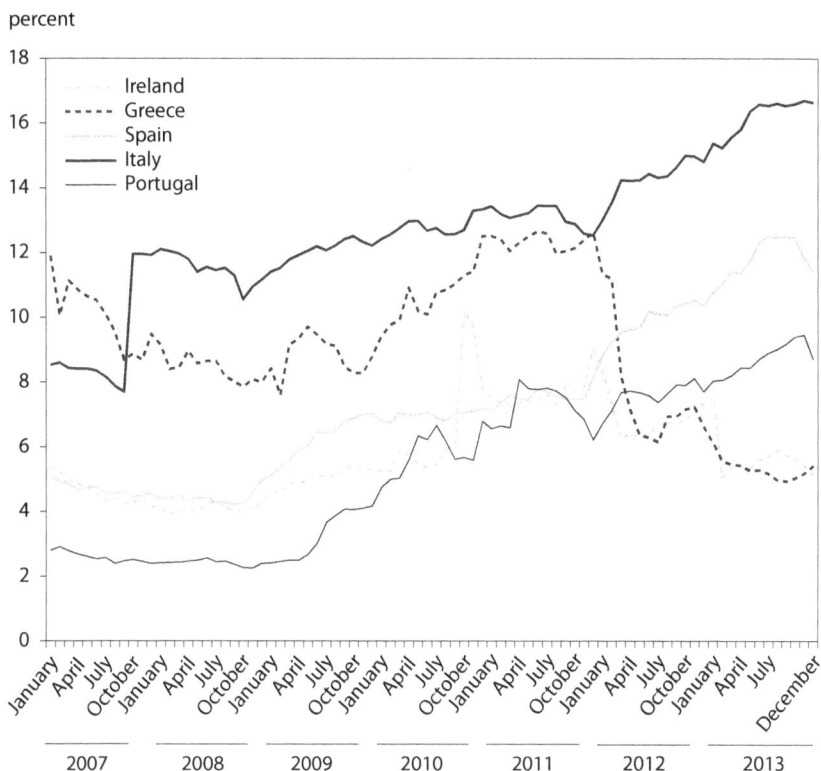

Source: ECB (2014c).

of one-third were imposed on bank holdings of sovereign debt. The impact would amount to about 5 percent of assets in Italy, 4 percent in Spain, and 3 percent in Portugal. These losses would represent about half of bank capital in Italy, about two-thirds in Spain, and about half in Portugal.[25] In contrast, the 6 percentage point drop in government obligations as a percent of assets for Greek banks as a consequence of the sovereign restructuring represented more than the entirety of capital, which stood at 5.8 percent in 2011.

Indirect vulnerability of the banks to the sovereign is likely to be large as well, however. To the extent that domestic firms are unable to borrow more

program countries, Ireland (34.4 percent; IMF 2013e, 42), and Portugal (38.6 percent; IMF 2013f, 32). In Spain, the amount borrowed from the ESM represented only about 4 percent of GDP.

25. Bank capital as a percent of total assets in 2012 (or 2011 if most recent) amounted to 6 percent in Portugal, 6.1 percent in Spain, and 9.4 percent in Italy. In comparison, this ratio was 11.3 percent in the United States, but only 4.4 percent in Germany (World Bank 2013).

cheaply than the sovereign, private sector borrowers may face a credit crunch and there may be an increase in defaults. More broadly, sovereign debt distress is highly likely to translate to greater uncertainty and slower growth in the economy, with adverse consequences for quality of bank loans to the private sector.

Bank and Sovereign Spreads Correlation

A comparison of the path of credit default swap (CDS) rates for major banks and for the sovereign provides a basis for considering the direction of causality in the debt "doom loop" between the banks and sovereigns. Figure 3.4 presents these comparisons for the sovereign and two of the largest banks in each country; and, for both Italy and Spain, a third large bank. If the path of the CDS rate for the banks is consistently to the northwest of the path for the sovereign, the implication is that the contagion is from weak banks to the sovereign. If the path for the banks is consistently to the southeast of that for the sovereign, the implication is that the weak sovereign is causing contagion to the country's banks. In the benign, normal situation one would expect the CDS rate for the large banks to be slightly above that of the sovereign by a consistent but small spread. Even in this benign case, the reasonable presumption is that it is the sovereign spread that is dominant, so there is at least moderate contagion from the sovereign to the banks (in comparison with strong contagion in that direction when the bank spreads are systematically to the southeast of the sovereign spreads).

Figure 3.4 confirms the diagnosis that in Greece it was an imploding sovereign that imposed damage on the banks. The figure shows that the sovereign CDS rate reached 3,000 basis points in September 2011 and then went to much higher levels not shown on the chart. Two large banks followed the sovereign rate upward until mid-2011, but then became divorced from the sovereign rate and by early 2013 their CDS rates were back down to the range of 1,000 basis points. The opposite direction of contagion is similarly confirmed for Ireland. The CDS rates for two large banks soared to about 1,500 basis points in early 2011, when the sovereign rate was still only about 500 basis points. The bank rates remained far above the sovereign rates, even though both paths have come down substantially.[26]

In Portugal there is no obvious direction of strong contagion, either from banks to the sovereign or vice versa. The banks led the sovereign CDS rate through September 2011, but thereafter one of the two large banks actually had a lower rate than the sovereign, until the two converge again by June 2012.

In Italy, up until June 2012 the pattern was benign, with three large banks showing a modest and consistent spread above the sovereign CDS rate. In the

---

26. The path for one of the banks, Allied Irish, is discontinued after late April 2011 because an unchanged constant rate in the database for all dates thereafter suggests that the CDS no longer traded.

Figure 3.4   Credit default swap rates, five-year obligations: Sovereigns and major banks, 2008–14 (percent)

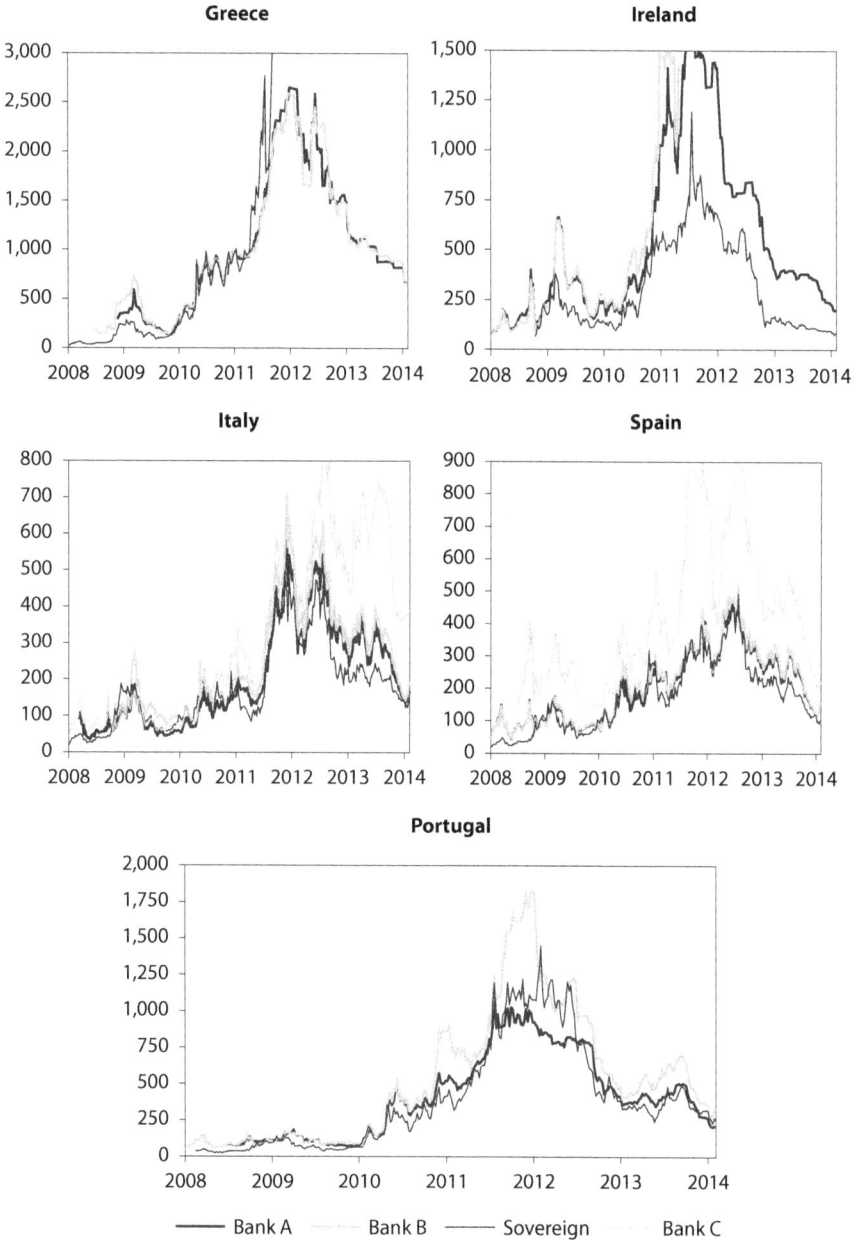

Note: Greece: A is the National Bank of Greece and B is Alpha Bank. Ireland: A is Bank of Ireland and B is Allied Irish. Italy: A is Intesa San Paolo, B is Unicredito, and C is Monte dei Paschi. Spain: A is Santander, B is BBVA, and C is Banco Popular Español. Portugal: A is Caixa Geral and B is Banco Comercial Português.

Source: Datastream.

second half of 2012 this gap widened even between the sovereign and the two strongest banks, and by much more against the third weaker bank (Monte dei Paschi). The pronounced decline in the sovereign spread that began with announcement of Outright Monetary Transactions (OMT) in July 2012 has outpaced the decline in the rate for the large banks; that is, favorable contagion from the sovereign to the banks has been incomplete. Even so, by the end of April 2013 the difference between the 300 basis point rate for the two stronger large banks and the 200 basis point rate for the sovereign was not particularly large, confirming the underlying benign pattern (and hence only moderate as opposed to strong contagion from the sovereign to the banks).

In Spain, the two largest banks once again display the benign pattern of closely tracking the sovereign at a slightly higher CDS rate. As in Italy (although to a lesser degree), for the two largest banks there is also some lag behind the sovereign in reduction of the CDS rate after the launching of OMT. The manifest difference for Spain, however, is in the behavior of CDS rates for another large bank, Banco Popular Español (the sixth largest bank). This bank's CDS rate has soared far above those of the two largest banks and the government, reaching 900 basis points in September 2011 and again in July 2012. The path of the CDS rate for Banco Popular lies everywhere to the northwest of that for the sovereign, marking the pattern for damage running from the banks to the state instead of vice versa.[27] The bank is illustrative of the pattern of a dichotomy between the strong largest banks and a substantial sector of weaker banks requiring recapitalization and the source of Spain's need to draw some €40 billion in lending so far from the ESM for recapitalizing the sector.[28]

Overall, the patterns in figure 3.4 show strong contagion from the sovereign to the banks in only a single case: Greece. The more general pattern is moderate contagion from the sovereign to the banks to the extent that typically bank spreads follow those of the sovereign (as capital markets tend to set a sovereign floor in lending to a country). The clear exception is Ireland, where the strong contagion was from the banks to the sovereign.[29]

Financial Fragmentation

One of the major consequences of the euro area debt crisis has been the fragmentation of financial markets, provoking higher borrowing rates for the

---

27. Banco Popular experienced large losses associated with aggressive real estate lending during the housing bubble.

28. Ilan Brat and Christopher Bjork, "Banco Popular Plans Large Rights Issue to Avoid EU Aid," *Wall Street Journal*, October 1, 2012.

29. The more dominant pattern in the figure is consistent with the finding in van Rixtel and Gasperini (2013, 25) that "regardless of a bank's credit rating, the difficulties faced by its sovereign became the arbiter of the bank's access to funding and its cost." The authors note that a sharp cutback in short-term funding from US money-market funds contributed to their funding difficulties (van Rixtel and Gasperini 2013, 13–14).

private sector in the debt-stressed periphery economies than in the core economies. Higher borrowing costs contribute to recession, providing a feedback loop to lower revenue and more sovereign debt stress. Reversing the process of euro area financial fragmentation in the private sector is a key goal of the move toward banking union, discussed below.

Figure 3.5 shows interest rates for bank lending to nonfinancial corporations (new business, all maturities).[30] In broad terms the lending rates confirm the perception of financial market fragmentation. The rates begin relatively close together and then fan out into three distinct paths, with private rates substantially higher in the debt-stressed economies. There are some surprises, however. Whereas the sovereign outcome has been far more severe in Greece than in Portugal, the (probably prime) lending rates to the private sector have been practically the same in Portugal as in Greece. Conversely, whereas Portugal and Ireland have been arguably relatively similar in terms of sovereign stress, there has been a large gap between private lending rates in the two economies. Ireland's private loan rates have been almost identical to those in Italy and Spain, even though Ireland had to enter an official lending program. Another somewhat surprising pattern is that the gap between private lending rates in the three middle-stress economies (Ireland, Italy, and Spain) did not begin to show a sharp increase above rates in the benchmark countries of Germany and France until about the first quarter of 2012, whereas sovereign risk spreads in Italy and Spain had spiked already in the second half of 2011. Perhaps the greatest surprise, however, concerns the moderate size of the gaps between the lending rates. At the height of the crisis in the second quarter of 2012, sovereign spreads in Italy and Spain reached 500 to 600 basis points above the German bund 10-year rate (chapter 2, figure 2.2). Yet the widest gap between the lending rates to the private sector was far smaller, at only about 150 basis points, and came later (in the second quarter of 2013).[31] For Italy, Edda Zoli (2013, 14) similarly finds that only about half of the change in the sovereign spread is transmitted to bank lending rates within six months. She also finds that only about one-fifth or less of the change in the sovereign spread is transmitted to bank CDS rates and bond rates (Zoli 2013, 11–12).

For interest rates, then, the evidence suggests that the transmission of financial fragmentation from the sovereigns to corporate borrowers occurred with a lag and in moderated rather than amplified form. A pattern of fragmentation tends to show up more forcefully in availability of bank lending, however, reflecting the phenomenon of credit rationing.[32] Raising interest rates charged

---

30. For Greece, the rate is for one-year loans, not just new lending.

31. Average maturities on the private loans may have been lower than the 10-year sovereign comparison. However, when default risk is high, the risk spread can be higher for a shorter-term loan than a longer-term one, because the amount of time to cover the given default risk is shorter and the risk-spread earnings have less time to accumulate and compensate.

32. The classic analysis of credit rationing is by Joseph Stiglitz and Andrew Weiss (1981).

Figure 3.5   Interest rates for new bank lending to nonfinancial corporations, euro area periphery, Germany, and France, 2007–13

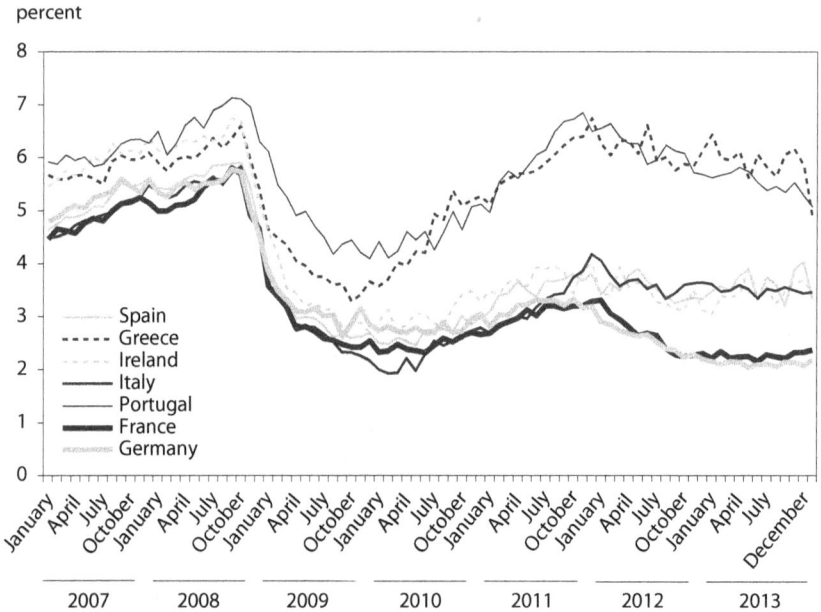

percent

Source: ECB (2014b).

to customer firms can cause adverse selection (with firms willing to pay high interest rates being less creditworthy) and distort incentives (toward projects with greater risk). Consequently, banks may curb lending volumes as a part of their response to facing higher interest rates in their own borrowing as a result of spillover from sovereigns.

ECB surveys on the difficulty of obtaining financing for small and medium enterprises provide some evidence of financial fragmentation. The percent of surveyed firms identifying access to finance as a severely pressing problem in April 2012–April 2013 stood at an average of 65 percent in Greece and about 52 to 55 percent in Ireland, Spain, Italy, and Portugal, but only 40 percent in France, 33 percent in Belgium, and 28 percent in Germany (ECB 2013a, 6).[33]

ECB data on net loan flows from financial monetary institutions to nonfinancial corporations similarly suggest substantial financial fragmentation, as shown in figure 3.6. In 2005–07 lending was extremely high in Spain and Ireland, but otherwise in a broadly similar range as a percent of GDP for France, Italy, Portugal, and Greece. During the Great Recession of 2008–09, net lending was low for all of the seven economies shown. Then during the

---

33. High "pressingness," 7 to 10 on a scale of 1 (not at all) to 10 (extremely pressing).

Figure 3.6   Net loan flows from monetary financial institutions to nonfinancial corporations, euro area periphery, Germany, and France, 2005–13

percent of GDP

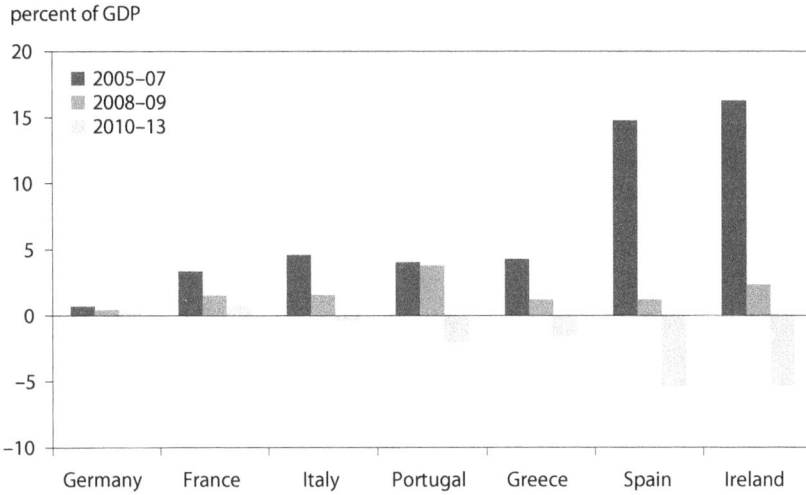

Source: ECB (2014c).

sovereign credit crisis in 2010–13 average net lending turned substantially negative in the five periphery economies but remained slightly positive in Germany and France.[34]

Overall, taken together the data on interest rates, net lending, and perceived difficulty of access to finance provide significant support for the diagnosis that financial fragmentation has been a serious side effect of the euro area debt crisis. Some would argue that this fragmentation should have been prevented by the ECB. However, it is highly unlikely that a generalized stance of greater monetary ease (including country-neutral quantitative easing) could have avoided the widening of sovereign risk spreads during the course of the crisis. Yet the strong (especially German) aversion to "monetary financing" and the time lag required to set up firewalls (the European Financial Stability Facility and the ESM) for conditional lending suggest that short-circuiting the crisis early on through forceful OMT would not have been a realistic option. Even going forward and with the help of a strong OMT capacity, complete financial integration defined as identical private sector borrowing conditions seems

---

34. The low levels of net lending in Germany at less than 1 percent of GDP even in 2005–07 suggest much greater reliance on internal funds and on funding from "other financial institutions" not taking deposits (such as financial subsidiaries issuing debt securities) than in the rest of the euro area; see ECB (2013b, 26). Note further that the negative net bank flows elsewhere in the periphery were at least partly offset by net bond issuance by corporations. Thus, in the year ending January 2013, bank credit outstanding in Spain fell by €80 billion but net bond issuance amounted to about €30 billion (IMF 2013b, 7). The pattern was similar though less pronounced in Italy.

likely to remain an elusive ideal in the absence of debt mutualization and/or political union that eliminates differential sovereign credit risk.

How Weak Are Euro Area Banks?

Going forward, a central question is whether existing bank weakness in the euro area is likely to impose major further increases in public debt burdens of debt-stressed periphery economies. Meaningful estimates of prospective additional public debt resulting from bank cleanups are difficult to assemble. The OECD (2012, 51) has suggested that a metric for bank recapitalization needs might be a target leverage ratio that ensures core tier 1 capital of 5 percent of total assets, rather than relying on the usual risk-weighted capital ratios (because of doubts about the reliability of risk weights). It found that prior to the recapitalization with official support at the end of 2012, banks in Greece would have needed to raise additional capital equal to 7.8 percent of GDP to reach this leverage ratio. The gap was smaller at 3.3 percent of GDP in Ireland and 1.8 percent in Spain, and only 0.15 percent in Italy and zero in Portugal. Ironically, the stronger northern economies were identified as having larger capital gaps than any of the debt-stressed periphery countries except Greece, with gaps ranging from 5 to 7.5 percent in Finland, the Netherlands, Germany, Belgium, and France.

A subsequent OECD study by Dirk Schoenmaker and Toon Peek (2014, 22–23) arrived at the following estimates of capital shortfalls to reach a 5 percent target for market value of equity relative to assets as of November 2013: Italy, 2.4 percent of GDP; Portugal, 3.5 percent of GDP; and Spain, 0.3 percent of GDP. In still another estimate applying a more stringent target of 7 percent for the ratio of equity to assets, Viral Acharya and Sascha Steffen (2014, 11) arrived at the following estimated capital shortfalls: Ireland, 1.0 percent of GDP; Italy, 0.6 percent; Portugal, 2.5 percent; and Spain, 2.6 percent of GDP.

If one considered these estimates as limits of prospective incremental sovereign debt resulting from bank recapitalizations, the implication would be that there is little remaining problem running from banks to sovereigns, because the gaps for the debt-stressed economies are too small to change public solvency by much. For example, in Ireland, the ratio of public debt to GDP stood at 117 percent at the end of 2012 (IMF 2013g). If only 3 percent of GDP bank recapitalization were required, and even if the entire additional amount were to come from public funding, the consequence would be only a minor change in the debt ratio. As for the case of Greece, the OECD estimate did not take account of the recapitalization finance provided by the end-2012 official support package (discussed in chapter 7), which substantially exceeded the OECD's 7.8 percent of GDP estimate of the capital gap. Of course, the OECD estimates may understate. Thus, the 1.8 percent of GDP identified for Spain would be only about €18 billion, yet as noted above, Spain has already received about €40 billion in ESM support for bank recapitalization subsequent to the OECD estimates.

An alternative set of estimates developed in appendix 3A casts even more doubt on the need for large additional bank recapitalization, especially after taking account of some €100 billion in loan writedowns taken by Spanish banks in 2012. At the height of the global financial crisis, the IMF periodically published estimates of likely bank losses.[35] These estimates and the method used to prepare them provide the basis in the appendix for considering potential scope for debt that could be imposed on sovereigns going forward because of bank recapitalization needs. The April 2010 IMF report (2010a, 12) estimates serve as a point of departure, because they reflect the situation before the euro area sovereign debt crisis began in earnest. In those estimates, the Fund calculated euro area bank losses at €665 billion. Of this total, it estimated that Germany accounted for €65 billion (mainly in Landesbanken and savings banks) and Spain €63 billion (IMF 2010a, 16–17). If the remaining €537 billion are allocated by country in proportion to bank assets, the estimated writedowns (realized and pending) at the beginning of 2010 amounted to €11.6 billion for banks in Greece, €31.1 billion for those in Ireland, €82.7 billion for Italy, and €14.2 billion for Portugal.[36] The IMF report in October 2010 (IMF 2010b, 13) indicated that three-fourths of the euro area bank losses for 2007–10 had already been realized (recognized in banks' accounts) by June 2010.

To arrive at these estimates, the IMF estimated a statistical model of bank provisions as a function of GDP growth and the unemployment rate. Appendix 3A applies this model to estimate similar bank writedowns that would have been expected to arise in 2011–13. The estimates find surprisingly that writedowns already taken *exceed* those that would be predicted using the IMF-based model. Large loan loss provisions and (especially) writedowns for loan impairment were taken in Greece and Italy in 2011 and in Spain in 2012. For the three-year period 2011–13, cumulative actual writedowns substantially exceeded the model predictions, leaving no room for hidden losses.

If the largest of the OECD (2012), Schoenmaker-Peek (2014), or Acharya-Steffen (2014) estimates are instead used as a more conservative basis, the resulting recapitalization needs are 3.3 percent of GDP in Ireland, 2.4 percent in Italy, 3.5 percent in Portugal, and 2.6 percent in Spain. Considering that some or most of this recapitalization would come from private sources, and considering that baseline public debt ratios are in the range of 90 to 130 percent of GDP, the incremental impact on public debt from bank recapitalization needs in the four periphery economies would be relatively small.

---

35. Thus, in October 2009 the Fund estimated that bank losses during 2007–10 would amount to $1.02 trillion in the United States and $814 billion in the euro area, or 9.1 percent of end-2007 assets for US banks and 2.3 percent for euro area banks (Cline 2010b, 241).

36. Shares in total euro area bank assets in June 2012 stood at 1.3 percent for Greece, 3.5 percent for Ireland, 9.3 percent for Italy, 1.6 percent for Portugal, 26.7 percent for Germany, and 13 percent for Spain (ECB 2014a).

Role of the Banking Union

In June 2012, the European Council launched the movement of the euro area toward banking union. In December 2012, it adopted a three-step process to achieve this goal (Véron and Wolff 2013). The first step is the concentration of supervision and regulation in an SSM, to be the responsibility of the ECB. The second step is the adoption of legislation set forth in two proposals of the European Commission: the Bank Recovery and Resolution Directive (of June 2012) and the Deposit Guarantee Schemes (DGS) Directive (of July 2010). The third step is the creation of a Single Resolution Mechanism once the BRR and DGS legislation is in place. Nicolas Véron and Guntram Wolff (2013) identify the need for a fourth step: to go beyond the Single Resolution Mechanism in the areas of insolvency, resolution, and deposit insurance.

An IMF policy study highlighted three objectives of banking union: reducing the fragmentation of financial markets, stemming deposit flight, and weakening the "vicious loop of rising sovereign and bank borrowing costs" (Goyal et al. 2013). It recognized that the December 2012 agreement on the SSM centered at the ECB was an important step, but argued that without common resolution and safety nets, an SSM would do little to weaken sovereign-bank vicious-circle links. The authors called for early recapitalization of "frail domestically systemic banks" by shareholders, creditors, the sovereign, and the ESM, and the winding down of frail nonsystemic banks (Goyal et al. 2013, 4).

In October 2013, the European Union adopted the SSM in a regulation that gave the ECB the power of supervisory review and authority to impose "additional own funds requirements" (EU 2013, 1287/75-76). National authorities were to retain responsibility only for "less significant" institutions with assets smaller than €30 billion and less than 20 percent of national GDP, placing some 130 large banks under direct supervision by the ECB. The SSM entered into effect in November 2013.

The status of direct recapitalization had advanced significantly in June 2013 with a Eurogroup decision on the framework for ESM recapitalization of banks, discussed below. However, the time horizon for implementation was likely to be late 2014 or 2015.

On bank resolution, in July 2013 the European Commission had proposed a Single Resolution Mechanism for restructuring and bailing out failing banks, run by Commission and ECB appointees, with a corresponding Single Resolution Mechanism Fund based on contributions from the banking sector.[37] In December 2013 the trilogue (representatives of the European Parliament, European Commission, and European Council) agreed on key features of the Bank Resolution and Recovery Directive (EC 2013a). Costs of bank failures are to be allocated first to bank shareholders and credi-

---

37. European Commission, "Commission Proposes Single Resolution Mechanism for the Banking Union," press release IP/13/674, July 10, 2013.

tors. In addition there is to be backing from resolution funds sourced from the banking sector itself, in amounts to accumulate over 10 years to reach 1 percent of total assets. All deposits of €100,000 or less would be exempt from resolution costs. Larger depositors would have seniority over all secured creditors.[38] The mechanism is to take force at the beginning of 2016. The agreement recognized that although the objective of the regime was to "place the responsibility of losses on private investors in banks and the banking sector as a whole," there would nonetheless be a need for "flexibility to depart from this principle in case of systemic crises" (p. 2).

Véron (2013) seeks to sharpen the policy sequence that will be needed to arrive at banking union. He emphasizes the importance and complexity of the transfer of supervisory authority for most of Europe's banking system to the ECB, probably by the second half of 2014. This transfer will require a prior comprehensive assessment of bank balance sheets and correspondingly the development of restructuring plans for banks found to be undercapitalized.[39] In the longer term, European treaties will need to be changed to strengthen the legal basis for the banking union.

The ESM and Bank Recapitalization

In June 2013, Eurogroup leaders agreed on the nature of and scope for bank recapitalization directly from the ESM (Eurogroup 2013a, 2013b). They determined that a limit of €60 billion out of the ESM's total resources of €500 billion would be placed on direct bank recapitalization. A subsidiary of the ESM was to be established for this purpose. It would provide capital to banks in the form of common equity shares, and would exercise commensurate influence on management of an institution being recapitalized. Bail-in burden sharing from existing shareholders and creditors would be expected. National governments would be responsible for any initial recapitalization amounts needed to bring the bank to the Basel III capital requirement of 4.5 percent of risk-weighted assets. National governments would additionally be expected to provide capital amounting to 20 percent of capital provided by the ESM subsidiary. The agreement left open the possibility of retroactive application of the instrument on a case-by-case basis, by implication primarily for Ireland and Spain. The bank recapitalization instrument would not be available until

---

38. In earlier discussions, EU finance ministers had further agreed that a minimum bail-in of 8 percent of total liabilities would be required before resolution funds could be used. Above that minimum, countries would have the option to use government resources to recapitalize a bank while protecting other creditors, but with a ceiling of 5 percent of the bank's liabilities for such support and subject to European Commission approval. See Alex Barker, "EU Reaches Deal on Failed Banks," *Financial Times*, June 27, 2013.

39. In May 2013, the European Banking Authority indicated that it would delay its bank stress tests originally planned for 2013, deferring to the ECB to make its own asset quality review prior to its assumption of supervisory authority. Ben Moshinsky, "EU Bank Stress Tests Delay Makes Way for ECB Supervisor," Bloomberg, May 16, 2013.

the Bank Recovery and Resolution Directive is agreed with the European Parliament and the SSM is in place.

In announcing the decision, Eurogroup president Jeroen Dijsselbloem stated that the new instrument would "help remove the risk of contagion from the financial sector to the sovereign, thus weakening the vicious circle between banks and sovereigns as called for by the Euro Summit last year" (Eurogroup 2013a). The terms for eligibility were strict in principle, requiring that "the requesting ESM Member is unable to provide financial assistance to the institutions in full without very adverse effects on its own fiscal sustainability... [and] that other alternatives would have the effect of endangering the continuous market access of the requesting ESM Member and consequently require financing of the sovereign needs via the ESM." To receive support an institution would have to have "a systemic relevance or [pose] a serious threat to the financial stability of the euro area as a whole or the requesting ESM Member" (Eurogroup 2013b).

The initiative appears to seek potential leverage through mobilizing "external and private capital investment alongside the ESM." In the absence of such parallel capital injection, however, the limit of €60 billion means that the instrument will be limited, representing for example only about one-tenth the magnitude of the US Troubled Asset Relief Program (TARP) set up in the 2009 financial crisis.

Gauging the Progress toward Banking Union

By early 2014 the outlines of banking union in practice were as follows. First, the ECB was on track to establish single supervision of the large banks in the euro area (about 130 banks with balance sheets exceeding €30 billion, comprising about 85 percent of the European banking sector (Ubide 2013, 3). The ECB would assume its new supervisory responsibilities within the SSM by late 2014 following the ECB's asset quality review (and a stress test by the European Banking Authority). Second, ultimate funding responsibility for failed banks remains largely at the national level for the next few years. Third, there is a relatively austere stance requiring bail-ins of creditors in the effort to avoid socialization of bank losses. Fourth and related, the ESM recapitalization mechanism is small and heavily constrained.

Ángel Ubide (2013) judges that although there has been progress, the prospective state of banking union is dangerous because it involves only a minimal euro area backstop and forces national bail-ins of creditors. He urges in particular that resolution funds of banks supervised by the ECB be consolidated with the direct recapitalization instrument at the ESM. He also urges that where a recapitalization is precautionary (as opposed to a default workout), required contributions be limited to junior and hybrid instruments. His fear is that otherwise there will be a counterproductive flight by private creditors. More generally he judges the banking union to be a poor substitute for eurobonds as the mechanism to address the sovereign debt crisis.

If the calculations of appendix 3A are anywhere near correct, nonetheless, the proximate strains on what may be seen as a fledgling and still inadequate banking union may be small. The key question would then be whether the resulting relief from banking crisis would be used fruitfully as providing the time needed for institutional change, or instead lead to a stalling out of reform because of the easing in crisis pressures.

Appendix 3A
Estimating Bank Recapitalization Needs

In 2009, the IMF (2009, 56) reported a simple statistical model relating euro area bank losses to macroeconomic conditions. Its estimating equation was:

$$P_t = 0.161 - 0.074g_t + 0.062u_t \qquad (3A.1)$$

where P = provisions and writedowns as percent of assets, g = GDP growth (percent), and u = unemployment rate (percent). In the spring of 2010 the Fund downscaled its loss estimates to about four-fifths the amounts indicated by this equation (from a total of $810 billion to $665 billion; IMF 2010a, 12). The corresponding adjusted equation by implication would be:

$$P_t = 0.132 - 0.06g_t + 0.051u_t \qquad (3A.2)$$

The adjusted writedown equation (short for provisions and writedowns) can be applied to the five debt-stressed periphery economies during the period 2011–13 to estimate the likely further losses experienced in the key period for the euro area debt crisis. These expected losses can then be compared against the amounts that banks in these countries actually set aside in provisions or wrote down as losses. If there are excesses of expected losses over reported losses, the difference can be interpreted as hidden losses that will eventually require recapitalization.

Table 3A.1 reports the results of this exercise. The first panel reports the application of equation (3A.2) to the growth and unemployment rates in 2011–15 (with 2013 through 2015 the forecasts in IMF 2013g). The second panel translates these loss rates into absolute amounts by applying the rates to consolidated bank assets outstanding at the end of the previous year. The third panel then shows the amounts actually written down or set aside as provisions by domestic banks during 2011 through 2013 (with the 2013 rate estimated as twice the actual amount for the first half). The fourth panel then reports the excess, if any, of the equation-estimated losses and the bank-reported losses, for each year in question.

It turns out that in all five economies the writedowns during 2011–13 exceeded equation-predicted levels needed. The writedowns were especially large in 2011 in Greece and Italy and in 2012 in Spain (where more than €100 billion was written off or set aside in provisions in 2012 alone). The surprising finding of this exercise, then, is that based on a previous IMF model of loan losses in relationship to GDP growth and unemployment, the domestic banks of the five periphery countries have no unaccounted losses at all and therefore should not pose a source of contingent liability that will add to the burden of public debt. As discussed in the main text, the OECD arrives at alternative estimates showing capital shortfalls, but even those estimates are small relative to existing sovereign debt.

Table 3A.1   Hidden bank losses implied by predicted versus reported writedowns, euro area periphery, 2011–13

Country	2011	2012	2013	2011–13 sum
A. Projected writedown rates (percent)				
Greece	1.19	1.43	1.44	—
Ireland	0.61	0.71	0.65	—
Italy	0.44	0.67	0.72	—
Portugal	0.70	0.92	0.92	—
Spain	1.01	1.23	1.29	—
B. Implied writedown amounts (billions of euros)				
Greece	5.8	6.0	6.1	—
Ireland	3.3	3.3	2.8	—
Italy	13.7	20.9	22.8	—
Portugal	3.6	4.5	4.3	—
Spain	43.1	54.3	56.8	—
C. Actual provisions and writedowns (billions of euros)				
Greece: Provisions	0.51	0.43	0.02	—
Impairments	43.59	10.17	7.56	—
Total	44.10	10.60	7.58	—
Ireland: Provisions	−0.42	0.09	0.02	—
Impairments	14.67	6.56	3.90	—
Total	14.25	6.65	3.92	—
Italy: Provisions	1.60	1.14	0.88	—
Impairments	49.38	29.63	21.20	—
Total	50.98	30.77	22.08	—
Portugal: Provisions	0.19	0.20	0.38	—
Impairments	5.73	5.91	4.94	—
Total	5.92	6.11	5.32	—
Spain: Provisions	4.09	7.89	4.76	—
Impairments	39.80	94.79	34.44	—
Total	43.89	102.68	39.20	—
D. Implied hidden losses (billions of euros)				
Greece	−38.3	−4.6	−1.5	−44.4
Ireland	−10.9	−3.3	−1.1	−15.3
Italy	−37.3	−9.9	0.7	−46.5
Portugal	−2.4	−1.6	−1.0	−5.0
Spain	−0.8	−48.4	17.6	−31.6

(continues on next page)

Table 3A.1   Hidden bank losses implied by predicted versus reported writedowns, euro area periphery, 2011–13 *(continued)*

Country	2011	2012	2013	2011–13 sum
Memorandum: Bank assets, end of prior year (billions of euros)				
Greece	394.7	343.0	346.0	—
Ireland	447.5	381.3	351.6	—
Italy	2,535.6	2,547.3	2,602.7	—
Portugal	414.1	398.9	384.5	—
Spain	3,498.4	3,604.5	3,594.9	—

Sources: ECB (2014a); author's calculations.

4

External Adjustment and Breakup Costs

Fiscal imbalances (especially in Greece) and banking crises (especially in Ireland) contributed to the sovereign debt crisis in the euro area periphery. Large external current account deficits (except in Italy) did so as well, by creating vulnerability to a cutoff in external financing once a break in confidence in sovereign creditworthiness had occurred. This chapter examines the role of the external imbalances both in causing the crisis and in influencing its resolution going forward. One of the prominent constraints in correcting the imbalances is the inability to depreciate the exchange rate because of membership in the single currency. This chapter thus concludes with a review of the likely costs involved if the euro were to break up.

The evidence suggests that large current account deficits (except in Italy) prior to the crisis contributed to sovereign risk by imposing a financing squeeze once foreign capital flows reversed. However, by 2012–13 these deficits had been largely eliminated, and not solely through contraction of imports because of recession but also from rising exports. Going forward, large additional increases in current account balances do not seem necessary to reestablish sovereign creditworthiness; nor would even heroic surpluses make much difference in sovereign risk spreads based on their limited observed relationships to the net international investment positions. The analysis also places greater emphasis on competitiveness on a trade-weighted basis including with the rest of the world, whereas the more usual analysis focuses more narrowly on the past loss of competitiveness of the periphery vis-à-vis Germany. With respect to a euro area breakup, a review of the various quantitative studies tends to support the mainstream view that the consequences could be extremely costly, justifying the case for doing "whatever it takes" to maintain the euro.

Current Account Deficit, Sudden Stop, and Sovereign Liquidity Squeeze

Before either the Great Recession or the euro area debt crisis, current account deficits reached relatively high levels in four of the five periphery economies. In 2007–08, the current account deficit averaged 14.8 percent of GDP in Greece, 11.4 percent in Portugal, 9.8 percent in Spain, and 5.5 percent in Ireland. The deficit was smaller in Italy, an average of 2.1 percent of GDP (IMF 2013n). Private capital inflows were the counterpart of the current account deficit. A substantial portion of these inflows helped finance government deficits, especially in Greece. Foreign capital has the wrong "home bias" from the standpoint of a borrowing government. Several of the periphery economies were thus vulnerable to a sudden-stop liquidity squeeze once the euro area sovereign debt crisis caused a collapse in confidence. As noted in chapter 3, in the case of Greece, the outflows of foreign bank claims on the government from end-2009 to the third quarter of 2011 (before the private sector involvement [PSI] haircut) amounted to 62 percent of the short- and long-term government debt coming due in 2010–11, exerting great pressure on the government to obtain alternative financing.

Figures 4.1a and 4.1b are suggestive of the dual influences of the precrisis external imbalance on the one hand and the level of public debt on the other in causing the sovereign debt crisis in the periphery. The severity of the debt crisis is measured on the vertical axis by the level of the sovereign risk spread on 10-year bonds (above the German bund) on average in 2012, the year of the most severe crisis. As causal factors, the horizontal axis shows the average current account balance as a percent of GDP in 2007–08, in figure 4.1a, and the ratio of gross public debt to GDP in 2012, in figure 4.1b. For Greece, the debt ratio is for 2011, prior to the PSI haircut. Both panels suggest a meaningful influence of each of the respective causal variables on the severity of the sovereign debt distress.

As shown in figure 4.1a, all of the countries that reached distressed levels of sovereign spreads had sizable current account deficits in 2007–08 (except Italy), whereas of the 11 large euro area economies, none of those with current account surpluses entered into sovereign debt stress. In figure 4.1b, it is also evident that based on public debt alone, France and Belgium might have been expected to encounter greater difficulty than Spain, but they did not, so the additional explanatory role of the external deficit is needed.

A simple regression using the data in the figures yields the following results (with t-statistics in parentheses):

$$s = -4.6 - 0.33\ CA + 0.077\ D;\ \text{adj.}\ R^2 = 0.85 \qquad (4.1)$$
$$(-1.7)\ (-2.5)\quad\ (2.6)$$

where s is the sovereign risk spread in percentage points above the 10-year

Figure 4.1a   Sovereign risk spreads, 2012, and current account balance, 2007–08

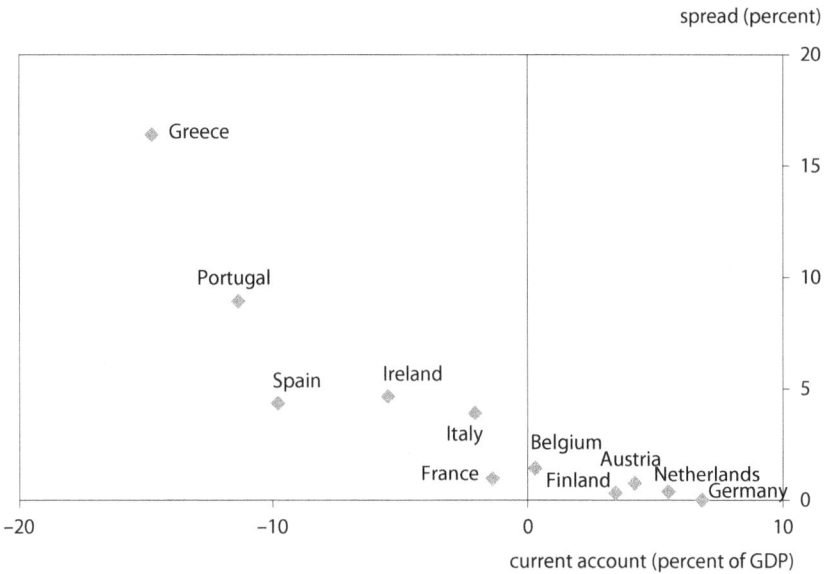

Note: For Greece, spreads are as of 2011.

Source: Datastream; IMF (2013n).

German bund, *CA* is the current account balance as a percent of GDP (2007–08), and *D* is gross public debt as a percent of GDP (2012 or, for Greece, 2011). Both the current account and debt variables are statistically significant at the 5 percent level. An additional percentage point of GDP in the current account deficit boosts the risk spread by 33 basis points. An additional 10 percent of GDP in public debt boosts the spread by 77 basis points. In short, the evidence seems relatively strong that both the potential vulnerability to a sudden stop associated with a large precrisis current account deficit and the relative level of public indebtedness played a role in the differential severity of the sovereign debt crisis in the euro area.[1]

Despite the influence of the precrises external deficits, there are good reasons for judging that the impact of the "sudden stop" of foreign capital inflows was not as predominant as in past emerging-market debt crises. In the context of the euro area, a key component of the sudden-stop shock is missing. The cutoff of external capital from the private market does not

---

1. David Greenlaw et al. (2013, 20) also find that for 20 advanced economies in 2001–11, the current account deficit mattered for the sovereign borrowing rate, with a nonlinear interaction with the debt-to-GDP ratio. At a debt ratio of 100 percent of GDP, their corresponding estimate is that in this period an extra percentage point of GDP in the current account deficit boosted the risk spread by 64 basis points, about twice as much as the estimate here.

Figure 4.1b Sovereign risk spreads and gross public debt, 2012

spread (percent)

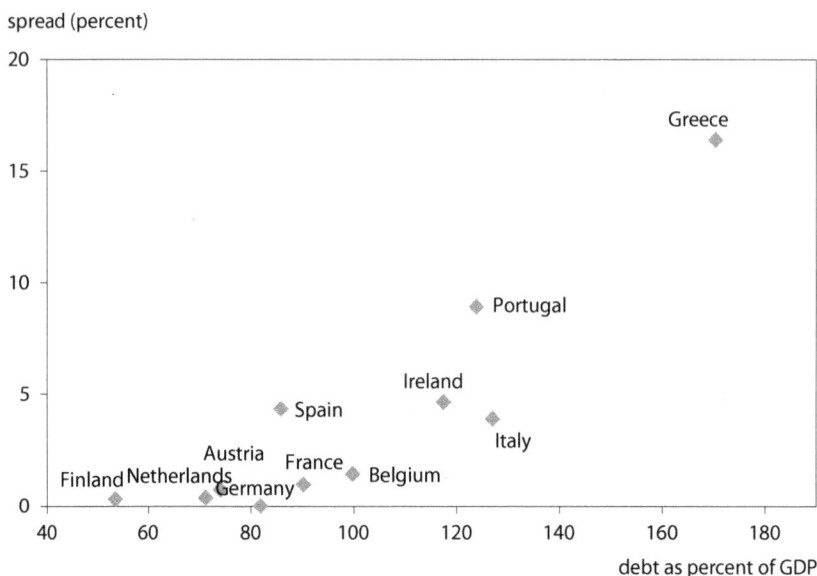

Note: For Greece, spreads are as of 2011.

Source: Datastream; IMF (2013n).

trigger a currency depreciation so long as the economy remains in the euro. As a consequence, the adverse balance sheet effect that features prominently in emerging-market sudden stops, whereby debt (including of the government) is denominated in foreign currency and suddenly becomes much more expensive in domestic currency, is missing. Moreover, the monetary arrangements within the euro area provide automatic sources of financing for the current account deficit—if not to the government directly—through "Target2" liabilities in the bank clearance system and through European Central Bank (ECB) financing of country banking systems. So the "stop" associated with the cessation of private foreign capital inflows has been neither as sudden nor as severe as, for example, those in the East Asian currency crises of the late 1990s, or the Argentine default at the end of 2001. The parallel implication is that the crisis either was not as severe (which has broadly been the case except for Greece) or that there was a greater role of vulnerability of government credit risk (as suggested by contrasting the periphery experience with that of Korea in 1998, where government debt was never in doubt).

Role of Current Account Adjustment in Resolving the Crisis

Several authors emphasize the presence of large external current account deficits in euro area periphery economies as having been a major factor in causing their sovereign debt crises (for example, Guerrieri 2012, Merler and Pisani-Ferry

2012b, Sinn and Valentinyi 2013, Gros 2013). Some correspondingly see major reversals of intra-euro-area competitiveness and current account imbalances as essential to resolution of the crisis. Paolo Guerrieri (2012, 10) provides a sharp articulation of this point of view:

> A smooth adjustment of the intra–euro area divergences in competitiveness and macroeconomic imbalances is key to the solution of the Eurozone crisis… increases in savings and exports in Eurozone deficit countries need to be offset by equal increases in spending and imports in surplus ones. Peripheral Europe cannot possibly succeed in reducing its borrowing substantially unless surplus countries such as Germany pursue policies that allow their surpluses to contract.

Even though the financing squeeze provoked by a sudden stop for countries with large current account deficits contributed to the sovereign debt crisis, the analysis below will suggest that going forward a sharp further improvement in the current account adjustment beyond that already achieved by the periphery is not needed for debt sustainability. The basic reason is that once confidence can be reestablished by the overall adjustment program, especially including progress toward primary fiscal surplus targets, government borrowing conditions should normalize and not face further pressure from capital flight of foreign lenders. Moreover, the large current account deficits of the periphery economies have already disappeared, so the force of the concern about external imbalances going forward must depend on a diagnosis of whether these corrections are illusory and transitory and stem solely from recession and its curbing of import demand, or whether instead more sustainable adjustment is on track. Analyses such as that by Guerrieri (2012) also would appear to attribute too much weight to the north-south imbalances and intra-euro-area real effective exchange rates and too little weight to the overall (global) balances and real effective exchange rates of the periphery in identifying corrective policies.

Going forward, the main role of the external imbalance would seem instead to be in its influence on domestic growth, and through growth, on the sustainability of debt. The principal problem is that in the single currency, there is no scope for currency depreciation as a means of carrying out growth-oriented adjustment based on expansion of exports and substitution of imports. Domestic demand previously financed by private capital inflow, particularly in the nontradable sector (especially housing construction), is thus difficult to replace with new demand from an increase in net exports. So far the effort to arrive at a workable substitute for exchange rate flexibility has focused on "internal devaluation," through the curbing of domestic labor costs and such mechanisms as "fiscal devaluation," whereby (for example) labor taxes are replaced by the value-added tax (VAT) in an effort to reduce domestic unit labor costs.

It turns out that there has been considerable adjustment in the external imbalances already, despite the straitjacket of the single currency. This adjustment has included a sizable contribution from export gains, rather than stemming solely from compression of import demand as a consequence of falling incomes. In broad terms, it would appear that the obstacles to sovereign debt recovery posed by external imbalances are not insurmountable, and are less severe than some analysts have suggested.

Current Account Balances and Trade Performance

Figure 4.2 shows the course of current account balances for the five debt-stressed economies as well as France and Germany, from the mid-1990s prior to the single currency through 2012, and International Monetary Fund (IMF) estimates for 2013. The advent of the single currency was indeed associated with a large swing into current account deficit in Greece, Portugal, Spain, and to a lesser degree Ireland. The debt crisis has also been associated with a sudden stop in the sense that there has been a sharp reduction in these current account deficits and the foreign capital inflows that financed them. Thus, the deficit in Greece reached 14.9 percent of GDP in 2008, but fell to 2.9 percent in 2012 and narrowed to 0.3 percent in 2013. The path for Portugal was similar, with the deficit reaching 12.6 percent of GDP in 2008 but narrowing to 1.5 percent in 2012 and a surplus of 0.1 percent of GDP in 2013. Much of the discussion of the role of external imbalances does not seem to have caught up with the faster than expected elimination of the deficits despite the lack of exchange rate flexibility.[2]

Nor is the recent improvement in current accounts solely attributable to a reduction of imports. Adjustment only on the import side would be a sign of deterioration rather than improvement because it would reflect falling demand as economies entered recession. For the five debt-stressed economies shown in figure 4.3 (all except France and Germany), aggregate real exports of goods and services (deflating by GDP deflators) rose by 8.4 percent from 2006–08 (before the Great Recession) to 2011–13. Real exports rose the most in Ireland (23.6 percent), Spain (17.4 percent), and Portugal (14.6 percent).

Real imports also rose over this period for Ireland (by 9.7 percent). However, for the five periphery economies in the aggregate, real imports declined by 6.5 percent. This decline was almost the same as their combined decline in real GDP, amounting to 5.8 percent (2006–08 to 2011–13; IMF 2013n). The overall picture is thus that about half of the external adjustment was accomplished in a positive fashion—on the export side—whereas the other half was the consequence of the negative influence of recession in compressing imports.[3]

---

2. An exception is Raphael Auer (2013, 1), who notes that rapid improvement in the current account deficits of Greece, Italy, Spain, and Portugal mean that "a key requirement for a return to a post-crisis Eurozone is thus on its way to being met."

3. Average annual aggregate real exports of goods and services for the five economies (deflating by GDP deflators) rose from €903 billion to €978 billion from 2006–08 to 2011–13, whereas aggregate real imports fell from €988 billion to €925 billion.

Figure 4.2   Current account balances for euro area periphery, Germany, and France, 1994–2013

percent of GDP

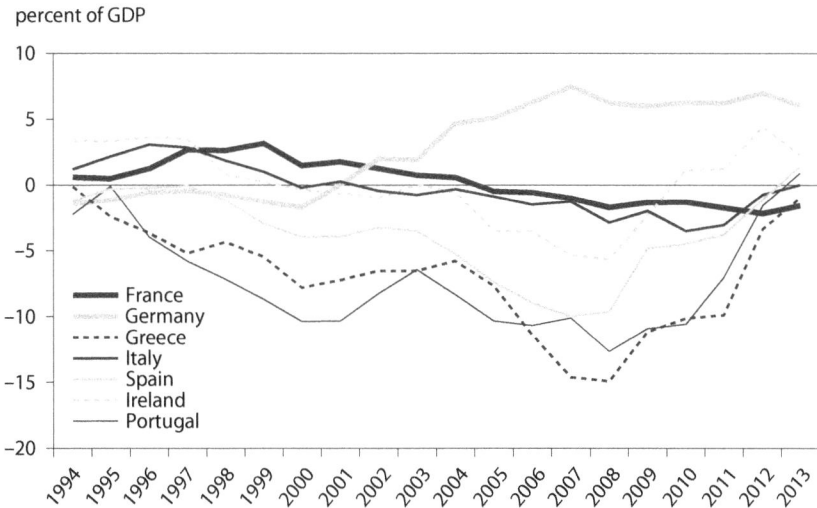

Source: IMF (2013n).

Once again Greece proved to be the exception to the general pattern. From 2006–08 to 2011–13, real exports of goods and services in Greece fell by 6.7 percent instead of rising. Real imports fell by even more: by 30.2 percent. Real GDP fell by 18.4 percent from 2006–08 to 2011–13. So far, then, the external adjustment in Greece does indeed conform to the diagnosis of recession-based import compression rather than export expansion. It is only a slight consolation that despite falling, exports have held up much better than the economy as a whole.

Real Exchange Rates

The stylized facts about external imbalances within the euro area describe a process in which the entry of the single currency was accompanied by price increases in the periphery that caused it to experience a severe loss of competitiveness relative to the north and Germany in particular. Figure 4.4 presents what had become a popular graphic in euro area policy circles circa 2011 (see, for example, Wolff 2012, 239), showing a serious rise in unit labor costs, relative to the euro area 15-country average, for the periphery, and a major decline in relative unit labor costs for Germany. The process of adjustment has involved significant real depreciation in the periphery economies subsequent to the crisis, however. An update of this chart through 2013 shows substantial correction in this divergence. Thus, whereas by 2008 the ratio of the individual country index to the index for Germany stood at 153 percent for Ireland, 139 for Spain, 132 for

Figure 4.3 Trade performance of euro area periphery, Germany, and France, 1999–2013

a. Exports (goods and services)

index of real euro values, 2005 = 100

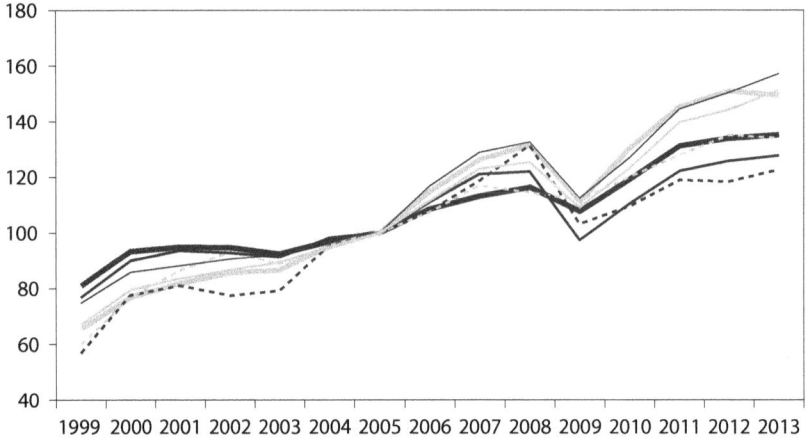

b. Imports (goods and services)

index of real euro values, 2005 = 100

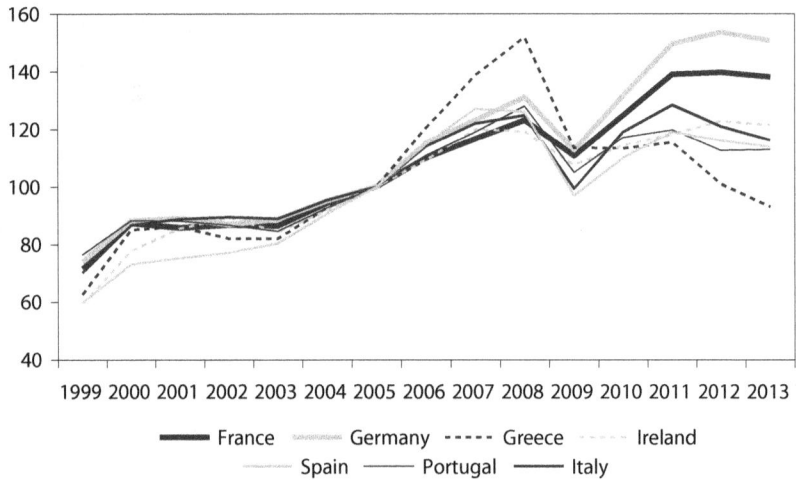

France   Germany   Greece   Ireland   Spain   Portugal   Italy

Source: IMF (2014).

Italy, 129 for Portugal, and 127 for Greece, by 2013 the ratios had fallen to 121 for Ireland, 119 for Spain, 117 for Portugal, and only 104 for Greece—although the ratio remained almost unchanged at 131 percent for Italy.[4]

---

4. These ratios can be seen in figure 4.4 by comparing each country line to the line for Germany.

Figure 4.4 Real effective exchange rate: Unit labor costs (total economy) relative to euro area 15-country average (European Commission data), 1999–2013

index, 1999 = 100

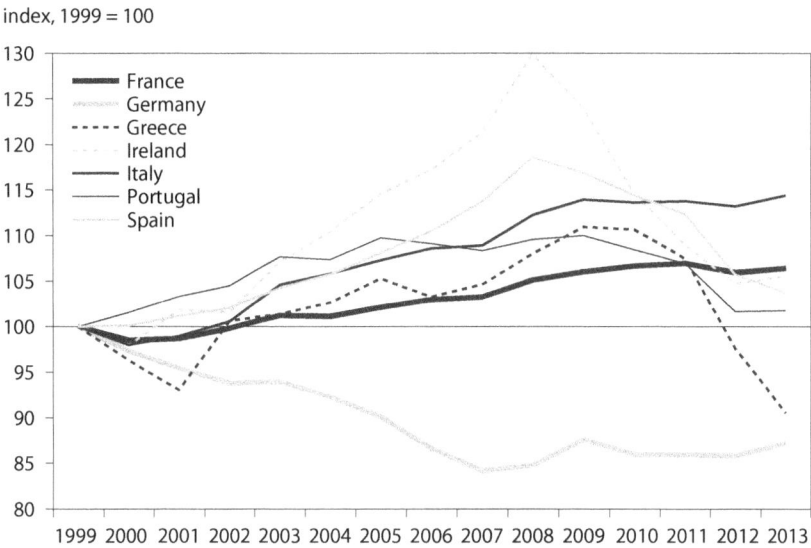

Source: European Commission (EC 2014).

If consumer prices are used as the deflator, and if the periphery countries are compared with a broader group of "northern" euro area countries, the picture is similar if less extreme in the divergence phase, but also somewhat less encouraging in the most recent trends. Figure 4.5 consolidates the consumer price indices (CPIs) of six northern economies (Austria, Belgium, Finland, France, Germany, and the Netherlands) into a single index, weighting by GDP in 2005. The figure shows the ratio of the consumer price index of each of the peripheral economies to this consolidated northern price index, with 2005 = 100. This intra-euro-area comparison shows less acute deterioration of competitiveness than the well-known unit labor cost figure against Germany (figure 4.4). For example, from 1999 to 2008 the unit labor cost for Spain rises by 43 percent relative to that of Germany, but the consumer price index for Spain rose by only 13 percent relative to the consumer prices of the broad "north" of the euro area. However, figure 4.5 also strongly suggests that a rollback in loss of competitiveness has only happened in earnest in Ireland. By 2013 the relative price was about 2 percent higher than it had been in 2008 for Greece, Italy, and Spain, and almost unchanged in Portugal.

Some decline in the real exchange rate of the euro overall against world trading partners has partly provided competitive relief even for the periphery economies other than Ireland, however. Figures 4.6 and 4.7 show broader real effective exchange rate (REER) indices, rather than indices just against euro

Figure 4.5   Ratio of periphery economies' CPIs to weighted-average northern euro area CPI

index, 2005 = 100

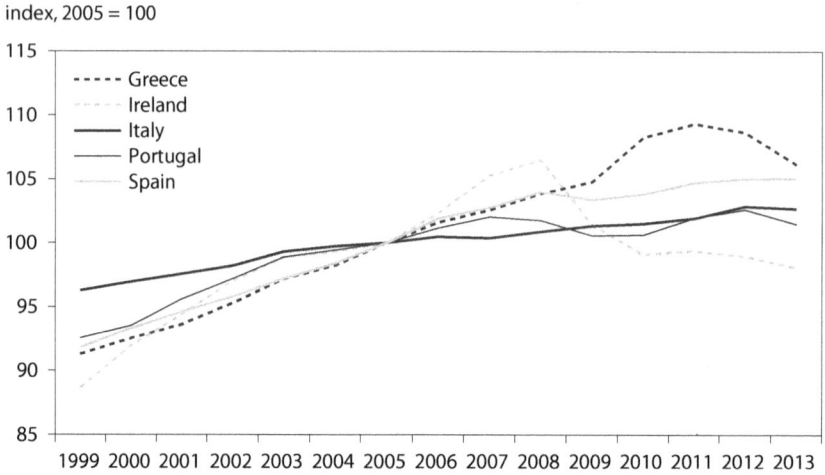

CPI = consumer price index

Note: The northern euro area economies are Austria, Belgium, Finland, France, Germany, and the Netherlands.

Source: IMF (2013d).

area partners.[5] The unit labor cost series used by the IMF to arrive at the REERs of figure 4.6 show even more dramatic cost adjustments for Ireland than the intra-euro-area REERs (figure 4.4). The falling relative labor costs in Ireland likely reflect the government's public sector wage cuts adopted in 2010–11 to deal with the crisis.[6] For Italy, the IMF unit labor cost series show a more pronounced long-term real appreciation than is apparent in the intra-euro-area REERs of figure 4.4.

The alternative REER series based on consumer prices (Bank for International Settlements [BIS]) tell an important story about the general trend of euro area real exchange rates against the rest of the world (figure 4.7). Namely, there was a substantial appreciation of all of the currencies from 2000 to 2008. The simple average REER index for the seven economies rose from a low of 87.9 in September 2000 (on the eve of the joint G-7 intervention to curb further decline in the new single currency) to a high of 105.1 in April 2008, a rise of 19.5 percent. Even the REER of Germany (BIS-CPI basis) rose 11.5 percent in this period, suggesting that the frequent interpretation contrasting

---

5. The BIS series is based on trade of 61 economies; the IMF series, 26 advanced economies and the euro area as a group.

6. Public sector wages in Ireland were cut by an average of 13.5 percent over two years, with net pay reductions as deep as 30 percent for those earning over €100,000 (IMF 2012e, 25).

Figure 4.6   Real effective exchange rate: IMF index deflated by unit labor costs, 1994–2013

index, 2005 = 100

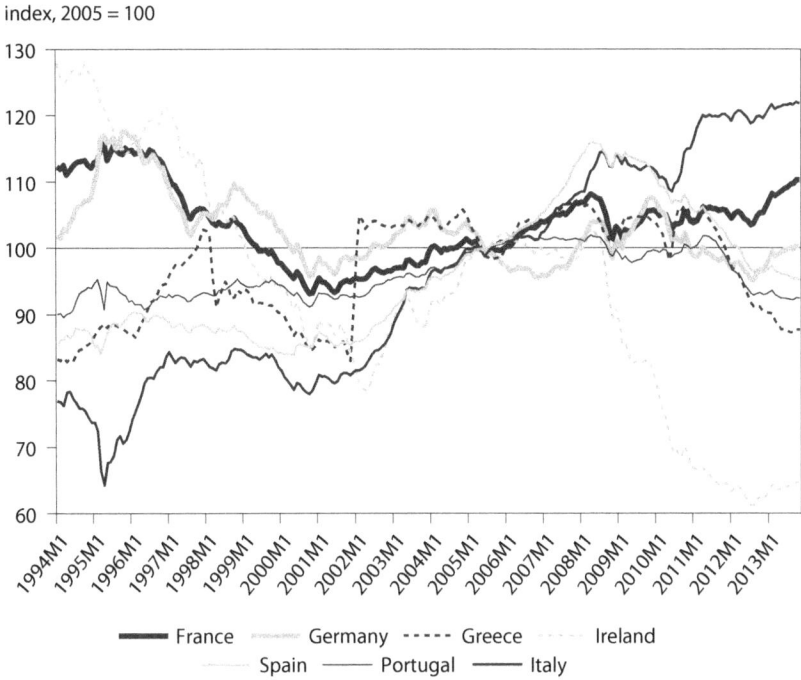

IMF = International Monetary Fund

Source: IMF (2013d).

German wage restraint against periphery laxity at the least oversimplifies as an explanation of widening external imbalances in the periphery.

Ruo Chen, Gian-Maria Milesi-Ferretti, and Thierry Tressel (2012) argue that the usual emphasis on intra-euro-area factors is "incomplete." They demonstrate that asymmetric impacts of external influences aggravated the intra-euro-area imbalances. The advent of strong competition from China disproportionately eroded the trade performance of peripheral economies such as Portugal while stimulating exports of investment goods from Germany.[7] The shock of higher oil prices adversely affected trade balances of the periphery but boosted investment-good exports from Germany. The authors also find that the bulk of the appreciation between 2000 and 2009 was accounted for by the rise of the euro against other currencies rather than rising costs in the periphery relative to Germany and the rest of the euro area north. Whereas

7. Pedro Lourtie (2012, 56) similarly emphasizes the loss of Portuguese competitiveness as the European Union entered the process of enlargement to include Eastern Europe and as competition from China and India in labor-intensive products increased.

Figure 4.7   Real effective exchange rate: BIS index deflated by consumer price indices, 1994–2014

index, 2005 = 100

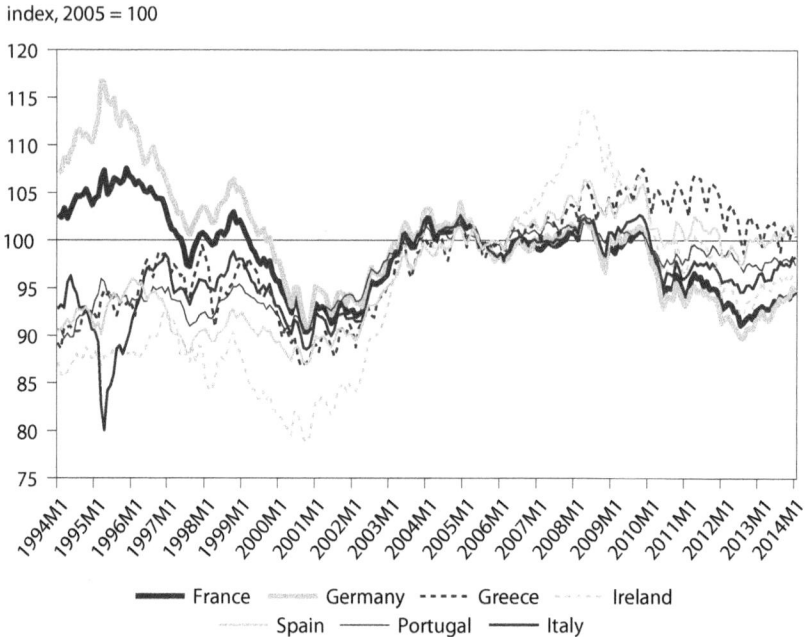

France ——— Germany ■■■■■■ Greece ----- Ireland ....
Spain ——— Portugal ——— Italy ———

BIS = Bank for International Settlements

Source: BIS (2013).

the trade shocks would have required real effective depreciations in the debtor periphery, intra-euro-area capital flows and the rising euro instead brought further real appreciation for the periphery.[8] Guerrieri (2012) also emphasizes the role of structural factors, citing the shift of Germany toward outsourcing its intermediate inputs to Eastern European countries, a process that was not replicated in the periphery and to some extent came at the expense of periphery country exports.

Figure 4.8 consolidates four of the five periphery economies into a single group, weighting by nominal GDP in 2005. Greece, Ireland, Portugal, and Spain all had major deteriorations in their current account balances from 2003 to 2008, and then major reductions in deficits from 2008 to 2012. (Italy was not representative in this dimension, as its external deficit never exceeded 3.5 percent of GDP in this period.) For the group of four, the weighted current

---

8. The authors also find that the periphery's external deficits were financed by capital inflows from within the euro area, especially France and Germany, whereas investors from outside the euro area primarily purchased French and German public debt, apparently considering periphery instruments to be poorer substitutes for such assets than perceived within the euro area.

Figure 4.8   Weighted average current accounts and real effective exchange rates (REERs) for four euro area periphery economies, 2005–13

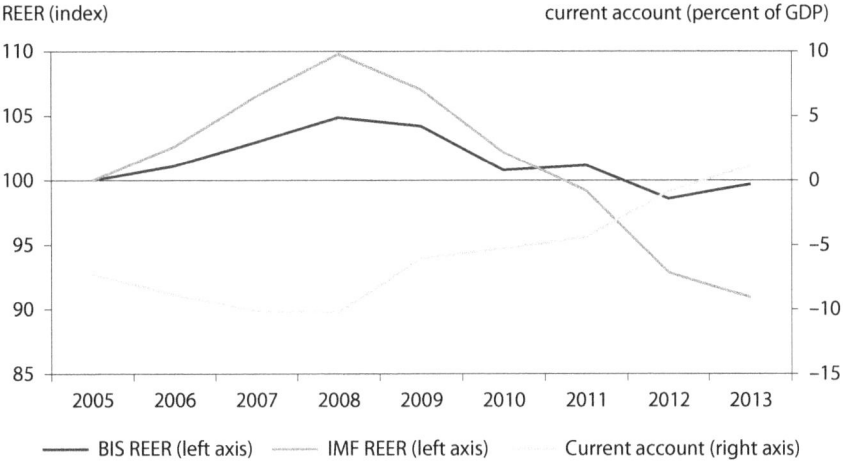

REER (index)   current account (percent of GDP)

— BIS REER (left axis)   ---- IMF REER (left axis)   Current account (right axis)

Note: The Bank for International Settlements (BIS) index is deflated by consumer price indices and the International Monetary Fund (IMF) index is deflated by unit labor costs. The four periphery countries are Greece, Ireland, Portugal, and Spain.

Source: BIS (2013); IMF (2013n, 2014).

account deficit stood at 7 percent of GDP in 2003 and deteriorated further to 10 percent of GDP in 2008. The deficit then declined rapidly to only 0.8 percent of GDP in 2012, and the current account was expected to show a surplus of 1 percent of GDP in 2013. Figure 4.8 also shows the weighted average of two alternative real exchange rate indices (BIS based on CPIs and IMF based on unit labor costs). With 2005 = 100, the two series peaked in 2008 at 105 and 110, respectively, and then proceeded to depreciate, reaching 99 and 93, respectively, by 2012. The sizable further current account adjustment from 2012 to 2013 reflects the lagged influence of the substantial real depreciation by 2012. In broad terms, there has been an external current account correction on the order of 11 percent of GDP over just five years. Over the same period there has been a strong price incentive to adjustment from the decline in the real effective exchange rate, also by about 11 percent. The impact is larger than would usually be expected from the real exchange rate change, undoubtedly reflecting the additional influence of domestic recession.[9]

---

9. For an economy the size of Portugal, a typical impact parameter would be 4 percent of GDP reduction in current account deficit for 10 percent real effective depreciation; for an economy the size of Spain, the corresponding typical impact would be 3 percent of GDP. See Cline and Williamson (2011, appendix B).

Sovereign Risk Spreads and External Position Going Forward

Although the analysis above finds that large current account deficits before the crisis contributed to sovereign risk spreads after the sudden stop, going forward the role of further current account adjustment in reducing risk spreads is less obvious. Current account deficits have come down sharply and official support programs have bridged the sudden stop. It turns out that there seems to be little remaining influence of the current account on country risk spreads in the euro area based on actual 2012–13 current account balances and expected trends through 2016.

Figure 4.9 shows the average 10-year interest rate in 2013 for 10 major euro area economies. Greece is excluded because its debt restructuring with deep haircuts makes any bond yields incomparable to those on normal sovereign debt. The horizontal axis shows the average current account balance as a percent of GDP for 2012–16 as estimated by the IMF (2013n). Markets presumably take account of the recent actual experience (2012–13) as well as the expected future path (2014–16). As is evident, there is no clear relationship between the average long-term interest rate in 2013 (and hence the sovereign risk spread) and the current account balance. This time a simple regression yields a coefficient that is statistically insignificant but does show a mild influence (1 percentage point of GDP increase in the current account deficit boosts the spread by 10 basis points). The weakness of the relationship is illustrated by the fact that France, with an average current account deficit of 1.7 percent of GDP, has almost the same interest rate as the Netherlands with a surplus of 11 percent of GDP, with both interest rates at about 200 basis points.

In contrast, the second panel shows continuation of the expected relationship between the interest rate and the debt level. The horizontal axis indicates the average ratio of gross public debt to GDP for 2012–2016, again as estimated by the IMF. Higher public debt is associated with a higher interest rate (and thus sovereign risk spread). There is a statistically significant relationship despite the small number of observations.[10] This relationship indicates that the benchmark 60 percent Maastricht debt-to-GDP ratio would have been expected to translate to a 10-year sovereign yield of 125 basis points in 2013; and that for each additional percentage point of GDP in public debt, this yield would rise by 5.3 basis points, placing the expected rate at 443 basis points for a debt ratio of 120 percent of GDP.[11] With Germany's debt ratio averaging 77.5 percent of GDP for this period, by implication a debt ratio of 120 percent would mean a sovereign risk spread above the German bund of 218 basis points. The lack of a meaningful influence of the current account deficit on the sovereign yield in 2013 may in part reflect the changed environment in the euro area as

---

10. A simple regression yields: $R = -192 + 5.3\,D$, where R is the average 10-year government bond rate in 2013 and D is the average expected ratio of gross public debt to GDP (percent) in 2012–16, with t-statistic of 3.8 and p-value of 0.005 for the debt ratio, and adjusted R^2 of 0.59.

11. The same impact in equation (4.1) above is 7.7 basis points.

Figure 4.9   Average 10-year sovereign yield in 2013 versus average 2012–16 current account balances and debt/GDP ratios for 10 euro area economies

a. Sovereign yield versus current account balances

sovereign yield (basis points)

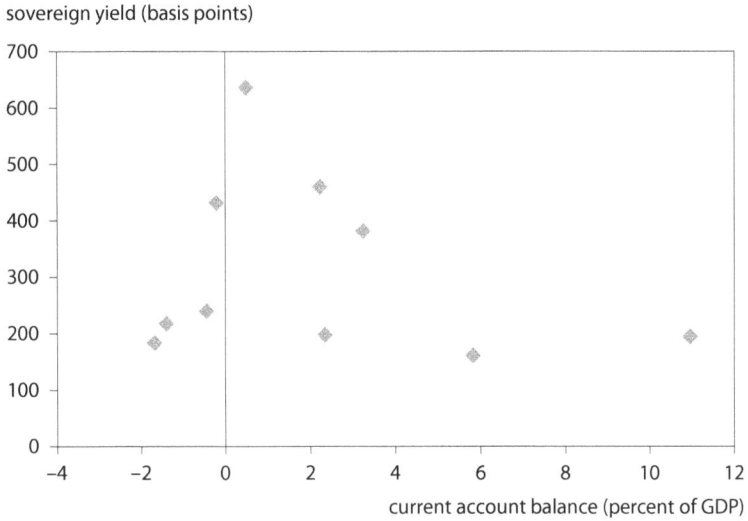

current account balance (percent of GDP)

b. Sovereign yield versus debt/GDP ratios

sovereign yield (basis points)

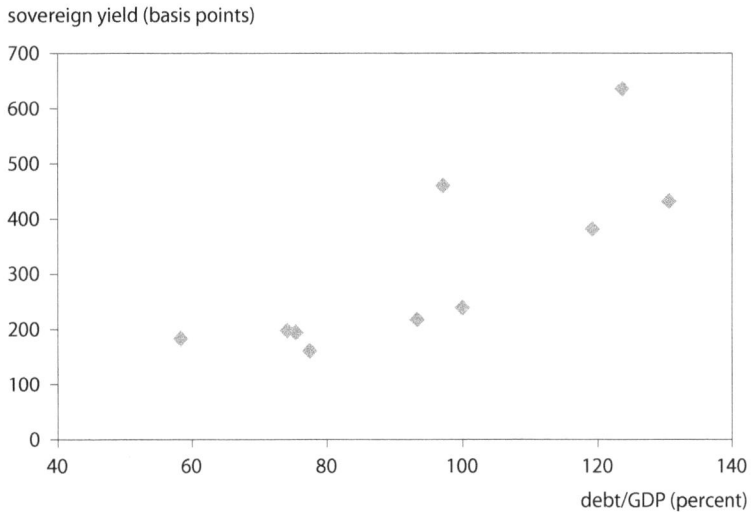

debt/GDP (percent)

Note: The 10 euro area economies are Austria, Belgium, Finland, France, Germany, Ireland, Italy, the Netherlands, Portugal, and Spain.

Source: Author's calculations.

a consequence of Outright Monetary Transactions (OMT). The combination of OMT and assured external finance through Target2 would seem a powerful institutional structure going forward for avoiding negative impacts of current account deficits on the sovereign risk spread. The corollary, however, is that policymakers should not view reaching a current account surplus as the means to reduce the sovereign risk spread. The comparison between France and the Netherlands again suggests that such a pursuit would be fruitless.

Those who emphasize the external dimension of the euro area debt crisis in its prospective resolution also tend to intermix two different concepts of debt: public fiscal debt, on the one hand, and countrywide net external liabilities, on the other. Some at least implicitly assume the sovereign debt crisis cannot be resolved without a sharp reduction in the net external liabilities of the countries in question. It is easy within such a framework to arrive at extreme pessimism about debt sustainability for the euro area debtor countries because the rigidity of the exchange rate is seen as an inherent obstacle to the necessary reduction in net external liabilities.

For the euro area, at first appearance there is indeed a substantial relationship between country credit risk and net international investment position (NIIP). Figure 4.10 shows that interest rates on 10-year government bonds in the first quarter of 2013 stood at an average of about 5 percent for Portugal, Ireland, and Spain, and their average NIIP was a large net liability position of 140 percent of GDP. In contrast, for Germany and the Netherlands, the average interest rate was only 1.6 percent, and the average NIIP, +46 percent of GDP. However, the case of Italy suggests that this relationship may be more circumstantial than fundamental. Italy's interest rate is far higher than would be expected if the principal influence were the NIIP, considering that Italy has only a moderate net international liability position (–25 percent of GDP), comparable to that of France. In contrast, Italy's debt metrics, with public debt at about 125 percent of GDP, are much more comparable to those of Portugal, Ireland, and Spain (averaging about 110 percent), strongly suggesting that it is the public debt characteristics rather than the NIIP that determine the sovereign risk spread. Credit default swap (CDS) rates provide a basis for considering the importance of the NIIP versus that of public debt in sovereign debt risk. Using a cross-section test for 18 industrial countries, an equation for average CDS rates on 10-year government obligations in the first quarter of 2013 yields the following equation:

$$r = 22.8 + 1.21\, D - 0.704\, NIIP + 317\, Pd - 202\, Jd; \text{ adj. } R^2 = 0.78 \qquad (4.2)$$
$$(0.5) \quad (1.96) \quad (-2.43) \qquad (4.1) \quad (-1.6)$$

where r is the credit default swap rate (in basis points), D is gross public debt as a percent of GDP in 2012, $NIIP$ is the net international investment position

Figure 4.10 Interest rates on 10-year sovereign bonds, 2013Q1, and net international investment position, selected euro area economies

interest rate (percent)

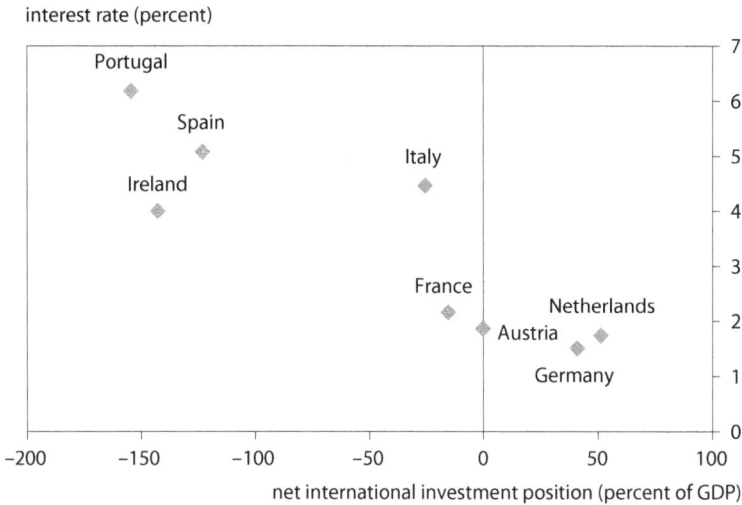

net international investment position (percent of GDP)

Source: Datastream; IMF (2013d).

as a percent of GDP in 2012, *Pd* is a dummy variable for Portugal, and *Jd* is a dummy variable for Japan.[12] *T*-statistics are reported in parentheses.

Although this equation does confirm an influence of the NIIP, the magnitude of this influence is limited. Thus, a country with net international liabilities of 100 percent of GDP will face a default risk premium that is only 71 basis points higher than a country with a zero NIIP position.[13]

---

12. Data are from Datastream and IMF (2013d, 2013g). The countries are Australia, Austria, Belgium, Denmark, Finland, France, Germany, Ireland, Italy, Japan, the Netherlands, Norway, Portugal, Spain, Sweden, Switzerland, the United Kingdom, and the United States. Greece is omitted because its postrestructuring status makes it unrepresentative. The significance levels (*p*-value) are 3 percent for NIIP, 7 percent for debt, 0.1 percent for the Portugal dummy, and 14 percent for the Japan dummy.

13. In contrast, Daniel Gros (2013, 507) finds a relationship that places this difference far higher, at 270 basis points. However, he includes Greece with a spread of 950 basis points in his February 2013 spreads data. Yet by that time Greek debt had been restructured with a deep haircut, making it not directly comparable to other euro area debt and removing the relevance of the previous current account deficits as a measure of postrestructuring foreign debt. The high spread represented investor distrust after the previous losses as well as fear of further haircuts, with private debt likely subordinate to official claims and with doubts remaining about Greek debt sustainability. In addition, Gros' use of the cumulative current account for 1995–2012 as a proxy for net international investment position seriously understates Ireland's net liabilities, which amounted to 151 percent of GDP in 2012 (IMF 2014) instead of 18 percent using the cumulative current account proxy. Removing the observation for Greece and shifting that for Ireland far to the left on the chart of spreads (vertical axis) against NIIP (horizontal axis) would make the relationship far more gently sloped.

Striving to reduce NIIP liabilities in the European periphery by pursuing large current account surpluses would therefore be a high-cost, low-return strategy for bolstering public debt sustainability. For example, Spain's NIIP is –96 percent of GDP. Suppose it achieved a current account surplus of 10 percent of GDP and sustained it over a decade, bringing net liabilities to zero. The reward would be to reduce its sovereign risk spread by 71 basis points. But the sustainability of Spain's public debt will turn not on 70 basis points, but rather on whether the risk spread is on the order of 600 basis points (as occurred in July of 2012), or instead some 300 basis points (the level in July 2013) or 200 basis points (the level by early 2014) or lower. In short, it seems unlikely that the right path to recovery of debt sustainability in the euro area periphery will need to involve large and sustained current account surpluses for the countries in question.

Real Exchange Rate, External and Internal Imbalances, and Growth

Whereas the direct influence of the NIIP and thus current account on the default risk spread is limited, the level of the exchange rate and the performance of the current account could still affect market perceptions of creditworthiness through an effect on prospective growth. In the classical framework of James Meade (1951), a country below full employment (below "internal balance") and with an excessive current account deficit (below "external balance") should pursue expansionary monetary and fiscal policy in combination with a depreciation of the exchange rate. In the Salter-Swan diagram of Meade's framework (figure 4.11), such an economy is at point *a* (Swan 1955, Williamson 2006). Its current account deficit places it to the northeast of the external balance equilibrium line. Its unemployment places it to the northwest of the internal balance equilibrium line. Depreciation of the currency would move the economy from point *a* to point *b*, providing some additional employment while swinging the external balance into surplus. Pursuing expansionary monetary and fiscal policy would move the economy from *a* to point *c*, largely eliminating unemployment but greatly increasing the current account deficit. The proper policy is a combination of depreciation and monetary-fiscal expansion, along the path *ad* to the intersection of the internal and external balance lines. The debt-stressed euro area periphery economy is, however, severely constrained from following the usual Meade prescription. A cutoff from debt markets makes it impractical to pursue fiscal stimulus; nor is monetary stimulus available because there is no independent monetary policy. A depreciation of the currency is not an option because of the single currency. Real depreciation may be possible to some extent through "internal devaluation" (e.g., wage cuts) or "fiscal devaluation" (shift from labor to product taxation), but the scope for effective depreciation may be limited.

Figure 4.11   The Salter-Swan diagram of Meade's policy framework

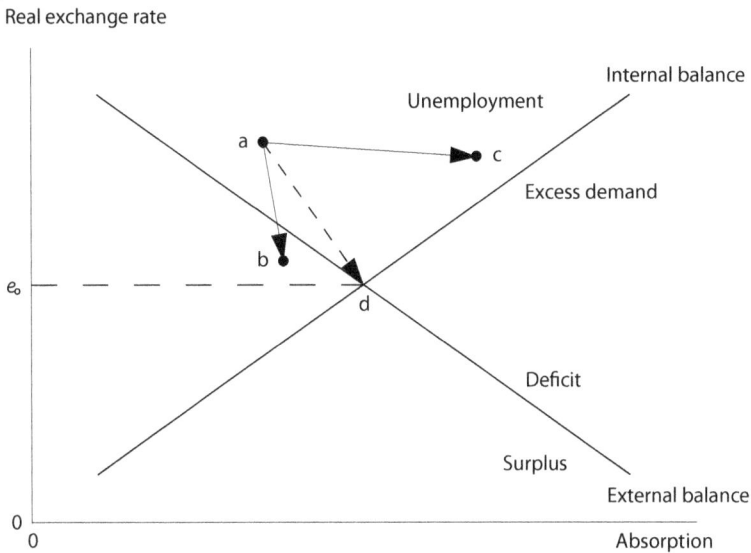

Real exchange rate

Source: Author's illustration based on Meade (1951).

Adjustment in the South or North?

One way out of the dilemma is to convince the euro area partners in the north to pursue fiscal expansion and the ECB to pursue monetary expansion (moving the economy from *a* toward *c*), and to encourage partners in the north to pursue aggressively expansive wage policy, providing a real depreciation for the periphery economy and moving it from *a* toward *b*. In this view, the Meade solution can be pursued, with joint application of the policies moving the economy toward *d*. But the policy changes have to be adopted by the euro area as a whole, with monetary expansion by the ECB and fiscal and wage expansion by the northern members. There are two problems with this solution, however. First, Germany and other northern countries will understandably be loath to embark on a path of high inflation. Second, if the principal source of the external imbalances was not an overvalued exchange rate relative to Germany but an overvalued exchange rate vis-à-vis the world as a whole (as suggested by the discussion above), the price of the strategy could be unduly high in terms of increased inflation in the north for a given amount of success in overall adjustment in the periphery.

Silvia Merler and Jean Pisani-Ferry (2012b) construct a calibrated model to examine the role of north-south imbalances within the euro area, and conclude that it is the differential fiscal stance between north and south that determines the real exchange rate, so the south cannot escape more austerity.

However, unless monetary policy aims at higher inflation in the north, the low inflation or actual deflation in the south necessary to achieve real depreciation becomes self-defeating for debt dynamics (by curbing the rise in the nominal value of GDP). They thus find that "Accepting more inflation at home is therefore a way for the North to contribute to restoring debt sustainability in the South" (Merler and Pisani-Ferry 2012b, 13).[14]

The model the authors develop, however, seems questionable. Output is made a function of the real exchange rate, the primary surplus (with a negative parameter that is a constant multiplier), and the real interest rate (negative coefficient). This framework would seem to tie growth excessively rigidly to the real exchange rate. Although there is some support for this presumption from the Meade framework, the fixed relationship makes no allowance for growth focused in the nontradables sector. Inflation is determined by a Phillips curve, so that faster growth boosts prices. There is no room in the model for real exchange rate change other than through the macro price-level effects. As shown in figure 4.6, Ireland has managed to achieve sharp reductions in its unit labor costs, indicating that linking the real effective exchange rate solely to the macro price level may be misleading. Moreover, the model ignores the real exchange rate relative to the rest of the world, yet this has been more important than the real rate between euro area partners in determining current accounts (as noted above). For its part, the Phillips curve seems an outdated framework, and inherently leads to the recommendation of slow growth in order to achieve real depreciation.

It is difficult to conceive of Germany and other economies of the euro area north accepting inflation any higher than, say, 3 percent over a five-year period in order to help the south. During the past quarter century, inflation of 3 percent or higher occurred in only three years (IMF 2013a). If inflation in the south stayed at 2 percent, the cumulative 5 percent real depreciation of the south relative to the north would boost output in the south by 0.5 percent to 1.5 percent, applying the coefficient range used by Merler and Pisani-Ferry, or 0.8 percent based on an alternative statistical estimate.[15] These changes

---

14. Guerrieri (2012, 1) has taken a similar position, sharpening the critique to argue that "The official policy...is that this adjustment should be entirely one-sided. Domestic spending must fall in debtor countries, with no offsetting expansionary policy in the creditors.... The right approach must combine more symmetrical macroeconomic fiscal adjustment with microeconomic policy measures aimed at encouraging productivity increases."

15. Merler and Pisani-Ferry use a range of −0.1 to −0.3 for the elasticity of output with respect to the real effective exchange rate. An effort to investigate this range yields the following results. Annual real growth is regressed on the real effective exchange rate index (BIS, 2010 = 100) lagged six months, using 1999–2012 data for the five periphery economies plus France and Germany, with dummy variables for the 2009 global recession and for the years of euro area debt crisis (2010–12 for Greece, 2011–12 for Ireland, Italy, Portugal, and Spain). A statistically significant coefficient of growth on the exchange rate is found, amounting to −0.21 or, after omitting outliers (Ireland in 1999–2000, Greece in 2010–11), −0.16. The (preferred) trimmed estimate is toward the lower end of the Merler and Pisani-Ferry range.

are too small to be decisive in a framework in which baseline debt ratios are falling by some 5 to 10 percentage points over a five-year period (see chapter 6). Doubling or even tripling the relative price change and hence the output effect would not fundamentally change this diagnosis.[16] Debt sustainability thus seems more likely to turn on whether the sovereign credit risk spreads can be held to moderate levels than on whether Germany and the rest of the north can be convinced to undergo a substantial period of unusually high inflation so the south can become more competitive.

In Cline (2013d) I examine the related question of whether Germany's large current account surplus (6 percent of GDP in 2013, projected at 4.6 percent by 2018) is a major source of inadequate demand and hence "a deflationary bias for the euro area" as charged by the US Treasury (2013) in its report to Congress on exchange rate policy. The question is whether plausible increases in Germany's fiscal deficit would boost German growth sufficiently to induce a sizable output expansion in the periphery. Model simulations by the IMF (2013o, 23) indicate that a German fiscal stimulus of 1 percent of GDP sustained for two years would boost real GDP of euro area partners by a maximum of 0.2 percent, with the effect concentrated in the Czech Republic, Austria, the Netherlands, and Belgium, rather than the debt-stressed periphery. Germany's economy is assessed by the IMF (2013n) to have an output gap close to zero, implying a real multiplier of close to zero for Germany itself. In Cline (2013d) I show that in order to adhere to the euro area rules of reducing the excess of debt above 60 percent of GDP by one-twentieth each year, Germany could only boost its fiscal deficit by 1.5 percent of GDP. By implication, even if the higher fiscal deficit were sustained for five years, the impact on the periphery would be to boost output somewhere on the order of 0.4 percent or less, too little for a decisive shift in the debt ratio.[17]

If Germany and the north are not going to reflate massively, however, the question then becomes: How can the periphery maintain the new balanced current account without the euro area as a whole imposing an unacceptable surplus on the world economy? The answer is essentially that the periphery economies are sufficiently small that the elimination of their deficits can relatively comfortably be accommodated within the global totals, especially considering that the surpluses of China and Japan have fallen substantially. Thus, from 2008 to 2013, the combined current account balance of the peripheral five economies will have swung from a deficit of $318 billion to a surplus of $29 billion, an increase of $347 billion. The surpluses of China and Japan will have fallen from $421 billion and $160 billion, respectively, to $238 billion and $64 billion, respectively, a combined reduction of $279 billion—on the same order of magnitude as the reversal in the euro area periphery balances. For

---

16. Tripling the impact, for example, by setting an inflation target of 4 percent annually for Germany and the rest of the north and only 1 percent for the periphery.

17. That is: somewhat less than the 0.2 × 2.5 two-year periods = 0.5 percent of GDP for the euro area as a whole, given the concentration of the impact on more northerly neighbors.

the euro area as a whole, the current account surplus will have risen from 0.16 percent of world GDP to 0.40 percent, whereas the combined current account surplus of China and Japan will have fallen from 0.95 percent of world GDP to 0.41 percent (IMF 2013n).

Exit and Devaluation?

Hans-Werner Sinn and Akos Valentinyi (2013) are also among those who consider depreciation in the south to be essential to resolving the euro area debt crisis. They argue that the only question is whether the depreciation should be "internal or external," that is, accomplished through internal devaluation or through an exit of the periphery economies from the euro and effective devaluation of the replacement currency for each country in question. They observe that the formation of the euro involved an investment and credit boom in the periphery that represented a catching-up process financed by foreign capital and accompanied by rapidly rising domestic prices. The introduction of the euro eliminated exchange rate risk and "induced investors to disregard country-specific bankruptcy risks" (Sinn and Valentinyi 2013, 2). Moreover, the euro area generated optimism about convergence of the periphery with the core of the euro area. The authors show a close correlation between the average current account balance in 2002–07 and the level of per capita GDP in 1995. For example, Estonia, Slovakia, and Portugal had current account deficits in the range of 7 to 12 percent of GDP and per capita income at 30 to 65 percent of the euro area average, whereas Austria, Belgium, Germany, and the Netherlands had average current account surpluses of about 5 percent of GDP and per capita incomes of about 115 percent of the euro area average (Sinn and Valentinyi 2013, 2). By 2007–08, however, private capital financing the imbalances dried up and was largely replaced by ECB Target balances.

The authors maintain that "Internal devaluation through falling prices in the periphery can only be achieved through austerity programs that lead to a period of stagnation and mass unemployment in the periphery due to the downward rigidity of prices and wages" (Sinn and Valentinyi 2013, 2). The alternative of increasing inflation in the core countries could undermine the stability of the monetary union. The option of euro exit, however, would inevitably involve discussions, planning, distributing new currency, and so forth, in a fashion making it impossible to launch by surprise, but widespread anticipation of euro exit would provoke a run on assets. Balance sheets would then be mismatched and there would be negative balance sheet effects at the time of the devaluation. The authors are skeptical of the adjustment achieved by internal devaluation so far, judging that most of the improvements in current accounts have come from income effects rather than substitution effects resulting from a change in relative prices caused by internal devaluation. Nonetheless, they see little alternative to internal devaluation at present because "policymakers have excluded the exit option."

Figure 4.12   Relative consumer prices, periphery versus northern euro area economies, 2012–18

index, 2012 = 100

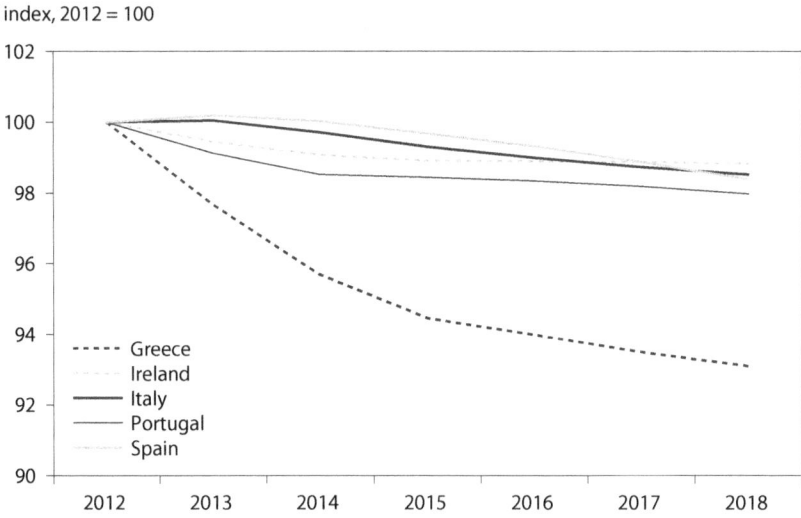

Note: The northern euro area economies are Austria, Belgium, Finland, France, Germany, and the Netherlands.

Source: IMF (2013n).

Once again, however, the prior questions have become: (1) How much more real depreciation is needed in the periphery, and (2) are the recent current account corrections sustainable or artificial because of dependence on depressed incomes?

IMF Forecasts of Real Exchange Rates and Current Account Balances

For its part, the IMF appears to see the imperative of further periphery depreciation as less urgent than the authors just discussed. Figure 4.12 repeats the relative consumer price calculation of figure 4.5, this time using 2012 as the base, weighting the "north" by 2012 GDP, and applying projections in the October 2013 *World Economic Outlook* (WEO) for inflation (IMF 2013n). Figure 4.13 correspondingly shows the WEO projections for current accounts and for growth. The broad picture that emerges is one of steady improvement, in which growth returns to moderate positive rates in 2014 and current account balances continue to improve (especially in Spain) or stay high (Ireland), yet these outcomes do not require sharp intra-euro-area depreciations as measured by the ratios of consumer prices to the aggregate consumer price index in the north. The exception is Greece, where the IMF anticipates that the process of internal devaluation will be more substantial. The 7 percent decline in consumer prices relative to the north in Greece for 2012–18 would approximately reverse the comparable increase from 2008 to 2012 shown in figure 4.5.

Figure 4.13 Growth and current account projections for euro area periphery, 2012–18

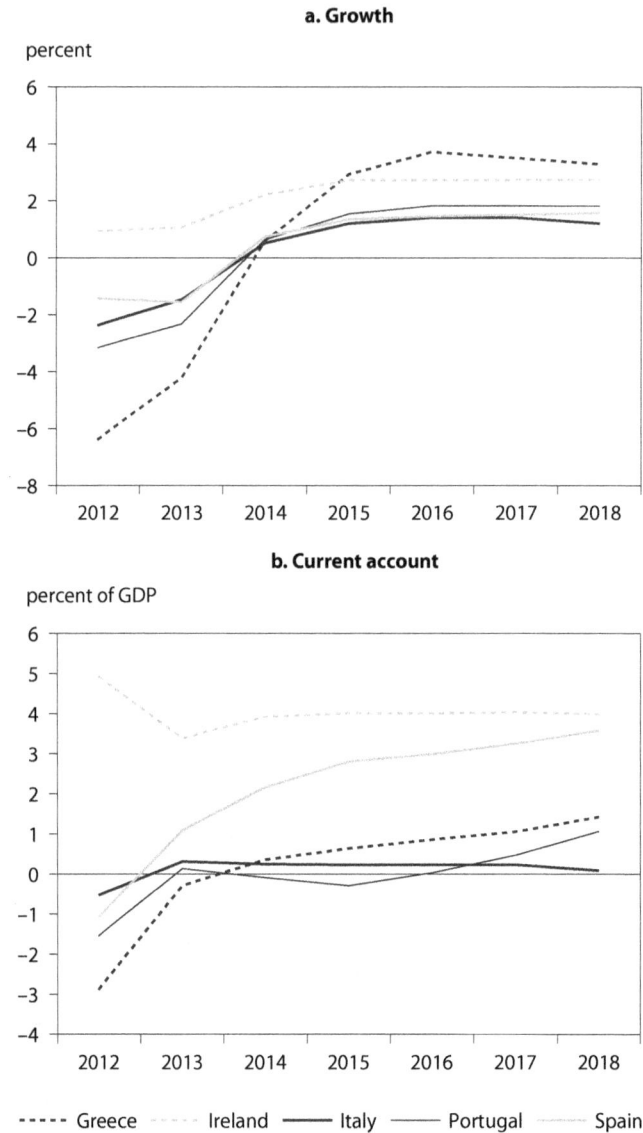

a. Growth

percent

b. Current account

percent of GDP

- - - - - Greece ⋯⋯ Ireland ━━━ Italy ─── Portugal ⋯⋯ Spain

Source: IMF (2013n).

If these projections turn out to be too optimistic, it would not be the first time, but they remain nonetheless the mainstream outlook.

Costs of a Breakup of the Euro

By 2013, the perceived risk of an exit from the euro by Greece or any other member had substantially receded. According to one measure, bets placed on the internet-based "InTrade," in late 2011 and again in the second and third quarters of 2012, the expected probability of a euro breakup, defined as the announcement by end-2013 by any euro member that it would exit from the currency, hovered in the range of 50 to 60 percent. This probability had fallen below 30 percent by the end of 2012 (Nordvig 2012, IMF 2013c).[18] A debate remains, however, on whether some form of breakup would be a good thing or a bad thing and, if the latter (the majority view), just how large the economic costs would be.

The Qualitative Debate

Among economists, prominent advocates of an exit from the euro by Greece and some other peripheral economies have included Martin Feldstein and Nouriel Roubini. Early in the crisis, Feldstein proposed a "holiday" from the euro for Greece, with the obligation to reenter later at a more competitive exchange rate.[19] His argument was that doing so would enable Greece to increase employment in exports and import substitutes to offset the loss of employment from cutting a large fiscal deficit (see figure 4.11). Roubini suggested in mid-2011 that the only feasible way for countries in the periphery to escape stagnation was to leave the euro and achieve massive real depreciations, even though this would impose trade and capital losses on the core.[20] Subsequently Arnab Das and Roubini argued that "Ideally, five distressed peripherals—Portugal, Ireland, Italy, Greece and Spain—would exit ...."[21] They contended:

> It is far better to restore competitiveness through devaluation than by changing relative prices with a fixed nominal exchange rate, which implies protracted debt deflation, potentially ending in disorderly defaults and exits in any case, or sustained inflation above target in surplus countries.... We

18. Note that in March 2013, the Irish firm InTrade ceased operations in the face of a suit by the Commodities Futures Trading Commission that it was enabling US citizens to place bets on commodities, illegal under US law. See Derek Thompson, "InTrade Shuts Down—Why?" *Atlantic*, March 10, 2013.

19. Martin Feldstein, "Let Greece Take a Eurozone 'Holiday'," *Financial Times*, February 16, 2010.

20. Nouriel Roubini, "The Eurozone Heads for Break Up," *Financial Times*, June 13, 2011.

21. Arnab Das and Nouriel Roubini, "A Divorce Settlement for the Eurozone," *Financial Times*, April 2, 2012.

would redenominate all contracts made under domestic laws into the new currencies at the time of exit.... Pursuing domestication prior to exit would reduce credit losses and currency risk.... However, doubts about the strategy might spark capital flight, requiring temporary bank nationalisation, curbs on deposit withdrawals, ... as well as temporary capital controls.[22]

The more usual diagnosis has been that an exit from the euro, especially by a major peripheral economy, would be extremely costly. Writing at the time of the first spike in sovereign risk spreads in Italy in November 2011, the *Economist* spelled out the risks as follows:

> What is vastly under-estimated by advocates of euro exit is the financial and social chaos that would ensue both in the departed country and in the rest of the world. A euro break-up would not, as some seem to believe, be a slightly messier version of the ERM crisis of 1992-93. It would be a gigantic financial shockwave. Once departure by Italy were a serious prospect, there would be runs on its banks as depositors scrambled to move savings to Germany, Luxembourg or Britain, in order to avoid a forced conversion into the new weaker currency. The anticipated write-down of private and public debts, much of which is held outside Italy, would threaten bankruptcy of Europe's integrated banking system. There would be runs on other countries that might even consider leaving. Credit would collapse.... Business short of [cash] would go under. Capital controls and restrictions on travel would be needed to contain the chaos. Once the recriminations start, the survival of the European Union and its single market would be under question.[23]

Similarly, writing before the euro area crisis, Barry Eichengreen (2010, 2) argued that a breakup of the euro could be "the mother of all financial crises." He notes that competitive gains from exit and depreciation would tend to be neutralized by labor union demands for compensatory wage increases, and exiting governments would have to pay higher interest rates on public debt. In principle labor market and fiscal reforms could overcome these induced adverse effects. But the fundamental problem remains that in a democracy very extensive discussion would have to precede redenomination of all contracts (including for wages, bank deposits, bonds, mortgages, and taxes), and time would be required for issuing new currency and coins and changing payment machines. In the interim, households and firms would shift funds to other euro area countries, provoking a systemwide bank run. Investors would shift to bonds of other governments, creating a bond market crisis. The ECB

---

22. By August 2012, Roubini had conceded that whether the eurozone is viable remained an "open question," especially "If Italy and Spain are illiquid but solvent...." He nonetheless argued that "A futile attempt to avoid a breakup for a year or two—after wasting trillions of euros in additional official financing by the core—would mean a disorderly end, including the destruction of the single market...." See Nouriel Roubini, "Delaying a Eurozone Breakup Could Make the Endgame Much Worse," *Guardian*, August 16, 2012.

23. "Breaking up the Euro: How It Could Happen; Why It Would Be Horrible," *Economist*, November 10, 2011.

would be unlikely to help because the country would be leaving the euro. If the government were already weak fiscally, it would not be able to borrow to recapitalize banks and repurchase its debt. Hence the mother of all financial crises would ensue.

Willem Buiter, chief economist of Citigroup, predicted in mid-2012 that with a high probability of 90 percent, Greece would leave the euro (see chapter 7). However, Buiter is among those who judge that even a partial exit of one country would be chaotic; and that if Spain and Italy were to exit, there would be a systemic financial collapse and global depression.[24] Anders Åslund (2012, 1, 12) argues, in part based on the experience in the dissolution of the Soviet Union, that "a Greek exit would not be merely a devaluation for Greece but would unleash a domino effect of international bank runs and disrupt the EMU payments mechanism," with the consequence that the euro area "would probably collapse altogether."

Yet some of the most powerful euro area politicians seem to have flirted temporarily with the notion of expelling Greece from the euro, only to return eventually to the tenet that the euro must be preserved "at all costs." In November 2011, German Chancellor Angela Merkel and French President Nicolas Sarkozy confronted Greek Prime Minister Andreas Papandreou over his intended referendum on the euro area support program. Failure of the referendum (cancelled after the meeting) could have implied an exit from the euro, and the comments of the German and French leaders were interpreted as, for the first time, breaking a taboo and placing the stability of the euro above Greece's ongoing membership in the currency.[25]

In early July 2012, Richard Portes pointed to this meeting as the moment when "Angela Merkel and Nicolas Sarkozy opened the door to a Greek exit." He warned that "Any country's exit, with the inevitable loss to depositors, would provoke bank runs elsewhere that could be stopped only with capital controls. And that would be the end of monetary union."[26] The watershed shift away from the specter of an exit from the euro came in late July 2012, when ECB President Mario Draghi stated that "the ECB is ready to do whatever it takes to preserve the euro. And believe me, it will be enough."[27] It was the announcement soon after of the ECB's OMT plan to purchase government bonds of countries in adjustment programs that gave force to this pledge.

---

24. Willem Buiter, "The Terrible Consequences of a Eurozone Collapse," *Financial Times*, December 7, 2011.

25. Stefan Simons, "Merkel and Sarkozy Halt Payments to Athens," *Spiegel Online*, November 3, 2011.

26. Richard Portes, "Market Forces Will Destroy the Euro If We Do Not Take Action Soon," *Financial Times*, July 10, 2012.

27. Mario Draghi, speech at the Global Investment Conference, London, July 26, 2012, www.ecb.int/press/key/date/2012/html/sp120726.en.html.

Alternative Cost Estimates

The most sanguine estimates of the benefits versus costs of a euro breakup have been those of a team led by Roger Bootle (2012) in a report that won the Wolfson Economics Prize. The competition for that year called for the best plan for a euro breakup that would minimize damages. The report averred that "a break-up of the euro is required to help unwind the structural imbalances" (p. 17). Their optimal reconfiguration would be a core northern euro area including Germany, Austria, the Netherlands, Finland, and Belgium. The peripheral economies, however, would not remain in a single but different currency, in view of their economic diversity and limited trade with each other.

The Bootle study makes estimates for the case of an exit from the euro by Greece. The authors suggest that Greece "would have to default heavily on its international debts," reducing the debt ratio to around 60 percent of GDP (pp. 27, 48), because otherwise redenomination of the currency and devaluation would impose heavy balance sheet losses. They recommend that all contracts would be redenominated in the new national currency at a rate of 1 to 1 euro. There would be an initial period during the printing of currency when noncash means of payment would be used for most transactions. Continued use of euros would be permitted, along with dual pricing. Banks and ATMs would be closed upon announcement of the exit. Capital controls would be applied if needed.

In the cost estimates, the report suggests that there would be 78 percent losses on government debt, 40 percent losses on loans to banks, and 20 percent on loans to private nonbanks (p. 51). Northern core countries would inject capital equal to 40 percent of losses of their banks. On this basis, Bootle and his colleagues estimate that the direct effect of a default and devaluation by the periphery would amount to 0.2 percent of GDP for Germany and France if Greece alone were to exit (and 0.1 percent of GDP for the Netherlands and Austria). If all five peripheral economies (Greece, Ireland, Italy, Portugal, and Spain) were to exit, the loss would amount to 1.5 percent of GDP in Germany, 2.3 percent in France, 1.8 percent in the Netherlands, 1.5 percent in Belgium, and 1 percent in Austria (p. 52). The authors judge that such losses "would not radically transform the public finances of core members," but recognize that "indirect losses might be much bigger, resulting from economic deterioration and market turmoil" (p. 53).

For the exiting country itself, the Bootle report makes the qualitative judgment that leaving the euro would "support an economic recovery through increased net exports" (p. 13), and that the alternative of adjustment through austerity and internal devaluation would be far worse. The report makes the key assumption that regardless of current EU legal documents, a country that exits the euro would not be thrown out of the European Union and lose its privileges of free market access for capital, labor, and goods. The Bootle report's central economic assumption is that the peripheral economies "unambiguously need a depreciation of their real exchange rate" for both external balance and full employment (p. 10), with needed real devaluations of 40 percent in Greece and Portugal, 30 percent in Italy and Spain, and 15 percent in Ireland (p. 48). Yet as argued above, the premise that a much larger current account adjustment is needed than has already happened is dubious. More generally, the casual fashion in which the report passes over likely costs to the exiting country itself from bank closures, contract revisions, and massive uncertainty associated with the exit leaves the case for breakup unconvincing. The principal value of the study is thus to contribute to the set of benchmark estimates of spillover effects on the rest of the euro area.

Among other prominent estimates of euro breakup costs, the most pessimistic is that of economists at Union Bank of Switzerland (UBS) (Deo, Donovan, and Hatheway 2011). They estimated that for a weak euro country exiting from the currency, the cost would amount to €9,500 to €11,500 per person during the first year (40 to 50 percent of GDP), and ongoing annual costs of €3,000 to €4,000 thereafter. For a strong euro member country such as Germany, they estimate that leaving the euro would cost its citizens €6,000 to €8,000 per person in the first year (20 to 25 percent of GDP), and €3,500 to €4,500 annually thereafter. Potentially greater than the economic cost, they argue, would be the political cost, as a breakup of the euro would eliminate Europe's "soft power" (p. 1).

The authors highlight five costs of a breakup. First, default on euro-denominated public debt would be almost certain, whether directly or through redenomination into a new national currency. Default would cause long-lasting economic costs from higher borrowing costs for the government. Parallel corporate default would be likely because of a forced change in the currency denomination of private debt. Corporate borrowing costs would rise because of the sovereign ceiling on credit ratings. Depreciation of the currency would be deep, sharply increasing the burden of debt left in foreign currency denomination.

Second, exit would likely trigger collapse of the domestic banking system, as depositors withdrew money from banks in the face of uncertainties about the new national currency. Only a closure of the banking system could prevent mass withdrawals. There would be contagion to other periphery economies as depositors there also would begin withdrawals. Third, an exiting country could not expect to remain a full member of the European Union. Negotiation to reenter the European Union, with partners sideswiped by spillover damage, would likely take years. Fourth, and most questionably, the authors assume that euro area partners would impose compensatory tariffs equal to the amount of the depreciation of the leaving member; they cite as illustrative a 60 percent depreciation and 60 percent tariff. Fifth, they posit that there could be civil disorder, and that leaving the euro could trigger further centrifugal forces within the country for fragmentation along ethnic or linguistic lines.

To arrive at their estimates, the authors assume a 60 percent depreciation of the currency against the remaining euro area; a 700 basis point increase in the risk premium for borrowing; a decline in trade volume by 50 percent;

a 50 percent runoff in bank deposits; and a 60 percent loss of value of the remaining bank deposits as depositors are forced to recapitalize banks. They do not provide equations or parameters that indicate how these assumptions generate the estimated costs.

For strong countries leaving the euro, there would be no default implications for the government; its fiscal position would improve as the burden of euro-denominated debt would be reduced from appreciation. However, banks would need to be recapitalized, because banks holding euro assets would have new national currency liabilities that would be appreciated. Strong countries would also face cutoff from the EU because the law permits no "halfway house." On trade, the authors contend that "The strong seceding country would effectively have to write off its export industry." Appreciation of the new currency would make exports uncompetitive, "exactly the issue that worried Germany pre-Euro" (Deo, Donovan, and Hatheway 2011, 12). The appreciation would be large and rapid, spurred by capital flight from weaker euro countries to quality, the new currency of the leaving strong country.

Overall, the UBS estimates seem substantially exaggerated. The key assumption of a cutoff from the European Union seems implausible, despite the existing treaty provisions. It is even more implausible that (for a weak country leaving) there would be retaliatory tariff increases by partners, and EU tariffs are low enough even for most-favored-nation partners (which leavers would become) that the collapse in trade assumed by the authors would be unlikely. The study is perhaps more helpful in articulating main categories of damages, and in serving to remind that an exit by a strong country would be costly to that country, albeit less costly than the cost to a leaving weak country.

Economists at ING Bank have provided euro breakup cost estimates that are more moderate but still high. In an early study (Cliffe and Leen 2010, 9), the ING team calculated that if Greece alone left the euro, Greek output would fall against baseline by a cumulative 9 percent over three years; the corresponding output losses would be 2 to 4 percent in the rest of the periphery and 1.5 percent even in France and Germany. If there were a complete breakup of the euro, the three-year cumulative output loss against baseline would be 10 percent of GDP for the euro area as a whole, 7 percent in the United Kingdom, and 3 percent in the United States. The euro would fall to $0.85 in both cases, and temporarily to $0.70 in the complete breakup.[28] New currencies of the periphery economies would fall 50 percent, spurring inflation. The authors do not set forth the methodology they use to arrive at these estimates, however.

A subsequent study by the group focuses on the asset exposure of the core economies to the periphery economies (Cliffe, Vanden Houte, and van Vliet 2012). The authors first calculate that total official and banking sector

---

28. Although it is unclear what "the euro" would be in the complete breakup scenario. Implicitly the authors seem to refer to the new Deutsche mark. Their analysis differs from most, including especially that of the UBS group, in not featuring a strong appreciation of the core economies and especially Germany, and hence negative effects on their exports.

exposure in the "core" countries (Germany, France, the Netherlands, Belgium, Austria, and Finland) to the five periphery economies (Greece, Ireland, Italy, Portugal, and Spain) amounts to €2.2 trillion, or 36 percent of core economy GDP. Exposure of the official sector to the five economies amounts to a surprisingly uniform 20 to 22 percent of GDP for each of the six core economies. In contrast, French banks have much more exposure (20 percent of French GDP), as do Dutch banks (16 percent) and German banks (13 percent), than do banks in Belgium (10 percent), Austria (7 percent), and Finland (1 percent).

The authors emphasize the concentration of official exposure in the Eurosystem. Target2 liabilities of Ireland, Portugal, Spain, and Italy amounted to €832 billion as of mid-2012, and the ECB held an additional €175 billion in bonds of the four economies purchased over the two previous years.

They estimate that even if only Greece were to leave the euro, there would be a GDP growth loss (against the base case) amounting to 1.2 percent of GDP in the first year for the average core economy and 2 percent for the average peripheral economy (excluding Greece). They judge that a Greek exit could cause a wider exit of peripheral economies triggered by bank runs.

The ING study does not provide a formal model of breakup costs, however, and mainly bases its argument on the large numbers for stocks of exposure of core economies to periphery economies. Ideally there would be some methodology for translating these stocks into expected one-time and recurrent losses. The authors instead appeal to the argument that progress is being made, for example in the rapid reduction of Spain's current account deficit, and thus that fixing the euro is likely to be much cheaper than breaking it up.

For its part, the IMF has made illustrative calculations of the costs of a more limited breakup of the euro: the exit of Greece (IMF 2013c, 78). It judges that "Direct spillover risks have been receding, crisis preparedness in the euro area has improved greatly, and...contagion...risks have been falling.... [However] indirect spillover risks from a Greek exit remain substantial." Because exposure of the private sector to Greece has fallen sharply, direct financial losses from a potential default are a less likely source of spillovers than before. The Fund notes that in case of exit and default, there would be not only an output collapse but also a sharp depreciation of the exchange rate, and both would weigh heavily on Greece's capacity to service debt denominated in foreign currency. However, external liabilities have fallen to less than 1 percent of euro area GDP. Trade effects would be limited because Greece accounts for only 2 percent of euro area GDP, and for most European countries, exports to Greece are less than 1 percent of their GDP. For the official sector, total exposure to Greece is around 2 percent of GDP, so the scope of even deep writedowns of the Greek Loan Facility (bilateral) and European Financial Stability Facility loans and Eurosystem and ECB claims would be limited. (Exceptions include branches of Cypriot banks in Greece.)

The IMF notes that there has been a falling correlation between spikes in Greek CDS rates and those of other peripheral economies, indicating an easing of contagion risk. Even so, "the potential euro area output cost of a Greek exit is fundamentally uncertain and of a very large magnitude in certain scenarios" (p. 80). The IMF authors model the historical relationship of a financial stress index (FSI) to growth. The severity of the FSI shock in the event of Greek exit would depend on the effectiveness of the European firewall and the likelihood of bank runs. The IMF note estimates that if the FSI shock were similar to that in 1998 when Long Term Capital Management collapsed, euro area output loss could be 1½ percent of GDP for one year; if the shock were equivalent to that of the Scandinavian banking crisis in the early 1990s, the loss of output would be 3 percent of GDP for one year. But if the Greek exit proved to be as catastrophic as the collapse of Lehman Brothers, the model indicates that output loss would amount to 6 percent of euro area GDP in the first year, another 5 percent in the second year, and another 1 percent in the third year. The Fund concludes that "it is not possible to establish that contagion from euro exit would be limited and manageable" (p. 80).

It is striking that in the severe case, exit by Greece alone could cause damage amounting to 12 percent of euro area GDP over three years. So the real calculus for breakup involves a low (or perhaps not-so-low) probability, high-cost event. Correspondingly, the implication is that the right way to think about the problem is that it behooves the euro area to pay a modest insurance premium (call it "whatever it takes") to keep the euro intact in order to avoid the risk of a catastrophic outcome.

5

Eurobonds, Firewalls, Outright Monetary Transactions, and Debt Restructuring

This chapter seeks to round out the discussion of leading functional issues in the management of the euro area debt crisis, before turning to the model-based projections in the final chapters of this study. One policy area concerns the possible development of eurobonds as a vehicle for limiting debt costs to periphery economies by avoiding excessive sovereign risk premiums. A second policy area is that of the institutional firewalls in the euro area that can provide what amounts to lender of last resort support to debt-stressed periphery economies. A third policy area is that of debt restructuring arrangements and strategy, a theme that has taken on a higher profile both because of the Greek restructuring of 2012 and the apparent recent escalation of policy discussion within the International Monetary Fund (IMF) on more aggressive and preemptive debt reduction initiatives.

By far the most important policy instrument devised so far in managing the euro area debt crisis has been the European Central Bank's (ECB) program of Outright Monetary Transactions (OMT). By implication, it is important to ensure that the program remains in place and is not eliminated or debilitated by the recent German Constitutional Court challenge. Calls for debt mutualization through eurobonds have remained quixotic, although a practical alternative involving an insurance fund proposed here might be useful as a contingent instrument if the crisis returns to a more acute phase. The European Financial Stability Facility (EFSF) and European Stability Mechanism (ESM) firewalls have been helpful for the three program countries (Greece, Ireland, and Portugal). However, they have been limited to a size too small to deal with a crisis in Italy or Spain, should one arise. As for proposals for new financial architecture for euro area sovereign debt restructuring, they would seem counterproductive. The case for them has not been meaningfully strengthened by either the experience of Greece—which is best seen as a special case—or recent court decisions on Argentine debt.

Eurobonds

At least since mid-2011, it has been evident that the heart of the euro area sovereign debt crisis is the danger that escalating risk spreads on public debt will provoke a self-fulfilling prophecy of default.[1] There is essentially a "multiple-equilibrium" problem. In the good equilibrium, investors have confidence and interest rates remain only moderately higher than those of the risk-free base, German bund rates. In the bad equilibrium, investors fear default and the risk premium is far higher. At the higher interest rate, the same stock of debt that would have been manageable in the good equilibrium becomes unsustainable in the bad one, because the debt stock balloons as the deficits are much higher because of higher interest payments.

In 2011 and the first half of 2012 it became increasingly clear that there was a need for a firewall that could prevent interest rates on government debt in Italy and Spain from spiraling still further upward (for example, to the mid-2012 level of 12 percent for Portuguese debt) thereby causing the self-fulfilling prophecy of insolvency. The firewall needs to be large: Outstanding medium- and long-term public debt maturing in 2012–15 will have amounted to about €900 billion for Italy and Spain. There have been three well-known candidates for a large firewall: "eurobonds" of some type, in which sovereign risk is mutualized with joint and several liability across euro member governments; a sharp expansion of the ESM, which at its existing level of €500 billion is too small to deal with a potential crisis in Italy and Spain; and the lender of last resort to date, the ECB. The ECB lent about €1 trillion to periphery economy banks in late 2011 and early 2012, and more importantly announced its OMT program in early August of 2012, as discussed below. Over the following year sovereign spreads fell substantially in Ireland, Portugal, Italy, and Spain, but it remains to be seen whether the OMT will prove to be a permanent solution.

Germany has stoutly resisted a major scaling up of the ESM because it is the country most likely to be stuck with the bill in the event of losses. For the same reason, Germany has also resisted eurobonds in the absence of a far greater centralization of fiscal control, an institutional development that could take years. Also, whereas eurobonds might sharply cut interest rates on new bonds for periphery economies, mutualization of euro area debt would presumably raise borrowing costs for Germany and other core economies.

In mid-2012 prior to the launching of OMT, both the newly elected French president François Hollande and Italy's then prime minister Mario Monti

---

1. This section draws on William R. Cline, "A Better Euro Bond," *Wall Street Journal*, European Edition, June 7, 2012.

called for eurobonds as a means of resolving the crisis.[2] Germany's Chancellor Angela Merkel reiterated and hardened her opposition to eurobonds in late June 2012, stating that "eurobonds, euro bills and European deposit insurance with joint liability" were "economically wrong and counterproductive" and contrary to Germany's Constitution.[3] Then in the third quarter of 2012 the easing of risk spreads in periphery sovereign borrowing that followed the announcement of OMT substantially reduced the profile of eurobonds as a major policy option for dealing with the crisis.

Leading Eurobond Proposals

Given the solid opposition of the Merkel government, discussing various alternatives for eurobonds may be as useful as debating the gender of angels.[4] With this caveat, the leading eurobond proposals are the following. (For a useful survey, see Claessens, Mody, and Vallée 2012.)

The first prominent proposal for eurobonds, by Jacques Delpla and Jakob von Weizsäcker (2010), would convert euro area sovereign debt into two classes. The first, blue bonds, would be mutualized, with joint liability of all euro area governments. An amount of debt up to 60 percent of a country's GDP would be eligible for conversion into blue bonds.[5] Any debt in excess of this amount would be ineligible for joint guarantee, or red bonds. In principle this approach would have the benefit of creating a deep market for secure euro area bonds (about $8 trillion, approximately two-thirds the size of US treasury debt held by the public), strengthening the position of the euro as a reserve currency. It would also provide a price incentive for countries to avoid debt above the 60 percent of GDP threshold, because red bonds would pay higher, country-specific interest rates. But in the context of the present debt crisis, that would be a problem rather than a solution, because the peripheral economies all have debt far in excess of 60 percent of GDP, and high borrowing rates on new debt are the problem rather than a form of salutary discipline. Moreover, most of the existing stock of public debt from the past was contracted at a time when there were minimal risk spreads, so that conversion of the first 60 percent of GDP tranche to mutualized status would provide little interest rate relief (Cline 2012a, 219).

A second major approach has been proposed by the German Council of

---

2. Heather Stewart, "Hollande Pushes Case for Eurobonds," *Guardian*, May 22, 2012; Rachel Cooper, "Angela Merkel and Mario Monti Clash over Eurobonds," *Telegraph*, June 2, 2012.

3. Tony Czuczka, "Merkel Hardens Resistance to Euro-Area Debt Sharing," Bloomberg, June 25, 2012.

4. Although the leading German opposition candidate has called for eurobonds and an end to ECB bond purchases. Tony Czuczka, "German SPD Seeks Euro-Area Debt Pooling in Anti-Merkel Platform," Bloomberg, March 12, 2013.

5. The proposal subsequently was formulated to provide that the exchange for blue bonds would be completed over three to four years (Claessens, Mody, and Vallée 2012, 9).

Economic Experts: a European Redemption Fund (ERF) (see Bofinger et al. 2011). First suggested in the November 2011 annual report of the Council and subsequently fine-tuned, the proposal would have the ERF purchase all public debt of euro area members (including Germany) in excess of 60 percent of the GDP of each country in question. During the phase-in period of the first six years, rather than rolling over maturing debt in financial markets, countries would replace it with debt to the ERF at the lower interest rates it would be able to offer because of mutualization (except for Germany and some others who could borrow more cheaply on their own). Debt to the ERF would reach an estimated maximum of €2.8 trillion by 2018. The redemption phase would then begin, with complete repayment over the 20-year redemption phase. Countries would be expected to identify earmarked sources of revenue for redemption payments, and to pledge collateral in gold, foreign exchange reserves, or covered bonds amounting to 20 percent of their debt to the ERF. In return for access to the ERF, euro area member countries would implement German-style constitutional "debt brakes" to ensure adherence to the fiscal pact already agreed in December 2011. Managers of the ERF could boost the interest rate spread above its borrowing cost to sanction countries not meeting fiscal commitments, or lower this spread to reward countries performing well on fiscal targets. Countries would be expected to develop structural reform programs as part of the broader European Redemption Pact.

A third approach is that suggested by the euronomics group of European economists (Brunnermeier et al. 2011a). In this proposal, a European debt agency would purchase on the market euro area government bonds amounting to a total of 60 percent of euro area GDP, with the bonds of a given country limited to 60 percent of that country's GDP. The authors place this total at €5.5 trillion. The agency would finance these purchases by issuing a senior security, European Safe Bonds (ESBies), and a junior security. Each would be composed of a portfolio of euro area government bonds (in proportion to each country's GDP), and hence would not involve joint and several liability but instead some risk to the security from losses on a portion of its holdings. This is an exchange traded fund (ETF) structure, rather than a debt incurred and guaranteed by a supranational entity. The authors calculate that 70 percent of the portfolio could be in ESBies, and that even the subordinate remainder would have investment-grade ratings. Any default losses on the portfolio, however, would come at the expense of the junior security, which would pay a higher interest rate (6 percent in normal times). Countries with debt higher than 60 percent of GDP would be borrowing at the margin on their own national rating, "sending the right signal to the country's government" (Brunnermeier et al. 2011b).

Like the red bonds of the blue-red proposal, however, this structure would broadly leave the problem of high borrowing rates of peripheral economies unaddressed. Indeed, the authors seem to be more concerned about creating a truly liquid euro area public bond asset, the ESB, for two purposes: (1) providing euro area banks an alternative to holding their sovereign's bonds, curbing the "doom loop" between banks and sovereigns, and (2) creating "a large pool of safe assets" about half the size of the US treasuries, which would "stabilize and diversify global capital flows." However, it seems doubtful that Spanish banks (for example) have been increasing their holdings of Spanish government bonds (see chapter 3) because they cannot find any other safe assets. Instead, the banks of a given country in effect internalize external benefits from the shoring up of their own sovereign and hence their home economies that are missing when they invest in obligations of other sovereigns.[6] The availability of safe assets, the main objective of the ESB apparently, thus seems nongermane to the principal problem. Similarly, although strengthening the global financial system by creating a new large pool of safe assets is a worthy goal, it seems tangential to the euro area debt problem, which turns on a problem that the creation of this exchange traded fund would not address—reducing the marginal borrowing cost of peripheral countries.

A fourth proposal is that by Christian Hellwig and Thomas Philippon (2011). They propose a blue-red structure but one with mutualized blue debt (issued by a euro area debt management office) limited to short-term eurobills and set at about 10 percent of GDP (the level for treasury bills in the United States). The debt would be jointly and severally guaranteed. Although the authors do not explicitly say so, considering that the peripheral economies have debt ratios exceeding 100 percent of GDP, and that the short-term portion already pays a lower interest rate than the average, any interest savings would inherently be limited. Instead of overall interest cost savings, the authors emphasize that their approach would "help with crisis management as well as financial regulation … while minimizing the risks of moral hazard" (p. 1). They judge that the assured availability of short-term debt would prevent liquidity crises, providing indirect benefit to the economies (and indirectly easing long-term rates as well).

Strong countries would have to participate, and all euro countries would abstain from issuing their own debt of less than two years maturity. The authors add that the eurobills would be the ideal asset for meeting new Basel III liquidity requirements. They also stress that limiting the term of the instrument is an indirect means of making it senior to other government obligations. Perhaps the central question about the eurobills proposal, however, is whether it would be sufficient to do much good. In the Greek debt crisis, in 2009 the runoff in short-term public debt amounted to 5.7 percent of GDP, whereas the gross borrowing need amounted to 30 percent of GDP (IMF 2011a, 49). On the other hand, in Portugal, the stock of short-term debt (about 11 percent of GDP) accounts for fully half of annual gross borrowing requirements. The mechanism might thus provide some crisis management benefits, although it is not clear that Germany and other core states could be convinced to give up issuance of their own short-term government debt. Overall, the proposal

---

6. Thus, in mid-2011 the *Economist* judged that "Since Greek banks have a natural interest in holding up the sovereign, they are likely to participate" in voluntary rollover of debt. See "Greek Debt: Everyone's Problem," *Economist*, June 22, 2011.

appears to amount to a "small steps" approach along the road to debt mutualization.

A Eurobond Insurance Fund

I have proposed an alternative approach that combines debt mutualization with the payment of bond insurance premiums by the borrowing countries at rates reflecting their long-term creditworthiness.[7] A bond insurance fund would provide a cushion insuring against potential losses for German and other euro area members taking on the responsibility of a share in the guarantees. With the cushion of a sinking fund based on bond insurance premiums and controls such as these on member country access, it is conceivable that German authorities would be prepared to go ahead with eurobonds. A key difference between the bond insurance fund approach and the blue-red bond proposal is that the insurance approach would ensure that a reasonable ceiling would be set on the cost of new borrowing in the peripheral economies, whereas their borrowing on the red-bond market would make them vulnerable to surges of interest rates to unsustainable levels.

Based on past relationships of country ratings to sovereign risk spreads, I have calculated that the interest rate on a eurobond might be expected to be about 45 basis points above the German 10-year bund.[8] If the German bund were to return to 2.5 percent, placing the eurobond base rate at about 3 percent, there would be room for an additional sovereign risk spread of up to, say, 250 basis points for a less creditworthy euro area member, still leaving eurobonds as a means of borrowing at a sustainable rate, if not exactly a bargain rate. Over a decade, at 250 basis points the insurance premium would build up a sinking fund of 25 percent of the face value, available to cover losses before the guarantors of the eurobond would be called upon to make good on losses. The arrangement would set insurance premiums at lower rates for more creditworthy countries (those with lower debt, deficits, and external deficits) with the premium presumably at zero for Germany under current conditions (should it decide to borrow in eurobonds).

To arrive at country ratings for determination of the insurance premium bracket applicable to each country, a weighted average vote of all members except the one being rated would be applied (again using weights reflecting ESM contribution shares or otherwise reflecting potential liability shares). For this purpose the executive board of the insurance fund could take into account existing sovereign ratings by major private international rating agencies. It could also invite technical analysis by IMF staff regarding how countries would be rated based on past international statistical patterns, while avoiding formal

---

7. William R. Cline, "A Better Euro Bond," *Wall Street Journal*, European Edition, June 7, 2012.

8. Cline (2012a, 219). The estimate is based on a cross-country relationship of sovereign risk spreads to country credit ratings, on the one hand, and the existing profile of credit ratings across the euro area member countries, on the other.

IMF board approval of such analysis. The arrangement could also provide that a country could be disqualified from borrowing in a given year if at the time the government had strayed substantially from fiscal policies consistent with meeting its fiscal pact obligations. Such a determination of eligibility again could be made by a weighted average vote of members except the country in question, or alternatively, by a subgroup of countries whose shares in potential liability exceeded their shares in outstanding eurobonds.

The insurance premium approach to the eurobond proposed here would seem considerably more feasible and start at a much more moderate scale than especially the ERF. The ERF would be a "big bang" alternative that, for example, could involve immediate assumption of about €1 trillion in debt just for Italy alone. Instead of relying on some form of tax sequestration as in the ERF approach, the bond insurance approach would deal with the joint risk assumed by building up a sinking fund based on reasonably calibrated country insurance premiums. Importantly, the insurance approach would directly limit interest rates paid at the margin on new debt, whereas none of the four major eurobond proposals discussed above would do so.

By early 2014, sovereign risk spreads were back down to the vicinity of 200 basis points for Italy and Spain and even lower for Ireland (although they remained on the order of 330 basis points for Portugal). As a result, the bond insurance fund might most usefully be seen as a contingent instrument for renewed consideration in the event that the euro area sovereign debt crisis returns to a more acute phase in the future.

Firewalls

In the initial financial rescue package for Greece in May 2010, the euro area and other EU members responded with bilateral loans through the Greek Loan Facility (GLF), alongside lending from the International Monetary Fund. The GLF lending was to reach €80 billion through 2013, and IMF lending, €30 billion (EC 2013b). Also in May 2010, the Ecofin Council (of EU economic and finance ministers) created the European Financial Stability Facility as a temporary rescue mechanism. The EFSF was to provide lending capacity of €440 billion, which together with a potential €60 billion from the existing European Financial Stabilization Mechanism (EFSM) and potential IMF support then estimated at €250 billion, was seen as an overall firewall amounting to €750 billion.[9] In March 2011, the European Council (heads of state of the EU member countries) adopted a package of measures that included creation of a permanent crisis management vehicle, the European Stability Mechanism, which was to come into force in July 2013 (ECB 2011) and was ratified and inaugurated in October 2012.

Both the EFSF and then the ESM were to issue bonds on financial markets to raise capital. Whereas the EFSF relied on euro area member state guarantees,

---

9. "EU Announces 750 Billion Euro Crisis Shield with IMF," Reuters, May 10, 2010.

the ESM has total subscribed capital of €700 billion, of which €80 billion is paid in and €620 billion callable. The ESM's lending capacity is set at €500 billion. The EFSF had provided an opt-out option enabling a country in an assistance program to be excluded from the guarantee structure. This feature prompted critiques that the mechanism could implode from a cascading sequence in which contagion successively hit additional countries and at the same time thereby diminished the potential pool of support. Writing in the third quarter of 2011, Daniel Gros (2011) and others (e.g., Wolff 2012, 247) emphasized this weakness. As a solution, Gros proposed that the ECB issue a banking license to the EFSF, thereby giving it leveraged capacity to deal with the much larger financing needs that would arise if Spain, Italy, and even France were to need support and have to "step out" of the EFSF (Gros 2011).[10]

During the course of the subsequent year, the need receded for recourse to such devices for indirect action by the entity widely regarded to be the only one sufficient to the financing task if the crisis were to spill over to Spain and Italy: the European Central Bank. Instead, as the crises intensified in the second quarter of 2012, the taboo against monetary financing of government deficits gave way to the imperative to "do whatever it takes" to preserve the euro. Action by the ECB previously thought impossible, both in directness and scale, became the lynchpin of the euro area firewall in the form of OMT, discussed below.

In July 2013 the ESM replaced the EFSF, assuming its existing claims. The transition from the EFSF to the ESM involved several important changes, even though the size of the firewall remained unchanged. First, EU members not belonging to the euro were not asked to participate in the capital of the ESM. Second, there was a shift from guarantees with opt-out for program countries to a predetermined capital structure with some paid-in capital, a change the ECB considered favorable for reducing "migration risk" of potential downgrades in credit ratings of individual euro area countries. Third, the ESM is to have preferred creditor status (except on outstanding loans assumed from existing EFSF programs), subordinate only to the IMF. Fourth, the ESM eliminated the need for the donor country to pass the lending through its budget (as the paid and callable capital was to be viewed as acquisition of an asset in an international lending organization), thereby avoiding the awkward phenomenon whereby parts of the rising debt ratios of Italy and Spain were attributable to their EFSF-based support to the three other peripheral economies (ECB 2011). Fifth, as discussed in chapter 3, in mid-2013 Eurogroup leaders agreed

---

10. Similarly, in a war-game type simulation exercise convened in September 2011 by Bruegel and the Peterson Institute for International Economics, held in Chantilly, France, participants arrived at a proposal to have the EFSF purchase an initial €100 billion in Italian debt (for example), and then use it as collateral for a loan from the ECB; the new loan in turn would be used to make a second-round purchase of additional government bonds, and so forth, enabling the EFSF to expand its lending capacity some 7 to 10 times the initial €100 billion in this chain of repos, depending on the size of collateral valuation haircut applied by the ECB. See Cline and Wolff (2012, 247).

on enabling the ESM, through a subsidiary, to participate in bank recapitalization through purchase of equity shares, under rigorous conditions for bail-in burden sharing by existing shareholders and private creditors, as well as prior recapitalization contributions by the national government in question.

The question of private sector involvement (PSI) has been important in the evolution of thinking about the firewalls. Arising from the March 2011 meeting of the European Council, the "Term Sheet on the ESM" provided that ESM lending would require borrowing member states to seek private lender standstills maintaining their exposure (the "Vienna Initiative" approach) if a sustainability analysis showed that a macroeconomic adjustment program could restore debt to a sustainable path; and that "the beneficiary Member State will be required to engage in active negotiations in good faith with its creditors to secure their direct involvement in restoring debt sustainability" otherwise (European Council 2011, 30). The escalation of PSI anticipated for the ESM, in contrast to the absence of PSI in the earlier EFSF programs, in combination with the aggressive shift toward deeper private sector debt reduction in Greece in the second half of 2011, contributed to the rise in sovereign spreads in that period. In December 2011, the European Council backtracked from the earlier position on quasi-mandatory PSI. European Council President Herman Van Rompuy stated that "from now on we will strictly adhere to the IMF principles and practices. Or to put it more bluntly, our first approach to PSI, which had a very negative effect on the debt markets, is now officially over."[11] The "IMF principles and practices" were much more vague, including having skirted PSI in the cases of Ireland and Portugal.[12]

In August 2011, Germany rejected the call of the president of the European Commission for an increase in the size of the EFSF.[13] Nonetheless, two years later the sustained quiescence of sovereign risk spreads for both Italy and Spain (down to some 250 to 300 basis points in August 2013 in contrast to the 450 to 550 basis points a year earlier) in effect left the proximate need for a firewall primarily confined to the same three program countries that had been at the center of the debt crisis: Greece, Ireland, and Portugal. The scale of the ESM is adequate to deal with these three cases, especially if the success marked by Ireland's completion of its adjustment program by the end of 2013 and Portugal's progress toward completion of its program by May 2014 is not reversed by a new round of market deterioration. Total projected new borrowing in private medium- and long-term debt during 2014–16 amounts

---

11. Remarks by Herman Van Rompuy, president of the European Council, following the first session of the European Council, December 9, 2011, EUCO 155/11, Brussels, 1.

12. The only reference to PSI in the final ESM treaty was as follows: "In accordance with IMF practice, *in exceptional cases* an adequate and proportionate form of private sector involvement shall be considered" [emphasis added] (EU 2012, 6).

13. "EU Commission Chief Calls for Bigger Bailout Fund," France24, August 4, 2011; Bernd Radowitz and Terence Roth, "Germany Opposes Larger Rescue Fund," *Wall Street Journal*, August 8, 2011.

to about €35 billion for Ireland and €40 billion for Portugal (see chapter 6 appendix tables 6D.1 and 6D.2) and €9 billion for Greece (chapter 7 appendix table 7A.1). The total stock of EFSF/ESM claims on Greece, Ireland, and Portugal at the end of 2012 stood at €190 billion and was scheduled to rise to a peak of €245 billion in 2014 (tables 6D.1, 6D.2, and 7A.1). After adding €60 billion for lending to Spain for recapitalization of its banks, the total of about €300 billion already spoken for is three-fifths of the ESM's lending capacity. If the three program countries needed to replace new borrowing from private markets with official funding (because of a renewed round of market turmoil), and if the IMF provided one-third and the ESM two-thirds, the additional ESM lending in 2013–15 would amount to €56 billion. The fraction of total ESM lending capacity already outstanding would then rise to almost three-fourths.

For practical purposes, then, the ESM amounts to a firewall for the three existing program countries, and little else. At its present scale, it is not a meaningful vehicle for addressing liquidity if renewed market pressures were to emerge in Italy and Spain. Thus, new borrowing of medium-term debt in 2014–16 is projected at €587 billion for Italy and €484 billion for Spain (appendix tables 6D.3 and 6D.4), amounts that dwarf the €200 billion or so still available in the ESM.

Outright Monetary Transactions

Mario Draghi's "whatever it takes" speech occurred on July 26, 2012.[14] On August 2, 2012, the ECB announced that it would introduce a program of Outright Monetary Transactions in secondary markets for sovereign bonds, aimed at "safeguarding an appropriate monetary policy transmission and the singleness of the monetary policy" (ECB 2012, 1). In its technical description released on September 6, 2012, the ECB specified the following features of OMT. First, a condition for OMT would be "strict and effective conditionality" under an EFSF/ESM adjustment program or a precautionary program (Enhanced Conditions Credit Line of the EFSF), so long as the program included the possibility of EFSF/ESM primary market purchases. Second, the IMF would be involved for design of conditionality and monitoring. Third, eligible cases would include future EFSF/ESM programs, as well as existing EFSF programs when the countries in question are regaining bond market access. Fourth, there would be no quantitative limits set on the size of the OMT. Fifth, the bonds purchased would be toward the shorter end of the yield curve, one to three years. Sixth, the Eurosystem "accepts the same (pari passu) treatment as private or other creditors with respect to bonds issued by euro area countries" (p. 1). Finally, the previous Securities Markets Programme (SMP) was discontinued (and replaced by OMT) (ECB 2012).

Figure 5.1 shows the sovereign risk spreads above German bunds for

---

14. Mario Draghi, speech at the Global Investment Conference, London, July 26, 2012, www.ecb
.int/press/key/date/2012/html/sp120726.en.html.

Figure 5.1 Sovereign risk spreads, four euro area periphery countries, July 2011–January 2014

percent

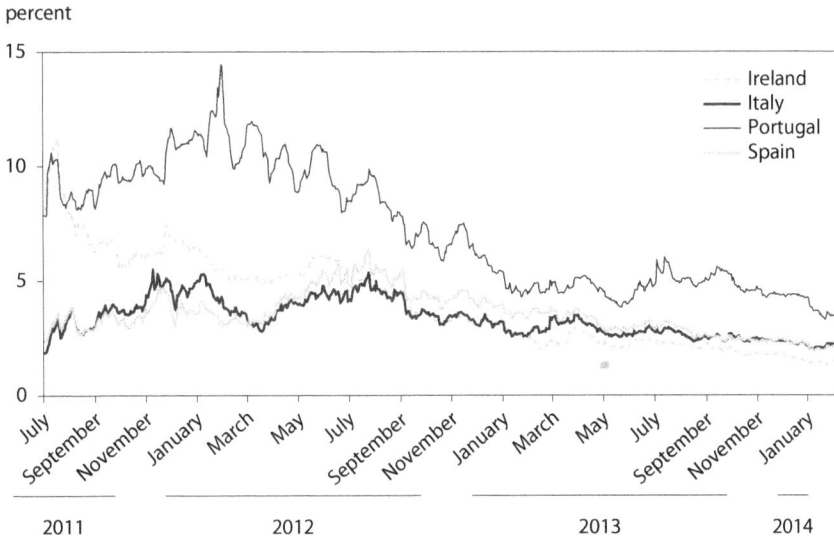

Source: Datastream.

10-year bonds of the four peripheral economies excluding Greece, from the beginning of July 2011 through the end of January 2014. For Italy and Spain, the peak of spreads was in late July 2012, before Draghi's speech. On July 20, 2012, the spread for Italy was 500 basis points; for Spain, 604 basis points. By September 7, after release of the technical details of OMT, the two spreads had fallen sharply, to 356 and 424 basis points, respectively. They continued to fall to 320 basis points and 396 basis points respectively by the end of 2012, and then to 215 and 220 basis points, respectively, by the end of 2013 and about 190 basis points by February 2014. There were similar declines for spreads for Ireland and (especially) Portugal—although the spread for Portugal rebounded significantly in the third quarter of 2013 in response to a government shakeup and as the US Federal Reserve announced the planned tapering of quantitative easing.

Figure 5.1 also shows the influence of an earlier episode of ECB intervention: the long-term refinancing operations (LTROs) provided to peripheral country banks at the end of 2011 and the beginning of 2012. This program had been less direct, as it provided liquidity to banks rather than representing potential purchases of sovereign bonds. It temporarily succeeded in reducing spreads (from about 500 basis points at the beginning of 2012 to 280 basis points in mid-March 2012, for Italy), but the spreads climbed once again in the second quarter of 2012 as the euro area debt crisis intensified with a risk of euro exit by Greece (in the face of new elections) and increasing concern about the Spanish banking system. By mid-2013, then, the mere announcement of the OMT appeared to have had a much stronger and longer-lasting effect than the approximately €1 trillion in LTROs. The crucial effect of the OMT has thus been to leap to the institutional resolution framework that had long been seen as necessary to deal with the crisis: forceful involvement of the ECB because it was the only institution large enough to deal with the crisis in the near term, whereas more comprehensive institutional reform of the euro area (such as fiscal union and/or banking union) would take years of negotiation (Cline and Wolff 2012, 2).

Draghi stated in July 2013 that "it's really very hard not to state that OMT has been probably the most successful monetary policy measure undertaken in recent time."[15] One tangible manifestation of the decline in spreads was that the IMF's baseline projection for Italy's interest payments by 2015 (for example) stood at 5.9 percent of GDP in its *World Economic Outlook* (WEO) of April 2012 but was cut to 5.4 percent of GDP in the corresponding WEO of April 2013, even though the projected debt ratio had escalated from 122 percent of GDP to 130 percent (IMF 2012h, 2013g).

OMT has faced consistent opposition from the Bundesbank.[16] On its website, the German central bank states: "The President of the German Bundesbank rejected the OMT in the ECB Governing Council because of its proximity to prohibited monetary financing of governments, with its associated consequences and perverse incentives."[17] However, German Chancellor Angela Merkel has supported OMT.[18]

As discussed in chapter 1, in early 2014 the German Constitutional Court challenged the OMT and referred its concern to the European Court of Justice. The benign market reaction suggested that the German court challenge would not derail the OMT (even though as noted in chapter 1, an eventual requirement eliminating pari passu could substantially weaken it). Even assuming that the OMT remains intact, a key question is whether this financial bazooka, which has proven to be so powerful so far, could actually be fired without backfiring. A structural risk is that if use of the OMT became necessary for either Italy or Spain, markets could fear the application of an adjustment program containing IMF funding, because that funding would raise the specter of subordination of private creditors to IMF credits. In view of recent IMF staff

---

15. Mario Draghi, Introductory Statement to the Press Conference (with Q&A), June 6, 2013, Frankfurt.

16. The Bundesbank reportedly submitted a highly critical report of the OMT to the German Constitutional Court in December 2012. Ambrose Evans-Pritchard, "Bundesbank Declares 'War' on Mario Draghi Bond Bail-out at Germany's Top Court," *Telegraph*, April 26, 2013.

17. Author's translation; see www.bundesbank.de/Navigation/DE/Bundesbank/Wissenswert/Glossar/Functions/glossar.html?lv2=32046&lv3=125056.

18. Brian Blackstone, "Germany, France Back Pledge to Save Euro," *Wall Street Journal*, July 27, 2012.

positions on debt restructuring (discussed below), and apparently heightened sensitivity within the IMF to going along with programs in which debt sustainability is uncertain following the rocky history of support to Greece, markets could also fear that full involvement of the IMF would raise the probability of some form of PSI. If so, the ECB pledge of pari passu treatment for OMT support might be trumped, in determination of market expectations, by the taint of forced recourse to the IMF. To minimize the risk of counterproductive market repercussions that might limit or thwart the effects of actual OMT purchases, it would thus seem highly desirable that if an IMF-associated program does become necessary for either of the two large economies, the IMF involvement should be solely in the form of technical advice. Technical advice creates no class of preferred creditor. Moreover, the advice would be considered, but not necessarily followed in all details (especially regarding PSI and debt reduction). Alternatively, the euro area could rely on its own adjustment program using the precautionary program structure first set up within the EFSF, the Enhanced Conditions Credit Line (EFSF 2011).

Debt Restructuring

IMF Reconsiderations

Despite the success of OMT in calming euro area periphery sovereign debt markets in the year from mid-2012 to mid-2013, in the same period there was a perceptible slide in international policy venues toward debt restructuring as a vehicle for addressing the crisis. Most notably, a self-evaluative review by the IMF found that the initial 2010 program for Greece was mistaken in providing large ("exceptional access") finance despite the lack of a high probability of debt sustainability. At the time a special exception had to be added to IMF rules to permit such lending under the alternative justification that there was a "high risk of international spillover effects" (IMF 2013h, 10). The report concluded that

> not tackling the public debt problem decisively at the outset or early in the program created uncertainty about the euro area's capacity to resolve the crisis and likely aggravated the contraction in output. An upfront debt restructuring would have been better for Greece *although this was not acceptable to euro partners* [emphasis added]. A delayed debt restructuring also provided a window for private creditors to reduce exposures and shift debt into official hands. (p. 28)

Euro area officials heatedly took issue with the Fund's critique. The EU Commissioner for Economic and Monetary Affairs and the Euro, Olli Rehn, stated that the IMF itself had not supported an early debt restructuring.[19] ECB

---

19. Jussi Rosendahl, "IMF Didn't Seek Early Greek Debt Restructuring: EU's Rehn," Reuters, June 7, 2013.

President Draghi shared the Commission's view that the IMF critique reflected hindsight bias.[20]

As for the amount of debt pushed onto the public sector by fleeing private creditors, a PSI stretchout began in July 2011 (and was replaced by a deep haircut in early 2012). So in practice the maximum runoff of private claims would have amounted to €6 billion in short-term debt and about €30 billion in maturities coming due from mid-2010 to mid-2011 (IMF 2010c, 28). So at the most, absence of an early, preemptive rescheduling caused the €130 billion in official support in the first program to be about one-third larger than it otherwise would have needed to be. Considering that the debt restructuring of early 2012 managed to capture about €200 billion in private claims, the leakage was small (and probably considerably less than the maturity-based maximum estimate).

A companion IMF policy review in April 2013 concluded more generally that "debt restructurings have often been too little and too late, thus failing to establish debt sustainability and market access in a durable way" (IMF 2013i, 1). That report spoke favorably of "preemptive" action when a country decides restructuring is needed (p. 11). Together, the reports suggest that IMF staff have been moving in the direction of more aggressive debt restructuring.[21] Yet implementing restructuring that can be avoided is likely to cause losses to both the borrowing country and creditors, especially if a haircut is imposed (with its effect of eroding the country's credit reputation and inflicting direct losses on creditors), and in the case of the euro area, risk serious contagion effects.

Euro Area CACs

A second and less known arena of recent policy change in the direction of restructuring has come from a Eurogroup agreement in November 2010, subsequently incorporated in the ESM treaty, that beginning in 2013 countries in the euro area would incorporate collective action clauses (CACs) in their international and domestic debt issues. The CACs are to provide for qualified supermajorities of two-thirds to 75 percent to enforce agreed restructurings on dissident bondholders. They include aggregation clauses, which prevent private investors from buying up just enough of a single specific bond issue to block the supermajority, as the voting is aggregated across all issues

---

20. He stated, "Often these mea culpa are a mistake of historical projection—you tend to judge things that happened yesterday with today's eyes. We tend to forget that when the discussions were taking place the situation was much, much worse. The fear of contagion and the high volatility." A Commission spokesman stated, "An uncontrolled default of Greece in 2009 or a debt restructuring early in the programme would have had devastating consequences not just for the rest of the euro area … but also for Greece itself." See Bruno Waterfield, "Brussels Dismisses 'Plainly Wrong' IMF Criticism over Greece," *Telegraph*, June 6, 2013.

21. One article in late 2013 indicated that "the I.M.F. is advocating a more aggressive approach to debt restructuring" but that it was "encountering stiff resistance … from European policy makers and … the United States government.…" See Landon Thomas, Jr., "I.M.F. Shifts Its Approach to Bailouts," *New York Times*, November 26, 2013.

(ECB 2011). In the past, advanced industrial countries have not used CACs, because of the implicit underlying assumption that they would never restructure debt. In 2003, the Group of 10 large industrial countries advocated inclusion of CACs as a standard for good practice for emerging-market economies issuing debt on international markets (primarily in New York and London). They did not consider CACs for their own debt in their own domestic currencies, however. The milestone of euro area CACs epitomizes two new realities: Advanced countries can experience sovereign defaults, and euro area countries are in effect borrowing in foreign currency when they borrow in euros.

Reviving the SDRM?

Following the previous major historical episode of sovereign debt crises—the East Asian crisis of the late 1990s and its eventual spillover to defaults in Russia and Argentina—the deputy managing director of the IMF at the time proposed a Sovereign Debt Restructuring Mechanism (SDRM).[22] The SDRM would give the IMF authority to approve a standstill, including foreign exchange controls, to bind minority creditors opposing a workout agreed to by a majority of creditors, and to grant preferred creditor status for new borrowing, broadly replicating the domestic bankruptcy process. The SDRM inherently posed some risk that debt workouts would become politicized and that a resulting weakening of creditor recourse could aggravate the central problem of sovereign lending—the absence of collateral (Eaton and Gersovitz 1981)—and thereby erode lending. The US Treasury opposed this "statutory" approach to debt resolution and called instead for a "contractual" approach based on CACs in bond contracts. Major borrowers such as Mexico were concerned that the SDRM could undermine their market access, and began implementing the alternative approach of CACs in their new international bonds. CACs allowing a qualifying majority (typically 75 percent or more of bondholders by value) to bind other dissenting bondholders in a restructuring agreement became standard, and by 2005 approximately 90 percent of new sovereign bond issues under New York law contained CACs (Committeri and Spadafora 2013, 17).

Until recently the emerging consensus was that the collective action problem in restructuring that the SDRM had sought to address had turned out to be much less serious than expected, and that even without the recent CACs, bonds had been successfully restructured in numerous cases where the exchange offers were perceived by creditors to be fair (Bi, Chamon, and Zettelmeyer 2011).[23] However, two new developments are seen by some of

---

22. Anne O. Krueger, International Financial Architecture for 2002: A New Approach to Sovereign Debt Restructuring, speech at National Economists' Club Annual Member Dinner, American Enterprise Institute, November 26, 2001. See also Cline (2006, 268-69).

23. One reason was that "exit consents" in restructuring agreements, using clauses that required only a simple majority, were found to be useful in degrading the existing bonds and making them less attractive for holdouts to retain (Buchheit 2012, 188).

the same experts as grounds for reviving something like the SDRM, both in the IMF and more specifically within the euro area: the experience of Greece, and new court rulings on Argentine debt.[24] A study by the Committee on International Economic Policy and Reform (CIEPR) has argued that the case of Greece shows that the problem is too much sovereign lending, not too little, that restructurings are too small and too late, and that CACs may not be sufficient without strong aggregation laws that overcome the problem of a sizable holdout minority in an individual bond (Buchheit et al. 2013). The same study argues that recent rulings on Argentina will make the holdout problem more severe by calling for pari passu (similar) treatment of payments to holders of restructured instruments and holdout owners of the original bonds.

The CIEPR study calls for the euro area to require that in any ESM support to a debt-stressed member country, if the country's debt-to-GDP ratio exceeds 90 percent the support should be contingent on a debt restructuring. Moreover, it recommends that assets and revenues of countries undertaking a debt restructuring be immune from legal action by holdouts if the restructuring were approved by the ESM (Buchheit et al. 2013, v). These would be the two key elements in a European Sovereign Debt Restructuring Regime (ESDRR). The authors consider this relatively aggressive architecture to be needed because euro area members are deprived of two usual adjustment mechanisms: exchange rate depreciation and inflation.

The central problem with any move to set up this mechanism or any other SDRM of this nature for the euro area is that it would risk doing far more damage than good. By far the most important task facing euro area sovereign debt management is ensuring that neither Spain nor Italy is forced into an unnecessary default. Yet setting up the ESDRR recommended by the CIEPR authors would unleash expectations that precisely such an event could become much more likely, given Italy's debt ratio of over 130 percent and Spain's debt ratio of over 90 percent. Doing so would also send the signal that sovereign insolvency can be expected with some frequency in the euro area. The consequences for sovereign risk spreads could hardly be favorable. Instead, a good case can be made that the Greek insolvency was unique, and that the other member economies of the euro area are solvent so long as there is not a destabilizing escalation of risk spreads that causes a self-fulfilling prophecy of insolvency. Indeed, it is this basic assumption that implicitly underlies the crucial decision of the ECB to eschew seniority in any purchases of sovereign bonds it makes in the OMT, a pari passu commitment that undergirds rather than undermines private sector confidence. The proposed ESDRR would do just the opposite, by preemptively calling for private sector restructuring as a condition for ESM support.[25] Although the CIEPR authors are aware of the danger

---

24. The "Greece and Griesa" problems (Judge Thomas Griesa issued the decisions), as I phrased it at an IMF meeting of experts. See Felix Salmon, "The IMF Revisits Sovereign Bankruptcy," Reuters, October 21, 2013.

25. The same study argues that recent court decisions on Argentine debt escalate the problem

of perverse expectational effects and therefore acknowledge that "In the short run … [it] could not be activated since it would trigger immediate instability" (Buchheit et al. 2013, 42), the projections in the present study suggest that even as late as 2020 the main periphery economies would not be below the 90 percent debt ratio, so the practical relevance of the proposal seems limited.

Greece as a Special Case

Chapter 6 sets forth projections using a probabilistic debt simulation model to determine whether debt is likely to be sustainable in the four peripheral economies that have not restructured debt: Ireland, Portugal, Italy, and Spain. Chapter 7 carries out comparable simulations to examine whether Greece will need still deeper debt forgiveness, this time by public sector creditors, in order to arrive at sustainable debt levels. For purposes of the more intuitive discussion of the present section, however, it is useful to consider broad indicators of the present status of debt to arrive at a preliminary and impressionistic view on sustainability by asking the following question: For each of the four nonrestructuring peripheral economies, does it more closely resemble France and Germany, or does it more closely resemble Greece? Figure 5.2 presents three summary indicators for this purpose. The first is the closely watched ratio of gross public debt to GDP; the second, the percent change in the nominal euro value of GDP from 2007 to 2013; and the third, the primary (noninterest) fiscal surplus as a percent of GDP (average achieved in 2012–13). Data are from the October 2013 *World Economic Outlook* of the IMF (IMF 2013n). The debt-to-GDP ratio for Greece is for end-2011, which reflects the level prior to debt reduction in the 2012 restructuring agreement. Two of the three summary indicators set Greece apart from all six of the other economies: the ratio of debt to GDP (170 percent for Greece at the end of 2011, versus 127 percent for the next highest country, Italy, at the end of 2012) and the performance of GDP growth from 2007 to 2013. There was a remarkable collapse of the nominal euro value of GDP by 18 percent in Greece, compared with a fall by 12 percent in the next-worst case (Ireland), about 2 percent in Portugal, about 3 percent in Spain, and a slight increase in Italy. In this dimension, however, the four nonrestructuring peripheral economies fared much worse than the

of holdouts. The decisions enjoin international banks from making payments to holders of restructured debt without making ratable payments to holders of original unrestructured debt (i.e., comparable fractions of the total obligation). However, the circumstances are extreme in the Argentine case (including Argentina's passage of a law in 2005 prohibiting any future settlement with holdouts, and the government's repeated ignoring of the court decisions). Especially considering that the language of the court decisions implies they would not set a general precedent, it would be highly risky for future holdouts in other restructurings to base their strategy on this case. See the comments about limited precedential implications by Charles Collyns and Anna Gelpern in the transcript of the release event for the CIEPR study, www.brookings .edu/~/media/events/2013/10/03%20sovereign%20debt/20131003_sovereign_bankruptcy_ transcript.pdf (30; 37).

Figure 5.2 Indicators of debt sustainability in euro area periphery, Germany, and France

a. Gross public debt, end-2012

percent of GDP

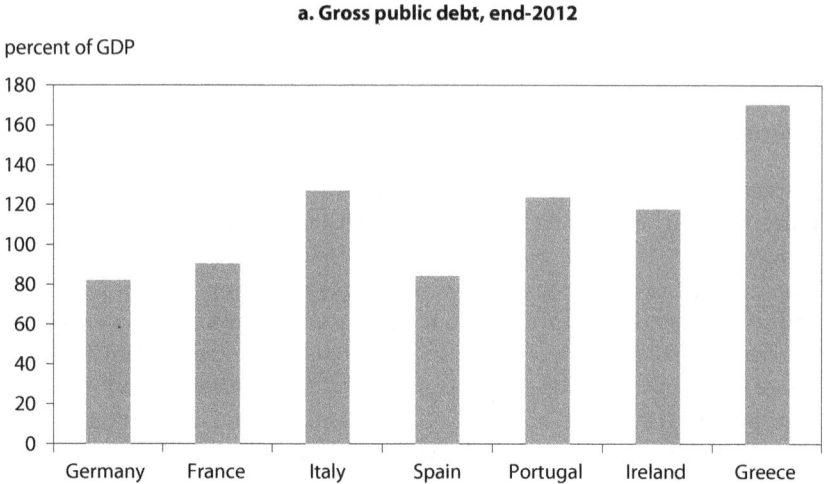

b. Change in nominal GDP, 2007–13

percent

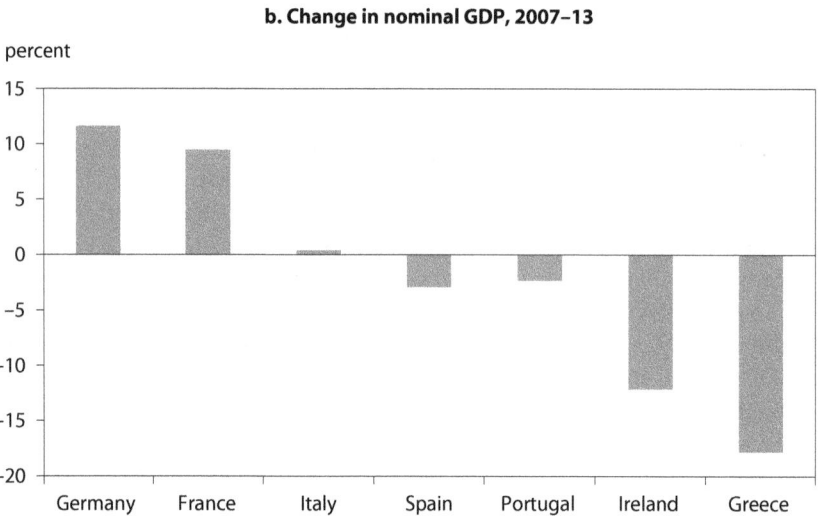

(continues on next page)

two core economies, as nominal GDP rose by about 9 percent (from 2007 to 2013) in France and 12 percent in Germany. On the third metric, the primary surplus, Spain and Ireland showed the worst outcomes, and in Spain it is the distance to go in closing the fiscal gap that is the greater problem than the level of debt already accumulated. Conversely, the relatively high level of the primary surplus in Italy tends to compensate for its high level of debt.

The informal implication of figure 5.2 could reasonably be that Greece has been *sui generis* because of its combination of a deep collapse in GDP with

Figure 5.2   Indicators of debt sustainability in euro area periphery, Germany, and France *(continued)*

c. Average primary surplus, 2012–13

percent of GDP

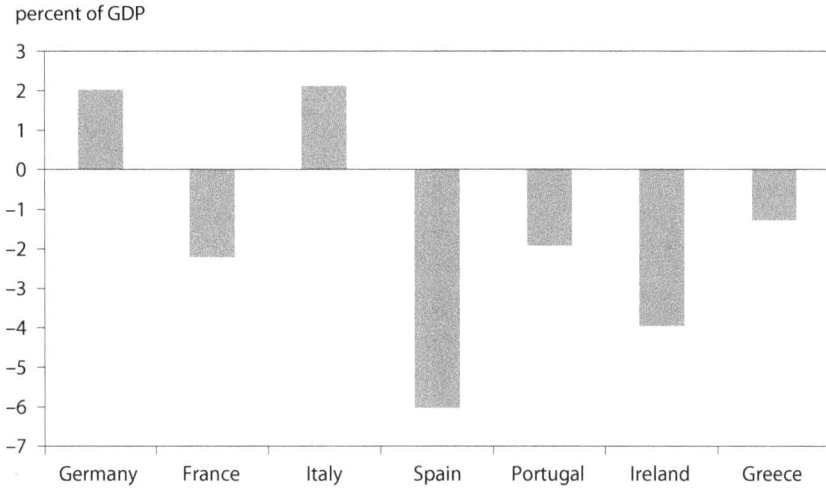

Note: For Greece, debt/GDP ratio is as of end-2011.

Source: IMF (2013n).

an exceptionally high ratio of debt to GDP. The model simulations of the following chapters examine more formally whether debt is likely to be sustainable, and hence whether restructuring is likely to be necessary or not, for the four other peripheral economies.

6

European Debt Simulation Model Projections: Ireland, Italy, Portugal, and Spain

The European debt crisis has been centered on a massive paradigm shift. For decades, it had been thought that the possibility of sovereign default for an industrial country was extremely remote; such defaults had not occurred since the 1930s.[1] As a consequence, when countries adopted the euro as a common currency in 1999, those among them that had faced higher interest rates because of higher inflation and currency risk were suddenly able to access capital markets at interest rates almost as low as those paid by Germany and other strong, low-inflation member economies. With the paradigm of negligible sovereign credit risk dominant in capital markets, there was no longer any reason for differentiation in interest rates given that there were no longer separate currencies.

The global financial crisis began to erode the presumption of identical sovereign credit risk and modest country spreads began to open up, but it was not until early 2010 that the paradigm shift occurred suddenly and dramatically, with news of far worse fiscal deficits in Greece than previously reported and new fears about the sustainability of Greek public debt (Cline 2012a, 208–209). By 2011–12, euro area member countries had become very much subject to the same type of scrutiny about sovereign credit that had previously focused on emerging-market economies.

It is widely recognized that the core conceptual underpinning for evaluating sovereign debt sustainability is that the fiscal balance needs to be sufficiently under control that debt does not spiral upward relative to GDP. Correspondingly, the central debt sustainability equation states that the

---

1. Although Germany remained in default on its World War I reparations until the London Agreement in 1953 cancelled half of its external debt, the default had begun in 1932.

"primary surplus" (noninterest expenditure minus noninterest revenue) must attain a level that reflects the competing influences of the interest rate (higher interest rate requires a higher primary surplus) and the growth rate (higher growth rate permits a lower primary surplus).

As discussed in chapter 2 and demonstrated in appendix 2A, the debt sustainability equation holds that if the ratio of debt to GDP is to be held constant (thereby avoiding an upward spiral out of control), the primary surplus π must essentially equal the existing debt-to-GDP ratio multiplied by the excess of the interest rate over the growth rate:[2]

$$\pi^* = \lambda(r - g) \tag{6.1}$$

where π^* is the debt-ratio-stabilizing primary surplus as a fraction of GDP, λ is the existing ratio of debt to GDP, r is the interest rate payable on the debt (in nominal terms), and g is the nominal growth rate of GDP.

Similarly, if there is a higher (lower) primary surplus, the ratio of debt to GDP will fall (rise), such that:

$$\Delta\lambda = \lambda(r - g) - \pi \tag{6.2}$$

That is: the change in the ratio of debt to GDP is equal to the debt ratio times the excess of the interest rate over the growth rate, minus the primary surplus. For example, if the ratio of debt to GDP is 1.20 (as in Italy in 2011), and the average interest rate on public debt is 5 percent, the nominal growth rate is 3 percent, and the primary surplus is only 1 percent, then the ratio of debt to GDP will be rising by 1.4 percentage point annually.[3]

The dynamics of debt sustainability mean that there is a high premium on avoiding an upward shock to interest rates, because eventually the higher interest rates can make insolvency a self-fulfilling prophecy. It was the surge of interest rates in the much larger economies of Italy and Spain in the second half of 2011 that suddenly transformed the European debt crisis from one of problems in minor member economies (Greece, Ireland, and Portugal) to a nearly existential threat to the euro area. Correspondingly, the perceived global risk from the crisis has ebbed and flowed with the various phases of sovereign risk spreads for especially these two large economies.

As shown in figure 6.1, crisis-level interest rates on government bonds afflicted Ireland and Portugal by the first half of 2011. Interest rates on 10-year bonds reached the stressed level of about 700 basis points in Spain and Italy by late 2011, then eased in early 2012 with a program of about €1 trillion in

---

2. The summary equation here is an approximation that ignores the cross product rg and the term g^2, which should approximate zero under modest inflation conditions.

3. That is, 1.2 (0.05 – 0.03) – 0.01 = 0.014.

Figure 6.1   Yields on 10-year sovereign bonds in euro area periphery and Germany

percent

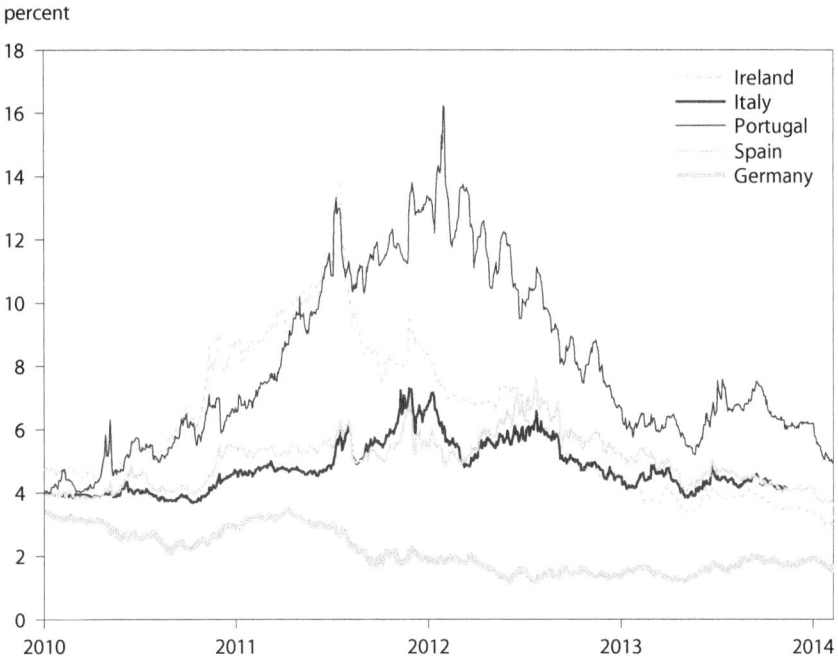

Source: Datastream.

long-term refinancing operations (LTROs) lending by the European Central Bank (ECB) to euro area banks. As political conditions deteriorated in Greece and concerns grew about Spain's banks, there was a return to higher interest rates for Spain and Italy in the second quarter of 2012, but the forceful mid-2012 announcement of ECB willingness to buy up to three-year government bonds in Outright Monetary Transactions (OMT) (ECB 2012), for countries entering into adjustment programs with the European Financial Stability Facility (EFSF) or European Stability Mechanism (ESM), brought a new phase of easing in market anxieties in the second half of 2012. These trends are evident in figure 6.1, which also shows the 10-year rate for the German bund, which has consistently eased as a result of the safe-haven effect. Consequently, the rates facing the debt-stressed economies have not risen as much as the corresponding sovereign risk spreads against the risk-free benchmark. The figure also shows an uptick in interest rates, especially for Portugal, in mid-2013 following the shift in US monetary policy toward proximate tapering off of quantitative easing and in the face of a government shakeup.

The sovereign debt simulation model applied in this study seeks to capture the dynamics of the debt sustainability equation by considering alternative scenarios for growth, interest rates, and the primary surplus, as well as taking into account privatization and bank recapitalization costs. This chapter applies the model to examine the public debt sustainability of Ireland and Portugal, two countries that have entered into adjustment programs with the International Monetary Fund (IMF) and euro area institutions, and the two crucial cases of Italy and Spain, which so far have not done so. The following chapter applies the model to the case of Greece, where sovereign debt restructuring has created considerably different circumstances.

Model Structure

The European debt simulation model (EDSM) combines assumptions about future paths of economic growth, fiscal performance, interest rates, debt incurred for banking recapitalization or other contingent debt, and privatization to arrive at the expected path of the public debt burden for each of five principal economies in the euro zone periphery. Earlier versions of the model were applied for Greece in Cline (2011), Italy (Cline 2012b), Spain and Italy (Cline 2012c), and again Greece (Cline 2013a). The study on Spain and Italy (Cline 2012c) introduced a method for identifying the probability distribution of the path of the ratio of debt to GDP, based on alternative scenarios for the key economic variables and taking into account the likely correlation of favorable versus unfavorable scenario alternatives (also applied for Greece in Cline 2013a). The present study applies this probabilistic version of the model, which is set forth in appendix 6A.

In the model, debt in a given year equals debt in the previous year, plus the fiscal deficit for the year in question, minus privatization receipts for the year, plus off-budget debt increases associated with bank recapitalization or other "discovered debt" (such as assumption of provincial arrears), plus any amounts used to purchase additional financial assets (or minus any drawdown in assets). The fiscal deficit equals net interest payments minus the primary surplus (or plus the primary deficit). Net interest payments are calculated applying relevant interest rates by broad category of debt to the respective amounts of debt outstanding at the beginning of the year, and deducting interest earned on government financial assets. The primary balance is assumed to be a particular target for the year in question.

The underlying objective of the projections is to assess the likely solvency or insolvency of each of the five principal sovereigns that have been affected by the European debt crisis: Greece, Ireland, Italy, Portugal, and Spain. A benchmark that has come into widespread use in recent years is that for euro area sovereigns, a ratio of gross public debt to GDP of 120 percent is the threshold below which solvency seems likely to be sustained and above which debt sustainability becomes increasingly questionable. As noted in chapter 2, the arithmetic of the debt dynamics above provides some support for this benchmark. Under normal conditions, a euro member country would likely be able to borrow at a real interest rate of 3 percent. It would be able to sustain real growth of at least 1 percent. With inflation at 2 percent, then a debt-to-GDP ratio of 120 percent would require a primary surplus of 2.4 percent of GDP to meet the sustainability equation (π^* in the first equation).[4] The benchmark might be too high for Greece, however, because markets could well be reluctant to return to financing a country with a damaged credit reputation except at lower debt levels.

Projections

The strategy of the projections is to apply the best central outlook for the key variables in the base case and plausible favorable and unfavorable values for each variable in the alternative scenarios, taking account of correlations across the scenarios. In most cases the baseline assumptions resemble those of the most recent IMF review of the country in question. However, there are some important differences, such as the use here of a more optimistic baseline for privatization receipts in Italy. Also, sovereign risk spreads tightened substantially in the second half of 2013 and first quarter of 2014, leading to somewhat smaller spreads assumed here than in the IMF Article IV reviews of Italy and Spain in the third quarter of 2013 (the most recent available).

The probabilistic approach set forth in this chapter deepens the projections by providing a robustness check even where the baseline itself closely resembles that of the IMF. This method, newly developed for the EDSM and first set forth in Cline (2012c), specifically takes account of the correlation between favorable and unfavorable states for alternative scenarios across the set of key economic variables. It thereby provides a more meaningful basis for arriving at a probability distribution of outcomes than would random combinations of favorable and unfavorable scenarios around the baseline.

Interest Rates

Except for Greece, where private sector debt restructuring occurred in March 2012 and official creditor restructuring was agreed in November 2012, the central dynamic in debt sustainability will be the return to (Ireland and Portugal) or maintenance of (Italy and Spain) capital market access at manageable interest rates. The baseline projections below calculate the interest rate for new (post-2012) medium- and long-term debt as the projected rate for the 10-year German bund plus a sovereign risk spread.

Table 6.1 reports the baseline outlook for the benchmark 10-year German bund for 2013 through 2020, along with the projected baseline country-risk spreads over this period. The bund rate for 2014–20 is based on the IMF's projection of average real 10-year government bond rates for the G-7 advanced economies, plus the IMF's projected annual inflation rates for Germany (IMF 2013g). Country sovereign spreads for 2013 are the actual averages for the year. These spreads were much lower than the corresponding spreads at the height of

---

4. Thus, $0.024 = 1.2 \times (0.05 - 0.03)$.

Table 6.1   Baseline interest rate benchmark and sovereign spreads, 2013–20

Country	2013	2014	2015	2016	2017	2018	2019	2020
10-year German bund (percent)	1.5	2.2	3.6	3.7	3.8	3.8	3.8	3.8
Sovereign spreads (basis points)								
Ireland	217	150	150	150	150	150	150	150
Italy	268	225	200	200	175	175	175	175
Portugal	472	350	300	250	225	200	175	175
Spain	295	225	200	200	175	175	175	175

Sources: For 2013: Datastream; for 2014–20: Author's calculations.

the crisis before the announcement of OMT.[5] For 2014 and beyond, all spreads eventually converge to a plateau of 175 basis points, except for Ireland, where the plateau is set at 150 basis points in light of levels already reached in early 2014. The higher initial spreads for Portugal will take longer to converge than those of Italy and Spain.[6] The central premise is that as the market shock from the European debt crisis continues to give way to medium-term normalization, sovereign spreads will consolidate further their recent trend of narrowing to more reasonable levels, although they will not return to their de minimis levels of the first phase of the euro area before the global financial crisis (2000-07).

For short-term debt (which stands at about 10 percent of total government debt in Portugal and Spain and about 7 percent for Italy, but less than 2 percent in Ireland), the interest rate is set at the projected inflation rate plus 0.5 percent for real return.[7] For the interest rate earned on government financial assets, a flat 2 percent is assumed over the period, below the benchmark 10-year German bund to reflect shorter average term.

For the adverse scenario, in all cases the baseline sovereign spread is increased by 150 basis points. For the favorable scenario, in all cases the baseline sovereign spread is reduced by 50 basis points.

The following discussion sets forth the other elements of the scenarios and the resulting range of projections for each of the four economies considered in this chapter. Detailed results of the baseline projection for each country are reported in appendix 6D. (Table 6D.1 shows projections for Ireland; table 6D.2 projections for Portugal; table 6D.3 projections for Italy; finally table 6D.4 has projections for Spain.)

---

5. Thus, average spreads in the second quarter of 2012 were as follows: Ireland, 560 basis points; Italy, 470 basis points; Portugal, 980 basis points; Spain, 420 basis points (Datastream).

6. The spreads in 2014 for Italy and Spain are slightly higher than those observed by February, allowing for some slowdown in the recent tightening of spreads.

7. For 2013 consumer price inflation is projected at 1.3 percent for Ireland, 2 percent for Italy, 0.2 percent for Portugal, and 1.9 percent for Spain. For 2014-20 the corresponding averages are 1.7 percent, 1.4 percent, 1.5 percent, and 1.5 percent, respectively (IMF 2013g).

Table 6.2   Scenario assumptions for Ireland

Scenario	2013	2014	2015	2016	2017	2018	2019	2020
	Real GDP growth (percent)							
1	—	1.0	1.8	1.8	1.8	1.8	1.8	1.8
2	0.1	1.7	2.5	2.5	2.5	2.5	2.5	2.5
3	—	3.0	5.9	5.9	5.9	5.9	5.9	5.9
	Primary surplus (percent of GDP)							
1	—	−1.3	1.0	1.7	2.2	2.7	2.7	2.7
2	−2.7	−0.3	2.0	2.7	3.2	3.7	3.7	3.7
3	—	0.2	2.5	3.2	3.7	4.2	4.2	4.2
	Privatization (billions of euros)							
1	—	0	0	0	0	0	0	0
2	0	1.0	1	1.0	0	0	0	0
3	—	1.5	2	1.5	0	0	0	0

Scenarios: 1 = unfavorable; 2 = baseline; 3 = favorable

Sources: IMF (2013p); author's assumptions.

Ireland

Table 6.2 shows the alternative scenarios considered for Ireland. The EDSM baseline is indicated as scenario "2." The unfavorable scenario is "1"; the favorable scenario, "3." For all three scenarios the values for 2013 are the best available estimates of actual outcomes. For 2014–18, the baseline adopts the growth and fiscal performance projections in the December 2013 IMF (2013p) review of the Extended Arrangement support program.[8] The 2018 rates are continued for 2019–20 (not included in the IMF projections). For growth, the unfavorable scenario is set at 0.7 percent below baseline. The favorable growth scenario for 2015–20 is set equal to the 60th percentile for annual growth observed in 1990–2012, which turns out to be 5.9 percent (IMF 2013g). The favorable rate for 2014 is set in between this favorable scenario benchmark and the 2013 outcome. The premise for the favorable growth scenario is that there is a potential for high snapback growth, subject to consistency with actual growth performance in the past. The large difference between baseline growth (reaching only 2.5 percent) and the favorable growth benchmark means that there is considerable "upside risk," or chance of a better-than-expected outcome.

The primary surplus baseline is set to rise from −4.5 percent of GDP in 2012 and −2.7 percent in 2013 to 0.3 percent by 2014 and a surplus of 3.7

---

8. This chapter applies the most recent available IMF growth projections for baselines. Estimates for actual growth for 2013 are from Consensus (2014). Estimates of actual 2013 outcomes for other variables are from the most recent IMF reviews for Ireland (IMF 2013p) and Portugal (IMF 2013q), and from the October *World Economic Outlook* (IMF 2013n) for Italy and Spain.

percent of GDP by 2017 (continued thereafter). It has been relatively little noticed, it would seem, that among the debt-distressed periphery economies, Ireland's 2012 fiscal performance ranks close to the bottom along with that of Spain (where the primary deficit stood at 7.7 percent of GDP in 2012, or 4 percent excluding bank recapitalization, and 3.3 percent in 2013; IMF 2013l). The unfavorable scenario places the primary balance at the baseline level minus 1 percent of GDP. Because the baseline already incorporates a relatively ambitious primary surplus (reaching 3.9 percent of GDP), the corresponding increment in the favorable scenario is instead set at 0.5 percent of GDP above the baseline. For Ireland, there is no inclusion of additional debt creation from bank recapitalizations or recognition of contingent debt, because the large bank recapitalization has already been carried out (see chapter 3). Public debt from these recapitalizations amounted to €52 billion over 2010–11, or 32.2 percent of 2012 GDP (IMF 2012d, 47). Nor is there any allowance for a possible shift of sovereign debt resulting from earlier bank bailouts onto the books of a euro area banking union. As discussed in chapter 3, although the June 2012 euro area decision to establish a banking union temporarily raised hopes that the ESM could inject capital to banks directly for Spain and perhaps do so retroactively for Ireland, opposition led by Germany soon ruled out this possibility for "legacy assets" and hence Ireland's bank-related sovereign debt. There is, however, a special treatment of interest on Ireland's debt associated with the bank recapitalization. As discussed in chapter 3, for €40 billion owed to the Central Bank of Ireland, the interest rate is a relatively favorable floating rate of 260 basis points above Euribor (see chapter 3).

For privatization, the government has stated the objective of privatizing €3 billion in state assets, mainly in electric power generation and gas. This amount is incorporated in the baseline scenario here. For the favorable case, the higher figure of €5 billion identified by an official advisory group in 2011 is applied.[9]

Figure 6.2 shows the results of the debt projections for Ireland under the scenarios of table 6.1. Details of the projections for the baseline are reported in appendix table 6D.1. In the baseline, the ratio of gross public debt to GDP, which had already risen from 44.5 percent of GDP in 2008 to 106.5 percent in 2011, will have peaked at 124 percent of GDP in 2013, and then will decline to 101 percent by 2020.[10] The figure also reports the 25th percentile (favorable low-debt path) and 75th percentile path (adverse), as well as the probability-weighted average of all 243 paths (the possible outcomes for five scenario variables with three cases each; see appendix 6A). Because of the inclusion of a favorable growth scenario with high growth (5.9 percent annually), the

---

9. Eamon Quinn, "Ireland Identifies State Assets for Sale," *Wall Street Journal*, February 22, 2012. Note, however, that the IMF (2013j) projects no privatization during this period.

10. The 2008 and 2011 levels are from IMF (2012d). In Cline (2011, 204) I estimate that about 40 percent of GDP in increased public debt stemmed from fiscal deficits (excluding bank support) in 2008–11, in comparison with about 30 percent of GDP attributable to the bank support.

Figure 6.2 Ireland: Gross debt as percent of GDP, 2011–20

percent of GDP

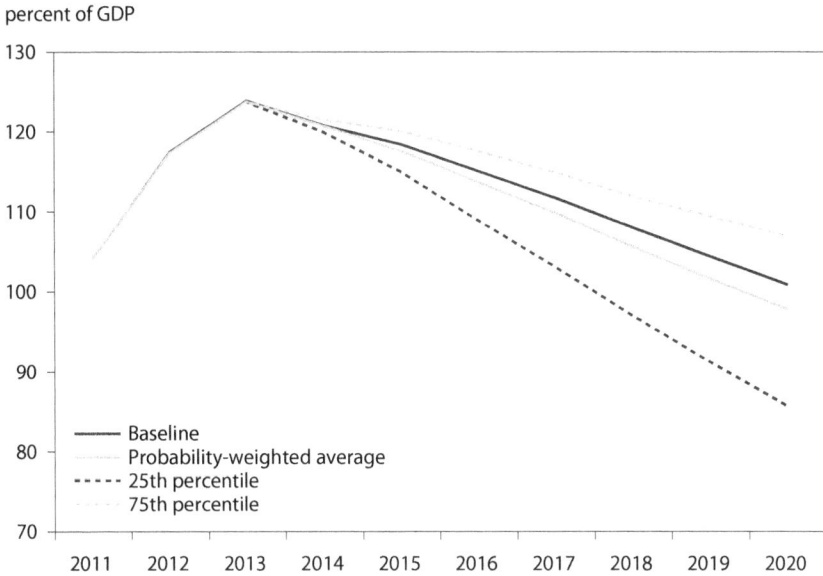

Source: Author's calculations.

probability-weighted outcome is considerably more favorable than the base case, and shows the debt-to-GDP ratio declining to 98 percent by 2020.

In December 2013, Ireland completed its program of official support. The government had already made a return to the private financial markets in July 2012, when it issued €5 billion in five-year bonds at an interest rate of 5.9 percent.[11] In January 2014, it issued €3.75 billion in 10-year bonds at a spread of only 140 basis points over German bunds.[12] Overall, the projections for Ireland suggest relatively robust prospects for debt sustainability and successful consolidation of its return to private markets, indicating that its exit from the official support program at the end of 2013 was timely rather than premature.

Portugal

Of the four major peripheral economies excluding Greece, financial markets have judged Portugal as remaining in the most precarious position. As recently as mid-2013, its sovereign spread on 10-year bonds stood at about 500 basis

11. Jamie Smyth and Ralph Atkins, "Ireland Returns to Global Bond Markets," *Financial Times*, July 26, 2012.

12. Conor Humphries and John Geddie, "Ireland Draws Bumper Demand for First Post-bailout Bond," Reuters, January 7, 2014.

points, the highest among the four economies (chapter 1, figure 1.1). By the end of 2013, however, the spread had fallen to 425 basis points, and by mid-February 2014 it had fallen further to only 330 basis points (Datastream). Soon after Ireland's early 2014 issue, Portugal returned to the bond market, issuing €3.25 billion in a five-year bond yielding 4.7 percent.[13]

Despite its higher spreads, especially in 2013, Portugal's cumulative decline in GDP from 2007 has been more modest than that of Ireland, its performance on the primary fiscal balance has been much better than that of Spain and Ireland, and its debt level relative to GDP is slightly below that of Italy and similar to that of Ireland (figure 5.2 in chapter 5). Portugal's unemployment rate of 17 percent in 2013 was well below Spain's level of 27 percent (IMF 2013n). Even so, as late as the third quarter of 2013 the *Economist* judged that "Markets are signaling disbelief that Portugal will avoid some form of second bail-out."[14] It cited IMF estimates that contingent liabilities from guarantees, public-private partnerships, and publicly owned firms could add debt of 15 percent of GDP.[15]

Despite adverse market perceptions at the time, the June 2013 IMF review of Portugal's adjustment program applauded the "strong progress in reducing economic imbalances—some two-thirds of the 10 percentage points of GDP structural primary adjustment required to stabilize public debt has been effected and the current account deficit has narrowed sharply" and noted that "Portugal was able to return to the international bond market in January for the first time since early 2011." In view of improving financing conditions and still high unemployment, the IMF support program was revised to ease the fiscal targets by 1 percent of GDP in 2013 and 1.5 percent in 2014. But the report judged that scope for more financing was limited and there was a "high risk that adjustment will continue to take place through more demand compression" rather than export expansion (IMF 2013f, 1). In its November 2013 report, the Fund cited political risks following the tensions within the ruling coalition that had spiked interest rates in mid-2013, and policymaking uncertainty associated with future Constitutional Court rulings (IMF 2013q, 1).

Table 6.3 reports the alternative scenarios assumed for Portugal. Baseline economic growth is set at the path in the IMF's November 2013 review (IMF 2013q), showing a return to slightly positive growth in 2014 and subsequent

---

13. Axel Bugge and Andrei Khalip, "Portugal Says Bond Issue Successful, Eyes Bailout Exit," Reuters, January 9, 2014.

14. "What Angela Isn't Saying," *Economist*, August 10, 2013, 60.

15. However, the *Economist* figure for IMF estimates of contingent liabilities is not present in the IMF's public documents. Its June 2013 review only noted that state-owned enterprises have debt of 9 percent of GDP that is not included in the general government debt figures (IMF 2013f, 14). The review then refers the reader to a prior country report for a "detailed discussion of contingent liabilities," but the referred report also does not contain a specific estimate of contingent liabilities, other than to mention that SOE debt amounts to 23 percent of GDP and only half is classified as general government debt (IMF 2012j, 18).

Table 6.3 Scenario assumptions for Portugal

	2013	2014	2015	2016	2017	2018	2019	2020
Scenario			**Real GDP growth** (percent)					
1	—	0.3	1.0	1.2	1.3	1.3	1.3	1.3
2	−1.6	0.8	1.5	1.7	1.8	1.8	1.8	1.8
3	—	1.0	3.1	3.1	3.1	3.1	3.1	3.1
			Primary surplus (percent of GDP)					
1	—	−0.7	0.8	1.4	1.8	2.1	2.1	2.1
2	−1.6	0.3	1.8	2.4	2.8	3.1	3.1	3.1
3	—	1.3	2.8	3.4	3.8	4.1	4.1	4.1
		Bank recapitalization and contingent debt recognition (billions of euros)						
1	—	4	4	0	0	0	0	0
2	0	0	0	0	0	0	0	0
3	—	0	0	0	0	0	0	0
			Privatization (billions of euros)					
1	—	0	0	0	0	0	0	0
2	1.0	0.5	0	0	0	0	0	0
3	—	1.5	1.2	0	0	0	0	0

Scenarios: 1 = unfavorable; 2 = baseline; 3 = favorable

Sources: IMF (2013q); author's assumptions.

growth of 1.8 percent by 2017 and after. The adverse case sets growth at 0.5 percent below baseline, approximately the same proportionate reduction from the medium-term benchmark as applied for Ireland. The favorable case is again set at the 60th percentile of annual growth rates from 1990 to 2012. In Portugal's case this higher-growth benchmark was only 3.1 percent, however. The IMF projections are also applied for the baseline path of the primary surplus. The favorable and adverse alternatives place the primary surplus 1 percent of GDP above or below the baseline.[16]

In the case of Portugal, the two other variables in the simulations—privatization on the favorable side and bank cleanup costs or other "discovered debt" on the unfavorable side—play an important role. Bank recapitalization costs for 2012 amounted to €7 billion to €8 billion (IMF 2012f, 40; IMF 2013f, 32), or 4.5 percent of GDP—not far from the more highly publicized bank recapitalization costs to the government of Spain (discussed below).[17]

---

16. With a more modest long-term baseline surplus, there is more scope for symmetric upside deviation for Portugal than in the case of Ireland.

17. In June 2012, the government of Portugal announced a total of €6.6 billion in recapitalization costs for three major banks (Ministério das Finanças 2012). Of the total, €5 billion was to be

The baseline IMF (2013q) projections do not show further recapitalization or discovered debt costs going forward. However, in the unfavorable scenario shown in table 6.3, it is assumed that a cumulative 5 percent of GDP in extra debt is added during 2014–15 because of costs associated with cleanup of state-owned enterprises (SOEs), considering that their gross debt is on the order of 23 percent of GDP.[18]

Receipts from privatization, which had amounted to €700 million in 2010 and €600 million in 2011, reached €2.2 billion in 2012 and were estimated at €1 billion in 2013 and projected at €0.5 billion in 2014 (IMF 2013q, 44). Assets being privatized have included airport operations, the state airline, and parts of the electricity sector.[19] Considering that the IMF review of June 2013 (IMF 2013f, 32) had anticipated €3.7 billion in privatization receipts in 2013 instead of the later estimate of €1 billion, the favorable scenario in table 6.3 places the cumulative privatization amounts in 2013–15 at €3.7 billion.

Figure 6.3 shows the results of the projections for Portugal. The baseline and the probability-weighted paths are close to each other, reflecting the broadly symmetrical assumptions used regarding the adverse and favorable scenarios in relation to the baseline. In the baseline, the ratio of gross debt to GDP declines from a peak of 127 percent in 2013–14 to 114 percent by 2020. Portugal's prospective debt path is somewhat less favorable than that of Ireland, and appears to have less possibility of a favorable surprise (the 25 percent favorable case yields a debt ratio of 108 percent by 2020 in comparison to 86 percent for Ireland; the probability-weighted outcome for Portugal is 114 percent in 2020 versus 98 percent for Ireland). Even so, Portugal has already begun a modest return to private market finance. Whereas its placement of Treasury bonds of greater than five years' maturity fell from €22 billion in 2010 to zero in 2011 and 2012 (although it placed €3.7 billion in bonds of one to five years in 2012), in July 2013 the government successfully placed €3 billion in 10-year bonds at an average interest rate of 5.7 percent, and in February 2014 it placed €3 billion in 10-year bonds at a yield of 5.1 percent.[20] It had also been able to continue rolling over short-term debt of about €20 billion annually even in 2011 and 2012 (IGCP 2013a, 2013b).

---

through the Bank Solvency Support Facility (BSSF) created in the context of the official (IMF and euro area) support program.

18. The SOEs of course also have assets. Simply adding the 9 percent of GDP in SOE debt not presently counted in general government debt while failing to somehow take account of the corresponding assets would be misleading, and another instance of the problem of focusing solely on gross rather than net debt.

19. In 2012, China Three Gorges bought 21 percent of Energias de Portugal for €2.7 billion; in February 2013, the French group Vinci bought airports operator ANA for €3.1 billion. Giles Tremlett, "Portugal to Hold Fire-sale of State Assets," *Guardian*, December 25, 2012; Henrique Almeida, "Portugal Seeks to Restart Sale Process for TAP Airline This Year," Bloomberg, July 18, 2013.

20. Peter Wise, "Portugal Draws Strong Demand in Debt Sale," *Financial Times*, February 11, 2014.

Figure 6.3 Portugal: Gross debt as percent of GDP, 2011–20

percent of GDP

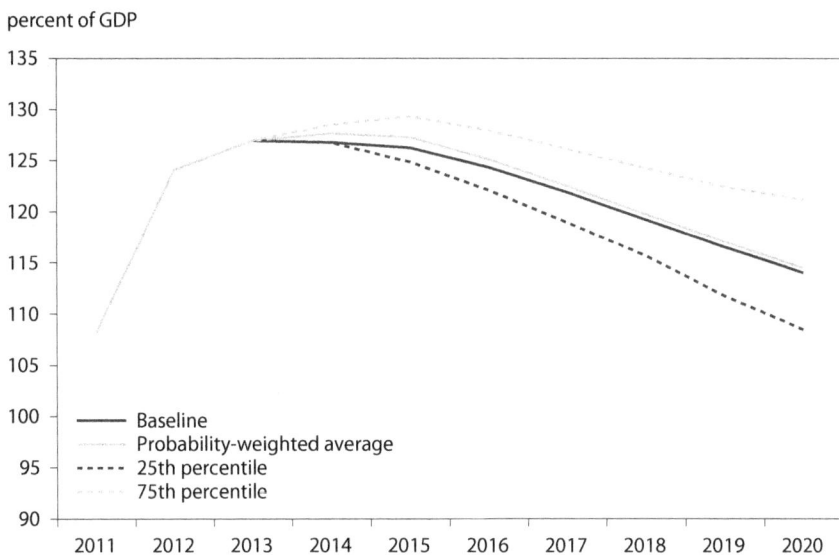

Source: Author's calculations.

Nonetheless, Portuguese sovereign spreads on 10-year bonds rebounded more in mid-2013 than did those of the other peripheral economies (excluding Greece), as shown in figure 5.1 in chapter 5. Spreads spiked in early July after resignation of the finance minister and foreign minister temporarily raised the specter of a collapse of the government.[21] More broadly, the beginnings of a shift of US monetary policy to taper off quantitative easing provoked a rise in US interest rates (from 1.7 percent for 10-year Treasury bonds in early May 2013 to 2.7 percent by mid-August; Federal Reserve 2014a). A corresponding shift in international capital markets reversing previous flows in search of yield in emerging markets and other higher-risk economies also began, and a second wave of emerging-market turmoil occurred in early 2014 in the face of a sharp depreciation by Argentina and political uncertainty in Turkey. As the peripheral economy with the highest sovereign spreads (excluding Greece), Portugal presumably stands in the most jeopardy from any broad increase in international capital risk aversion. Although during the first two months of 2014 continued improvement in its spreads seemed to reflect at least an immunity to and conceivably even a benefit from the emerging-market turmoil, it is unclear that this source of risk can be ruled out.

The projections here take account of the prospective rise in international interest rates (with a rising risk-free bund rate), and indicate that despite this

---

21. Phillip Inman, "Eurozone Crisis: Portugal Sends Stock Markets Tumbling," *Guardian*, July 3, 2013.

rise, Portugal's debt should be sustainable. Nonetheless, political uncertainty in early July 2013 prompted market concerns that private debt rescheduling could lie ahead if a second troika program proved necessary, and in light of the IMF's new call for earlier restructurings emerging from its self-critique of the outcome in Greece (see chapters 5 and 7).[22] By early 2014 market conditions facing Portugal had improved again (figure 6.1) and by then the proximate question facing Portuguese policymakers was whether and on what terms to enter into a new precautionary program as opposed to making a clean exit from the official support program when it reaches its scheduled end in May 2014.

Italy

Table 6.4 reports the scenario assumptions for Italy. Baseline growth projections are those of the IMF in its September 2013 Article IV Consultation report (IMF 2013m). The period 2019–20 maintains the growth rate for 2018. For 2013, actual growth is the estimate in Consensus (2014). For 2014–20, unfavorable growth is set at 0.5 percent annually below the baseline. The favorable growth path is again set at the 60th percentile of annual growth achieved in 1990–2012, which was 1.73 percent (IMF 2013g).

The baseline scenario for the primary balance is also that projected by the IMF (2013m). It calls for a high primary surplus that reaches 5.6 percent of GDP by 2018. For 2019–20 the estimate here reverts to the 4.6 percent figure for 2018 that had been used in the spring 2013 *World Economic Outlook* (WEO) (IMF 2013g). The Italian Ministry of Economy and Finance anticipates an even higher trajectory for the primary surplus, and its projection is thus applied as the favorable case scenario (Ministero dell'Economia 2013, 31).[23] Its primary surplus reaches 5.7 percent of GDP by 2017. For the unfavorable case, the primary surplus is set at 1 percent below baseline in 2014, and a flat 2.7 percent of GDP for 2015–20, the average actually achieved in 1990–2000 (IMF 2013g). Although the difference from the baseline is large in the unfavorable case, a narrower difference might not capture the full extent of downside fiscal risk in view of past experience.

Table 6.4 includes a panel for discovered debt that is relatively distinctive. Instead of bank recapitalization costs (as in Ireland and Spain) or SOE contingent debt (as in Portugal), in the case of Italy the main sources of new debt not created by current fiscal deficits are Italy's contributions to bilateral and EFSF assistance to Greece, Ireland, and Portugal, and payment of public sector arrears to private firms. New debt from assistance to euro area program countries amounted to 1.9 percent of GDP in 2012 and is projected at 0.8

---

22. Robin Wigglesworth, "Portugal's Political Turmoil Risks Debt Restructure," *Financial Times*, July 10, 2013.

23. Except for 2013, when the WEO estimate plus 0.5 percent of GDP yields a higher estimate and is therefore applied as the favorable case for that year.

Table 6.4 Scenario assumptions for Italy

Scenario	2013	2014	2015	2016	2017	2018	2019	2020
				Real GDP growth (percent)				
1	—	0.2	0.6	0.9	0.9	0.7	0.7	0.7
2	–1.8	0.7	1.1	1.4	1.4	1.2	1.2	1.2
3	—	1.0	1.73	1.73	1.73	1.73	1.73	1.73
				Primary surplus (percent of GDP)				
1	—	2.3	2.7	2.7	2.7	2.7	2.7	2.7
2	2.0	3.3	3.6	4.5	5.1	5.6	4.6	4.6
3	—	3.8	4.3	5.1	5.7	5.7	5.7	5.7
				Aid to euro area; discovered debt (billions of euros)				
1	—	22	0	1	1	0	0	0
2	20	22	0	1	1	0	0	0
3	—	22	0	1	1	0	0	0
				Privatization (billions of euros)				
1	—	0	0	0	0	0	0	0
2	0	11	16	17	17	0	0	0
3	—	15	20	21	21	0	0	0

Scenarios: 1 = unfavorable; 2 = baseline; 3 = favorable

Sources: IMF (2013m); author's assumptions.

percent of GDP in 2013 and 0.3 percent in 2014. (As discussed in chapter 5, any future aid through the ESM is not to be treated as debt-creating for the donor.) In addition, payment of arrears (Decree Law 35/2013) and statistical revisions amount to 0.2 percent of GDP in 2012, 0.5 percent in 2013, and 1.1 percent in 2014 (Ministero dell'Economia 2013, 31). The simulations do not include unfavorable and favorable variants from the baseline in this category.

Finally, privatization receipts in the baseline are the projections of the Ministry of Economy and amount to 1 percent of GDP annually for 2015 through 2017 (Ministero dell'Economia 2013, 31) and €11 billion in 2014 based on plans announced in late 2013.[24] In the unfavorable case, privatization receipts are zero. In the favorable case, they are placed 25 percent above the baseline.

Figure 6.4 shows the path of debt relative to GDP for Italy in the baseline, 25th, and 75th percentiles, and probability-weighted average outcome. In the baseline Italy's debt ratio peaks at 133 percent of GDP in 2014 and then declines to 115 percent by 2020. In the favorable 25th percentile the decline

---

24. Brandon Callahan, "Italy Seeking 10-12 billion Euros from the Sale of Shares in Eight State-owned Companies," *Dailypressdotcom*, November 22, 2013.

Figure 6.4   Italy: Gross debt as percent of GDP, 2011–20

percent of GDP

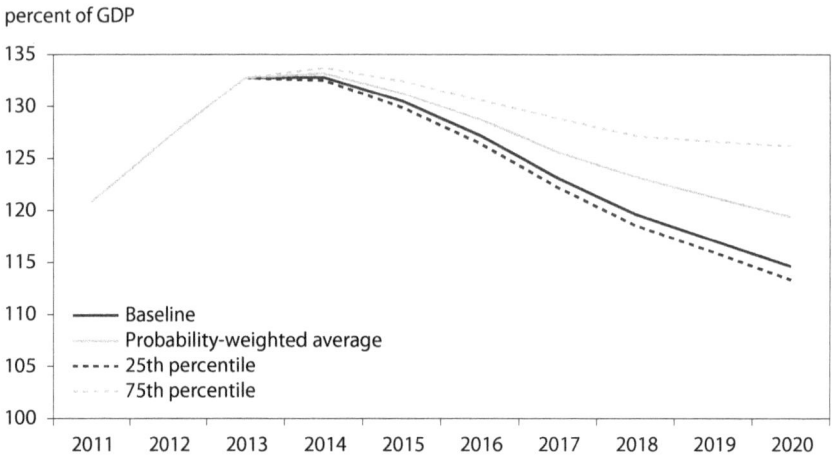

Source: Author's calculations.

would be to 113 percent. Even in the unfavorable 75th percentile the debt ratio would decline slightly, to 126 percent by 2020. The probability-weighted debt ratio declines from a peak of 133 percent in 2014 to 119 percent by 2020. The difference between the baseline and probability-weighted cases is substantial and reflects the asymmetry of a larger gap between the baseline and adverse case primary surplus (an average difference of 1.8 percent of GDP in 2014–20) than for the favorable case (0.7 percent of GDP).

The baseline projection for Italy's ratio of gross debt to GDP is qualitatively similar to, but modestly less favorable than, that in Cline (2012b), in which 2020 debt was projected to stand at 110 percent of GDP, and especially Cline (2012c), which placed the ratio at 104 percent. The less favorable outlook reflects primarily an already substantially higher debt ratio by end-2013 than had been anticipated.[25] The baseline path for the ratio of public debt to GDP here is somewhat more favorable than that of the IMF Article IV Consultation report (IMF 2013m); for 2018 that report places the debt-to-GDP ratio at 123 percent, compared with 120 percent here. An important difference is that the IMF makes no allowance for privatization; in contrast, the cumulative baseline privatization assumed here during 2014–17 amounts to €61 billion by 2017, or 3.5 percent of 2017 GDP.

The fact that the baseline lies so close to the 25th percentile optimistic case, and so far from the probability-weighted outcome, is a sobering indication

---

25. In Cline (2012c) the 2013 debt ratio was projected at 123.2 percent of GDP; the actual outcome was 132.7 percent. The difference primarily reflected the following cumulative effects during 2012–13: lower nominal growth (1.9 percent of GDP); lower primary surplus (0.9 percent of GDP); less privatization (0.8 percent of GDP); and especially discovered debt and aid to euro area economies not calculated in the earlier study (3.4 percent of GDP).

that policymakers may face more surprises on the downside than suggested by the baseline path. A factor weighing in the opposite direction is that nearly 3 percent of GDP in public debt is offset in principle by accumulated claims on Greece, Portugal, and Ireland in euro area assistance programs, arguably overstating the effective debt ratio.

Spain

Table 6.5 reports the alternative scenario assumptions for Spain. The baseline growth projections for 2014–18 are those in the IMF's most recent Article IV review (IMF 2013l, 35). (Actual growth in 2013 is from Consensus 2014.) These projections are surprisingly low, with growth during 2014–18 averaging only 0.6 percent annually, compared with the IMF's growth projections of 2.3 percent in Ireland, 1.5 percent in Portugal, and 1.2 percent in Italy over this period (tables 6.1 and 6.2 and IMF 2013g, respectively). Both the potential for high snapback growth following deep recession and Spain's own past record of high growth would seem to provide grounds for higher central expectations. In view of the seemingly pessimistic IMF baseline, the reduction from baseline in the unfavorable case is set at only 0.3 percent annually (rather than 0.5 percent in Portugal and Italy). For the favorable growth case, again the 60th percentile of annual growth performance in 1990–2012 is applied, yielding a benchmark of 3.7 percent (beginning in 2015, with 2014 half-way between the 2013 and 2015 estimates).

For the primary surplus, the IMF's Article IV review baseline is also applied (IMF 2013l, 37). The primary surplus of 1.7 percent of GDP by 2018 is not particularly ambitious by international standards, and is far below the prospective levels in Italy in particular. Accordingly, although the adverse scenario is set at 0.5 percent of GDP below the baseline (as in Portugal), the favorable scenario adds a full percentage point of GDP to the baseline.

For bank recapitalization, the baseline also applies the IMF estimates (IMF 2013l, 37). These show €38 billion in bank recapitalization costs in 2012 but zero thereafter. In view of market concerns about bank recapitalization costs in Spain (see chapter 3), it is noteworthy that the IMF anticipates no further increase to government debt from this source. As discussed in chapter 3, an exercise applying an earlier IMF model relating bank losses to unemployment and growth suggests that loan impairments already recognized by Spanish banks in 2011–13, and especially some €100 billion recognized in 2012 alone, should fully cover prospective losses. The €40 billion cumulative government cost from recapitalization in 2014–15 in the unfavorable scenario should thus be considered ample allowance for downside risk.

Finally, the privatization outlook is set at zero in both the baseline and unfavorable cases, but at a total of €15 billion over three years in the favorable scenario, based on earlier discussions of privatizing airports and the national lottery prior to the current government's suspension of such efforts because of

Table 6.5   Scenario assumptions for Spain

Scenario	2013	2014	2015	2016	2017	2018	2019	2020
	Real GDP growth (percent)							
1	—	–0.3	0.0	0.3	0.6	0.9	0.9	0.9
2	–1.2	0.0	0.3	0.6	0.9	1.2	1.2	1.2
3	—	1.2	3.7	3.7	3.7	3.7	3.7	3.7
	Primary surplus (percent of GDP)							
1	—	–2.8	–1.9	–0.9	0.1	1.2	1.2	1.2
2	–3.7	–2.3	–1.4	–0.4	0.6	1.7	1.7	1.7
3	—	–1.3	–0.4	0.6	1.6	2.7	2.7	2.7
	Bank recapitalization (billions of euros)							
1	—	20	20	0	0	0	0	0
2	0	0	0	0	0	0	0	0
3	—	0	0	0	0	0	0	0
	Privatization (billions of euros)							
1	—	0	0	0	0	0	0	0
2	0	0	0	0	0	0	0	0
3	—	5	5	5	0	0	0	0

Scenarios: 1 = unfavorable; 2 = baseline; 3 = favorable

Sources: IMF (2013l); author's assumptions.

unfavorable conditions.[26] Figure 6.5 shows the range of alternative projections for the ratio of gross public debt to GDP in Spain for the baseline, the paths at the 25th percentile and the 75th percentile across the 243 outcomes, and the probability-weighted average outcome. In the baseline, Spain's sovereign debt rises from 69 percent of GDP in 2011 to 84 percent in 2012 to 92 percent in 2013 and 111 percent by 2020. In contrast, in the probability-weighted outcome, the debt ratio plateaus at 107 percent of GDP by 2017 and after, almost the same as the 106 percent of GDP plateau in 2017–18 in the August 2013 IMF Article IV review baseline (IMF 2013l).

The higher baseline path for the debt ratio here than in the IMF review reflects a higher path of net interest payments, which reach 4.6 percent of GDP by 2016 (for example) versus 3.8 percent in the IMF projections. The corresponding implicit interest rates against gross debt at the end of the prior year are 4.6 percent here versus 3.7 percent in the IMF baseline. In the EDSM projections, interest rate data for outstanding stocks of Spain's public debt are taken from official national sources (described in Cline 2012c). It seems unlikely that interest rates assumed for new debt in the IMF's projections would be lower

---

26. Pablo Dominguez and David Román, "Spain Halts Plan to Privatize Main Airports," *Wall Street Journal*, January 24, 2012.

Figure 6.5   Spain: Gross debt as percent of GDP, 2011–20

percent of GDP

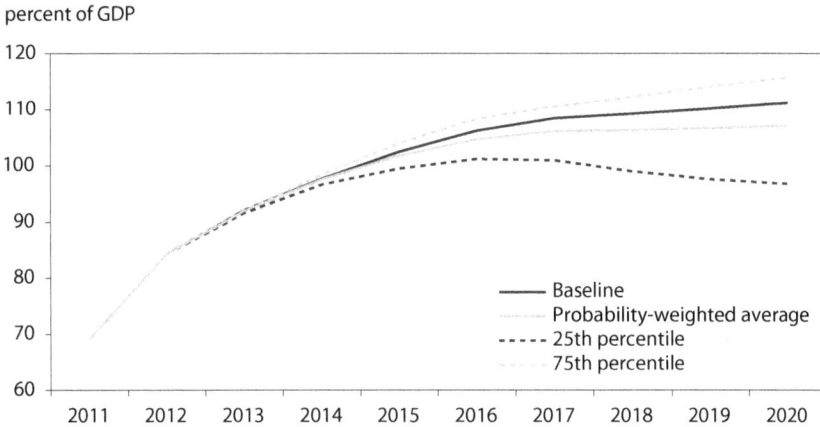

Source: Author's calculations.

than those in table 6.1. So it is unclear why the IMF's implicit interest rates for Spain are almost 100 basis points lower than those used here. An implication is that the projections here may be on the conservative side.

The fact that the baseline debt ratio has not quite leveled off by the end of the projection period does not reverse the conclusion that Spain is solvent. The probability-weighted path does indeed level off at 107 percent beginning in 2017. Even continuing the slight rising trend in the baseline after 2020, a pace of 1 percent of GDP per year, the debt ratio would not reach 120 percent until 2028. For the entirety of the next decade, then, Spain would remain at debt below 120 percent of GDP even in the baseline path, and well below that benchmark in the probability-weighted path.

Overview

Figure 6.6 presents the probability-weighted projections for the ratio of gross debt to GDP for the four debt-stressed euro area economies considered in this chapter. The striking pattern is that all four economies are on a path of converging to a debt ratio in the range of 98 to 119 percent of GDP by 2020. This range is within the benchmark limit of 120 percent dominant in policy discussions for the region (including in IMF guidelines) over the past three years, a benchmark that seems reasonable as discussed in chapter 2. In broad terms, the projections are consistent with a diagnosis of sovereign solvency for these economies.

These probabilistic projections are premised on the currently likely range of performance in the areas of fiscal policy, growth, and market interest rates. As shown for Italy and Spain in Cline (2012c), major slippage in which the adverse scenario began to be the most likely outcome, especially fiscal performance

Figure 6.6 Probability-weighted path of the debt/GDP ratio for Ireland, Italy, Portugal, and Spain, 2011–20

percent of GDP

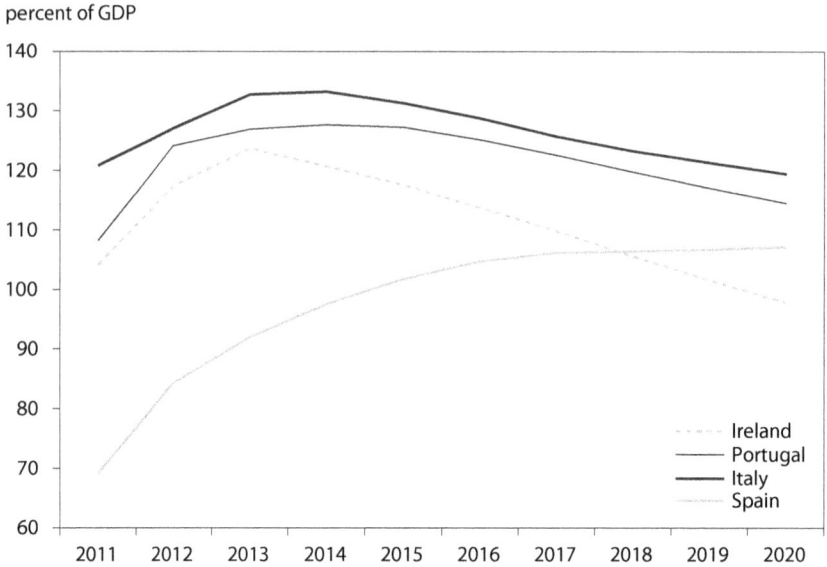

Source: Author's calculations.

but also growth and market interest rate conditions, could instead cause the debt ratios to remain at recent high levels or rise further, calling into question eventual solvency. The action of the ECB in its OMT initiative has gone a long way toward helping ensure that this slippage can be avoided in the sphere of market interest rates. The political will to persevere with medium-term fiscal objectives will be an essential condition for ensuring solvency.

The principal area in which political constraints could adversely affect the outlook for debt sustainability is the challenge of sustaining relatively high primary surpluses. It is thus useful to consider a final experiment in which a ceiling of 2.5 percent of GDP is placed on the primary surplus for each year of the projection period, 2014–20. This level would be relatively unambitious from the standpoint of past international experience with fiscal adjustment.[27] As shown in table 6.6, in the baseline projections the average primary surpluses in 2014–20 exceed this level for Ireland, Portugal, and especially Italy. The exercise reported in the final three columns of the table shows the impact of imposing the 2.5 percent of GDP ceiling. (This test is not relevant for Spain, because its primary surplus never exceeds this level in the baseline projections.) As shown in the next-to-last column, for Ireland and Portugal the effect is to moderate the progress in reducing the ratio of debt to GDP but not fundamentally change

---

27. The IMF (2013r, 25) finds that for 24 advanced economies in the period 1950–2011, the highest five-year moving average primary surplus had a median value of 4 percent of GDP.

Table 6.6   Impact of constraining the primary surplus[a]

	Actuals, 2013		Baseline projections		Constrained projections		
						Debt/GDP, 2020	
Country	Primary surplus	Debt/ GDP	Average primary surplus, 2014–20	Debt/ GDP, 2020	Average primary surplus, 2014–20	No spreads feedback	With spreads feedback[b]
Ireland	−2.7	123.8	2.7	100.8	2.0	105.4	107.6
Italy	2.0	132.7	4.5	114.6	2.5	129.5	134.4
Portugal	−1.6	126.9	2.4	114.0	2.1	116.2	119.0
Spain	−3.7	92.1	0.2	111.2	n.a.[c]	n.a.[c]	n.a.[c]

a. Constrained: Ceiling of 2.5 percent of GDP for primary surplus.
b. Adds 50 basis points to spreads on new borrowing.
c. Not applicable because no baseline primary surpluses exceed 2.5 percent of GDP.

Note: Primary surplus is in percent of GDP and debt/GDP ratio is in percent.

Sources: Appendix 6D and author's calculations.

the conclusion of substantial improvement over time. Thus, the debt ratio falls from about 124 percent of GDP in 2013 to 105 percent by 2020 for Ireland, not radically higher than the approximately 101 percent reached in the unconstrained baseline. The result is similar for Portugal, as the debt-to-GDP ratio by 2020 is not much higher than in the unconstrained baseline (116 percent versus 114 percent). For Italy, however, constraining the primary surplus would largely eliminate the progress in reducing the debt burden, which would fall from about 133 percent in 2013 to about 115 percent in the baseline but a substantially higher 130 percent in the constrained variant.

As shown in the final column, if financial markets were to exact an additional spread of 50 basis points because of the less ambitious fiscal targets, Ireland and Portugal would still achieve major progress in reducing the ratio of debt to GDP. Italy, however, would experience a slight increase rather than achieving a decrease, as the debt ratio would rise from about 133 percent of GDP in 2013 to about 134 percent by 2020. Under broadly favorable financial market conditions Italy could even then be judged solvent because the debt ratio would be essentially at a plateau rather than rising rapidly. However, Italy would presumably be more vulnerable to an adverse shift in market sentiment if it were to pursue this less ambitious fiscal effort.

The broad conclusion of this chapter is that the four periphery economies excluding Greece are solvent, with public debt that should be sustainable. This conclusion appears robust to political constraints on fiscal adjustment, with the caveat of somewhat greater risk from this standpoint for Italy, where high primary surpluses play a prominent role in reducing the high ratio of debt to GDP. The EDSM calculations suggest that there is a sound quantitative underpinning for the return of sovereign risk spreads to much more reasonable levels that had already occurred by early 2014.

Appendix 6A
The European Debt Simulation Model

A debt simulation model provides a useful basis for analyzing the sustainability of sovereign debt.[28] The basic premise is that if, under reasonable assumptions, the relevant debt ratios show a prospective path of moderation over time, or (for a country with a high debt ratio but nonetheless still able to access the capital market) at least avoidance of worsening over time, then a country is judged solvent and capable of carrying its sovereign debt load without restructuring or partial forgiveness. This study sets forth such a model, the European debt simulation model.[29] The model combines exogenous information, in particular on interest rates and the time profile of maturities coming due for long-term debt already outstanding, with alternative scenarios for key policy and market variables. The scenario variables apply alternative cases for real GDP growth rates, the primary fiscal surplus, the interest rate on new medium- and long-term debt, the amount of public outlay needed for bank recapitalization or other forms of "discovered debt," and the amount of prospective receipts from privatization. As discussed below, with three alternative states (base case, unfavorable, favorable) and five variables, there are 243 outcomes for the model. This study develops an approach to considering the correlation among the contingent states to provide a sense of the probability distribution of the various outcomes.

Model Equations

The horizon of the model is through 2020, or for year $t = 1$ to 8 for 2013 through 2020. Nominal GDP is calculated at:

$$Y_t = Y_{t-1}[1 + g_t][1 + \dot{p}_t] \tag{6A.1}$$

where Y is GDP in billions of current euros, g is the real growth rate, and p is the GDP deflator (with the overdot representing proportionate increase).

The fiscal deficit (DEF) for the year equals the net interest (INT) due on public debt minus the primary surplus (PS):[30]

---

28. This appendix is extracted from Cline (2012c).

29. Earlier versions of the model were applied in Cline (2011, 2012b, 2012c).

30. Standard international practice as represented by IMF methodology defines the primary balance as the total fiscal balance minus the balance on net interest payments. Even so, the Fund seems to devote little attention to interest earnings. In its lengthy manual on government finance, the primary balance and net interest are mentioned only briefly in a single box, which defines the "Primary operating balance" as the "net operating balance plus net interest expense" (IMF 2001, 46). Moreover, in some less complete IMF documents the mistaken impression is given that gross interest payments rather than just net interest payments are deducted in going from the total fiscal deficit to the primary balance. Thus, the IMF's 1995 pamphlet on the subject states that

$$DEF_t = INT_t - PS_t \tag{6A.2}$$

The net interest due is calculated as the sum across three public debt categories of the stock of debt at the end of the previous year multiplied by the interest rate applicable for the current year, with debt divided into short-term (one year or less), "old" medium- and long-term debt outstanding at the end of 2012, and "new" medium- and long-term debt incurred in 2013 and after. Thus:

$$INT_t = \sum_k D_{k,t-1} r_{kt} - FA_{t-1} r_{at} \tag{6A.3}$$

where D is the stock of debt, $k = 1$ to 3 is the category, FA is financial assets, and r is the interest rate.

The primary surplus is the scenario's postulated rate π as applied to nominal GDP, or

$$PS_t = \pi_t Y_t \tag{6A.4}$$

For the year in question, the net borrowing requirement (NBR) is then equal to the fiscal deficit plus the amount of extraordinary increase in debt attributable to recognition of arrears, capital payment in support of banks, or other nonbudgetary increase in debt, designated here as $DDIS$ for "debt discovery," minus the amount of receipts obtained from privatization, Z.

$$NBR_t = DEF_t + DDIS_t - Z_t \tag{6A.5}$$

The gross borrowing requirement will then equal the net borrowing requirement plus amortization (AMZ), plus the amount needed to cover the increase in public financial assets (ΔFA). For its part, amortization in turn will equal the sum of short-term debt to be rolled over (D_{1t}) plus the year's principal maturities on medium- and long-term debt outstanding at the end of 2012 (A_{2t}), plus amortization coming due on the outstanding stock of medium- and long-term debt newly incurred in 2013 and thereafter (A_{3t}):

$$GBR_t = NBR_t + AMZ_t + \Delta FA_t \tag{6A.6}$$

$$AMZ_t = D_{1t} + A_{2t} + A_{3t} \tag{6A.7}$$

The schedule of amortization on old medium- and long-term debt (A_2) is

---

"The *primary balance* excludes interest payments from expenditures" (IMF 1995, 14). In the case of European economies the distinction can be important, because there are sizable government financial assets.

known from Treasury data. It is assumed that the amortization due on newly acquired medium- and long-term debt is a fixed proportion θ of the previous year's outstanding post-2012 medium- and long-term debt, with the calculations applying $\theta = 0.1$ to represent 10-year maturities. The calculations also assume that short-term debt remains constant at $D_{1t} = D_{1,0}$, where $D_{1,0}$ is the amount outstanding at the end of 2012.

The amount of new borrowing of medium- and long-term debt (B_{3t}) will then be the gross borrowing requirement minus the amount of short-term debt being rolled over, or

$$B_{3t} = GBR_t - D_{1,0} \tag{6A.8}$$

The outstanding stock of short-term debt is constant at $D_{1,0}$. The outstanding stock of old medium- and long-term debt is the previous year-end total less the amount amortized during the year. Outstanding new (post-2012) medium- and long-term debt equals the amount at the end of the previous year, plus the amount of new medium- and long-term borrowing, minus amortization on this debt. Thus

$$D_{1t} = D_{1,0}; D_{2t} = D_{2,t-1} - A_{2t}; D_{3t} = D_{3,t-1} + B_{3t} - A_{3t} \tag{6A.9}$$

For their part, public financial assets at the end of the year equal the amount at the end of the previous year plus the increment during the course of the year: $FA_t = FA_{t-1} + \Delta FA_t$.

Equations (6A.1) through (6A.9) are accounting relationships that yield paths of debt, net debt, interest payments, and amortization, all of which when compared with GDP provide alternative indicators of the debt burden. The economic influences driving the accounting outcomes are, again, the key variables allowed to vary across the scenarios: growth, primary surplus, interest rate on new long-term debt, bank recapitalization and other debt discovery, and privatization.

Contingent State Correlation

Appendix 6B develops a method for taking into account the correlation of "contingent states" (good, bad, and central) across the key economic variables for purposes of identifying the relative probabilities of alternative outcomes. The point of departure is the specification of a base case for each variable (a time path of the central expectation for the variable, in this case for 2013 through 2020). An adverse "bad" time path and favorable "good" path are then identified, flanking the base case. With three possible states for five variable-time paths, there will be $3^5 = 243$ possible outcomes.

As developed in appendix 6B, there can be positive or negative correlation between pairs of states. For example, the "good" growth state is likely to be positively correlated with the "good" market interest rate case because as investors observe stronger growth performance they will be more willing to purchase government bonds at moderate interest rates. Conversely, a "good" state on one variable can be negatively correlated with that on another variable (i.e., correlated with that variable's bad state). For privatization, for example, if there is greater success raising the primary surplus there will be less pressure to raise funds through the substitute means of privatization. The "bad" state of less privatization receipts will be correlated with the "good" state of a high primary surplus.

The specification of scenario probabilities applied in this study is as follows. Other things being equal, the probability that a given variable will be at its "base" case is 40 percent; at its "good" case, 30 percent, and at its "bad" case, 30 percent. However, if another variable with which the variable in question is correlated (with coefficient unity) is at the same nonbase state as is the variable (both in their "good" states, for example), then the probability that the variable in question is in its good state is increased by an additive amount, and the probability that the variable in question is in its bad state is correspondingly reduced by this amount. As discussed in appendix 6B in the extreme case in which the variable's state is positively correlated with each of the other key variable states, and all of the variables are in the same nonbase state, the probability of the variable's nonbase state is at its maximum, set at 0.45, and the probability of the opposite nonbase state is at its minimum, set at 0.15. The scenario probabilities are then normalized so that they sum to unity.

The effect of calculating the scenario probabilities taking account of scenario correlation across the key variables is to provide a basis for examining the likely range of outcomes based on a particular criterion. For this purpose the estimates here consider the ratio of debt to GDP. The various outcomes are arrayed from best to worst and then the paths representing cumulative 25th percentiles and 75th percentiles are identified, as indicative of the most meaningful range of outcomes. The base case is also identified (in which each key variable has its base case path). Finally, the probability-weighted path is identified. Only by chance will it lie along the base case path.

The calculations in this study apply the correlation coefficients shown in table 6A.1, corresponding to the coefficient "ρ" in appendix 6B. The correlation coefficient between growth and the primary surplus is set to be positive but at a relatively low level of 0.2. The revenue outcome will tend to be strong when growth is strong, making for a positive correlation. However, in the context of fiscal adjustment with still relatively high unemployment, the effort to increase the primary surplus can have a negative impact on growth, eroding what would usually be a positive correlation.

Proceeding across the first row of the table, the correlation between the states (but not the levels, which are the reverse) for growth and interest rates is set at positive unity. As just suggested, investors are likely to take heart when they see stronger growth, and purchase government bonds with a lesser risk premium. Conversely, if they see severe economic contraction, they are more

Table 6A.1 Correlation coefficient between states for five economic variables

Variable	Growth (g)	Primary surplus (π)	Interest rate (r)	Bank recapitalization and debt discovery (DDIS)	Privatization (Z)
g		0.2	1.0	0.5	0
π	0.2		−0.5	0	−1.0
R	1.0	−0.5		1.0	0
DDIS	0.5	0	1.0		0
Z	0	−1.0	0	0	

Source: Author's calculations.

likely to insist on a high risk premium. The good states will be correlated with the good states and the bad ones with the bad ones. The correlation could be the other way around under more normal circumstances. Thus, when the economy is booming and refinancing public debt is not a problem but inflationary pressures are a concern, the central bank would likely increase interest rates.

Still in the first row, a positive correlation is posited between the growth state and the bank recapitalization and debt discovery state (again, state, not amount, which is the reverse). Stronger growth is likely to be associated with lesser need to bail out the banks, and lesser incidence of provincial fiscal gaps that need to be made up at the center. The good growth state will be associated with the good bank recapitalization state, and their respective bad states similarly associated. The correlation is set at less than unity, however, as legacy problems may leave substantial discovered debt (and bank recapitalizations) even in the good growth case.

For the final entry in the first row, countervailing directions seem sufficient to posit a zero correlation between growth and privatization. Although high growth would boost revenue and make privatization less urgent, the revenue effect is dealt with directly in the correlation between the primary surplus and privatization. There might be a weak association in the other direction: poor growth might raise the concern that any privatizations would be at fire-sale prices, so the "bad" state for growth would be associated with the "bad" state of low privatization effort. On balance the two are treated as neutral with respect to each other.

In the second row of the table, the first entry has already been discussed: the correlation of the growth state with the primary surplus state. The first new entry is for the correlation of the primary surplus state with the interest rate state. This coefficient is set at −0.5, meaning loosely that about half of the time the primary surplus will be in its good state (high) when the interest rate is in its bad state (high) but otherwise the two will not be associated. The motivation is that if the country faces higher interest rates, it will need to make a greater fiscal effort to compensate. The negative association between the states is moderated to the extent that investors reward the government with lower interest rates as they observe more ambitious fiscal effort. Once again the correlation could be in the opposite direction in the absence of debt stress, as unusually strong growth might prompt inflationary concerns and induce the central bank to raise interest rates.

The next entry in the second row of table 6A.1 indicates a zero correlation between the primary surplus and bank recapitalization (discovered debt). The final entry in that row indicates a correlation of negative unity between the primary surplus state and the privatization state, because the two are essentially substitutes as sources of cash available to the government.

In the third row of the table, the first entry not yet discussed is for the correlation of the interest rate state with the bank recapitalization state. This coefficient is set at positive unity, on grounds that banks are likely to be under greater stress when the sovereign is under greater stress from higher risk premiums in market interest rates. Finally in this row, the correlation between privatization and the interest rate states is set at zero, for reasons similar to those discussed above for a zero correlation of the growth performance with the privatization effort.

The final correlation not yet discussed is between the extent of bank recapitalization (and debt discovery) on the one hand and privatization on the other. The two are treated as being independent of each other (zero correlation coefficient).

Appendix 6B
Scenario Analysis with Correlated Contingent States

Many areas of policy analysis draw upon projections to evaluate the merits and feasibility of alternative policy choices.[31] For example, decisions about fiscal reform depend in part on projections of future ratios of public debt to GDP. Typically projection analyses will include a "baseline" central case, and one or more "alternative" projection paths under different assumptions for the key variables. When there are a number of crucial variables, and it is desirable to give reasonable consideration to alternative future "states" for each of them, the resulting number of possible outcomes multiplies quickly. Suppose, for example, that there are four key variables, and for each it is desired to take account of a central, bad, and good outcome. Then there will be $3^4 = 81$ possible scenarios.

A "fan diagram" can be used to indicate the range and likelihood of the likely time paths across the various scenarios. The extreme perimeter on the unfavorable side will be the scenario that combines all of the "bad" outcomes on all of the key variables. Conversely, the single scenario combining all of the "good" outcomes for the key variables will be the favorable perimeter. The base or central case will lie somewhere in between. For example, in a fan diagram with the debt-to-GDP ratio on the y-axis and time on the x-axis, the unfavorable perimeter might show a substantial increase in the debt burden over time; the baseline might show the debt ratio unchanged; and the favorable perimeter might show the debt burden falling over time.

The likelihood of a given range of scenarios can then be examined by the distribution of the scenarios around the central baseline scenario. Suppose for simplicity that the good, central, and bad cases on each of the variables are treated as having equal probability. The baseline scenario will be that combination for the "central" variant on each variable. Out of the 81 paths (for the example with four variables and three outcome states), there will be 40 paths less favorable than the baseline and 40 more favorable. Suppose the paths are arrayed from least to most favorable. Then the 20th path would represent the 25th percentile ($0.25 \times 81 \cong 20$), and the 61st path would be the 75th percentile. If each of the four variables were equally important in determining the outcome, the 20th path would be representative of the 16th through 31st paths, all of which would be identical in that they represent one central case, one good case, and two bad cases. Similarly, the 75th percentile would be representative of cases 51 through 66, all of which would have one central case, one bad case, and two good cases.[32]

---

31. This appendix is reproduced from Cline (2012c).

32. This can be seen by assigning the scores 1, 2, or 3 to bad, central, and good, respectively, for each of four variables, then enumerating the possible combinations, and then ordering by the average across the variables. The average score for the base (central) case is 2; for the 25th percentile it is 1.75; and for the 75th percentile it is 2.25.

In a real economic problem, the influences of each of the key variables will not all be equal. Importantly, their distribution of states will tend to show some correlation, rather than being independent of each other. For example, in arriving at a "good" outcome for the prospective debt ratio (stable or falling over time), the occurrence of the "good" state for economic growth as an influence will tend to coincide with the occurrence of the "good" state for the market risk premium spread (low spread) in so far as investors have more confidence when the economy is growing faster. There can also be negative correlation. Suppose for example that a larger trade deficit is perceived as "bad" for country creditworthiness. In this case there can be a negative correlation between the state for growth (good for high growth) and the state for current account (large deficit and hence "bad" when growth is strong). If in practice the states tend to be positively correlated (for most variables the good outcomes occur when the outcomes are also good on the other variables), then the distribution of outcomes will no longer be accurately represented by the random distribution discussed above. Indeed, in the extreme in which there is 100 percent positive correlation between all of the states, the distribution would collapse to three cases, one each for bad, base case, and good. If the states tend to be positively correlated, the gap will tend to be wider between the central baseline case and either the 25th percentile or 75th percentile cases, because the correlations of bad with bad cases and good with good cases will tend to generate greater clustering of outcomes close to the bad and good perimeters. Contingent case correlation will thus essentially widen the range of uncertainty around the central baseline. Conversely, if the state correlations are predominantly negative, the effect will be to push the 25th and 75th percentile outcomes toward the baseline.

The likelihood of a particular overall outcome will depend on the probabilities of the states for each variable and the correlations of these probabilities. In the simple case with three equally likely states for each variable and zero correlation across variables, we have the example given above for the 81 outcomes. Figure 6B.1 shows a histogram for these outcomes, where the measure of the outcome is simply the average score across the four variables with each variable at 1 for bad, 2 for base case, and 3 for favorable. The introduction of correlations across scenarios will alter the profile of the outcomes shown in the figure. What follows is an operational example of the identification of scenario probabilities for the case of five underlying economic variables and three states (bad, base, and favorable).

First, define an array of possible scenarios. With five variables and three states, there are $3^5 = 243$ possible scenarios. Using 1, 2, and 3 as the states for each variable, and using the first subscript to refer to the first variable, the second to the second, and so forth, then the first scenario will be S11111, the second scenario S11112, and so forth up to the final scenario S33333. For example, scenario S13211 will be the scenario in which the first variable takes the bad state (1), the second variable the favorable state (3), the third variable

Figure 6B.1 Frequency of average state scores for four variables, three states, and no correlation[a]

frequency

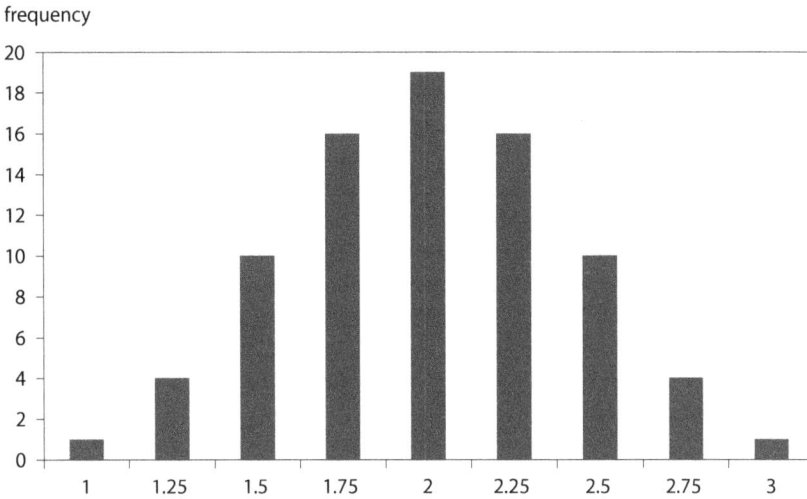

a. With scores of 1 = bad, 2 = central, 3 = good.

Source: Author's calculations.

the base state (2), the fourth variable the bad state (1), and the fifth variable the bad state (1).

A tractable if ad hoc way of proceeding is to posit that if a variable is at its base state, the probability of the case from the standpoint of that variable is a standard "central" probability, set for example at 0.4. However, if the variable is at either its bad or favorable state, then if all other variables are at their base states, its probability (from the standpoint of the single variable) will be the "alternate" probability, in this case 0.3 (that is: 0.3 bad + 0.4 base + 0.3 favorable = 1).

Correlation among variables can then be incorporated as follows. Let ρ_{ij} be defined as the correlation coefficient between the states of variable i and variable j. Define "δ" as the increment in the probability that a variable is in its bad (favorable) state when another variable with which it is positively correlated is in its bad (favorable) state.

The probability that a particular variable i will take a particular state s in a particular scenario k will then be calculated as:

$$p_{ik} = \alpha \; if \; s_{ik} = 2;$$
$$= \beta + \delta\sum_{j \in A}\rho_{ij} - \delta\sum_{j \in B}\rho_{ij} \; if \; s_{ik} \neq 2 \qquad (6B.1)$$

where A is the set of other variables that are in the same state as variable i (for example, at bad state 1 when for variable i the state is $s = 1$), and B is the set of other variables that are at the opposite state from that of variable i (in this example, at $s = 3$ instead of 1). Given the probability α for the baseline case, with two alternative scenarios (unfavorable, favorable) the term β must be $\beta = (1 - \alpha)/2$.

Calibrating the size of the probability increment δ will depend on the number of variables and on the desired ratio of the probability in the case that the variable in question is at the highest likely state when the other variables are in their nonbase states to the corresponding lowest probability. In the five-variable case, potentially there would be an additive amount of 4δ for the case in which the four other variables are all in their state that is associated with the good state of the variable in question. Suppose one seeks the maximum probability for a nonbase case, for the variable in question, to be three times the opposite-state nonbase probability. For the base probability $\alpha = 0.4$ and thus $\beta = 0.3$, this condition is met at $\delta = 0.0375$. That is, the high nonbase probability will be $0.3 + 4 (0.0375) = 0.45$; the low nonbase probability will be $0.3 - 4 (0.0375) = 0.15$.

Across the 243 scenarios (five-variable case), the unadjusted probability of the particular scenario k will then be:

$$p_k = \prod_i p_{ik} \tag{6B.2}$$

A final adjustment is then necessary to take account of the fact that it will only be by chance that the construction of the weighted probabilities taking account of correlations will yield a sum of unity probability across all scenarios. The final adjusted probability of the particular scenario k is then:

$$p_k^* = \lambda p_k \text{ where } \lambda = \frac{1}{\sum_k p_k} \tag{6B.3}$$

If there is some outcome variable that serves as a summary measure, such as the debt-to-GDP ratio in the terminal year, then the scenarios can be arrayed in order based on the value of this measure. The cumulative sum of the probabilities of the scenarios thus arrayed can then be observed to derive overall inferences from the projections. For example, It might be that in the full set of projections, with their weighted probabilities and taking into account likely correlations among the variables, the central estimate for the debt ratio will be 90 percent of GDP in 2020; the most favorable outcome, 70 percent; the least favorable outcome, 125 percent; and the 33rd and 67th percentiles in the distribution of outcomes, debt ratios of (say) 80 and 112 percent, respectively.

· The overall effect of this approach is to provide a somewhat greater sense of the realism of alternative outcomes than would otherwise be obtained solely by treating all of the possible variants as equally likely.

Appendix 6C
Comparison to IMF Baseline Projections

The debt projections of the IMF are an important point of reference. Greece, Ireland, and Portugal have financial support programs with official funding from the eurozone and the IMF. The Fund's judgments about debt sustainability determine whether it is willing to provide additional finance, and the support programs are premised on the central outlook for managing the debt on a sustainable basis. The IMF also prepares debt projections for Italy and Spain in its annual Article IV reviews.

The estimates of the present study thus take as their point of departure the baseline assumptions in the most recent IMF reports for each of the five peripheral economies. The estimates in the main text then introduce changes to the baselines only where there are major factors that seem important to add that are missing from the IMF projections. With the preferred baselines in hand, the calculations in the main text then explore the plausible range for alternative outcomes given the probabilistic approach developed in the European debt simulation model. This appendix reviews the extent to which the EDSM approximates or diverges from the IMF projections for the baselines, as a check on the model (and/or a basis for raising questions about the IMF projections).

Figure 6C.1 shows the comparison between the baselines of this chapter and those in the most recent IMF projections for Ireland, Portugal, Italy, and Spain.

The comparisons are simplest for Portugal and Spain, because in both cases there are no differences between the baseline set forth in this study and those in the IMF reports for growth, the primary surplus, discovered debt and bank recapitalization, and privatization. Nonetheless, by 2018 the EDSM projections place the debt-to-GDP ratio higher than the IMF baseline by 1.9 percent of GDP for Portugal and 3.7 percent of GDP in the case of Spain. In both cases (and especially for Spain), differences in the interest rates applied here and by the IMF appear to explain the divergences. Figure 6C.2 shows net interest payments as a percent of GDP in the IMF projections, obtained as the difference between the primary surplus and the total fiscal balance, and in the EDSM simulations of this study (applying the German bund base rate and country spreads shown in table 6.1). It is evident in the figure that for Spain the higher interest payments in the EDSM than in the IMF projection explain the divergence between the two projections of debt relative to GDP. Even for Portugal, where the interest paths are much closer, the cumulative difference in interest payments during 2013–18 is 0.7 percent of GDP, more than one-third of the total divergence between the debt ratios by 2018. Considering that the interest spreads in table 6.1 do not seem unreasonably high, the divergent projections suggest that for Portugal and especially Spain, the IMF baselines

Figure 6C.1   Comparison of EDSM to IMF baselines for gross public debt as percent of GDP, 2012–18

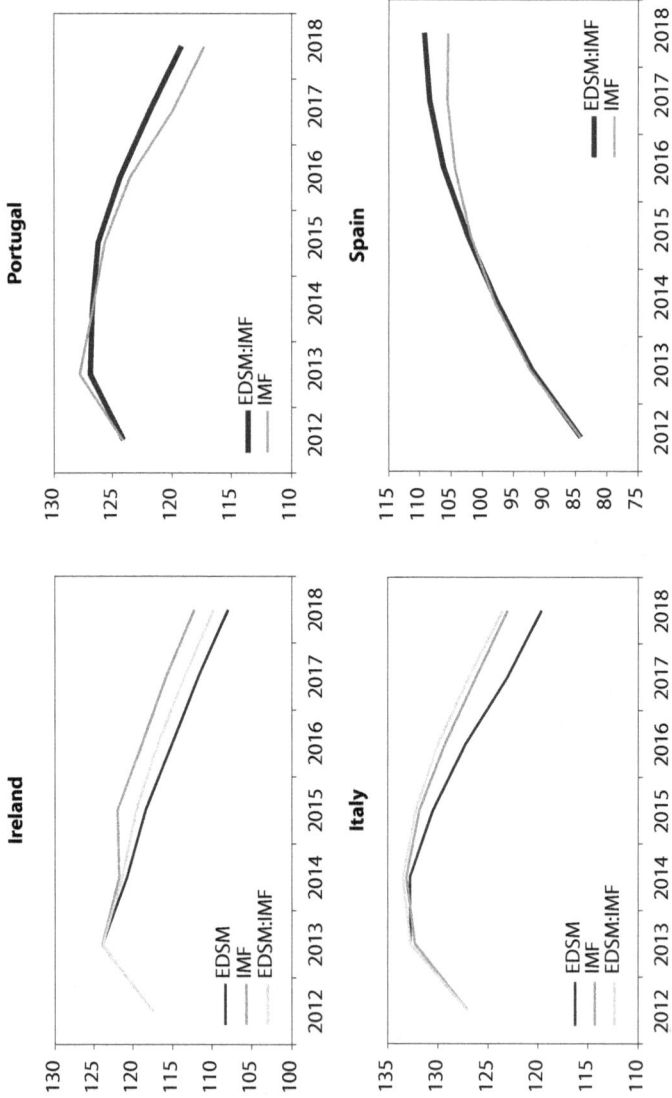

Ireland

Portugal

Italy

Spain

EDSM = European debt simulation model; IMF = International Monetary Fund

Note: EDSM:IMF refers to application of the EDSM to baseline assumptions identical to those used by the IMF.

Sources: IMF (2013l, 2013m, 2013p, 2013q); author's calculations.

Figure 6C.2   Net interest payments for Portugal and Spain, 2013–18

percent of GDP

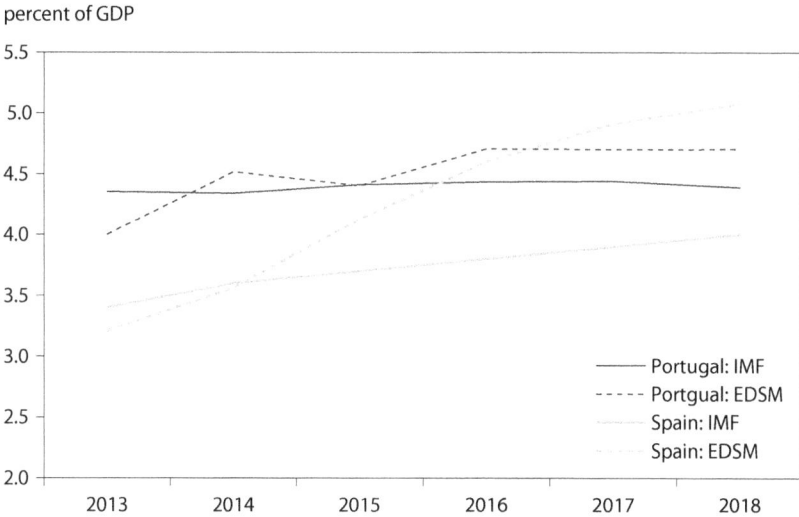

EDSM = European debt simulation model; IMF = International Monetary Fund

Sources: IMF (2013l, 2013q); author's calculations.

may be assuming interest rates that are on the optimistically low side.[33] The main implication for the two economies is that the projections of the present study may tend to be on the conservative side.

Returning to figure 6C.1, for Ireland and Italy the baseline assumptions in the present study are somewhat different from those in the most recent IMF reports. In these cases, then, "EDSM" refers to the baselines used here, whereas "EDSM:IMF" refers to application of the EDSM to baseline assumptions identical to those used by the IMF for growth, primary balance, bank recapitalization and discovered debt, and privatization. (The panels for Portugal and Spain show only EDSM:IMF because the baseline here is identical to those of the IMF in those cases.) It is evident that the baseline projections track those of the IMF relatively closely for Ireland and extremely closely for Italy when identical assumptions are made (suggesting that interest rate differences are less of a problem than for Portugal and Spain). Even after incorporating the change to the baseline assumptions for Ireland (inclusion of some privatization

---

33. For Spain, for example, in the IMF projections 2017 net interest is only 3.9 percent of GDP. End-2016 gross debt is 104.4 percent. End-2016 financial assets in the IMF's WEO amount to 13.2 percent of GDP (difference between gross and net debt; IMF 2013g). If earnings of 2 percent are imputed to assets, then net interest payments at 3.9 percent of GDP in 2017 imply an average interest rate on debt of only 4.0 percent (= [3.9 + {2 × .132}]/1.044). In the calculations here, the average rate on new medium- and long-term debt contracted in 2013–16 is 5.5 percent, and the average interest on end-2012 medium- and long-term debt, 4.4 percent; so the IMF estimate of 4.0 percent appears low.

receipts, absent in the IMF assumptions), the projection remains very close to that of the IMF. For Italy, the baseline projection is more optimistic than that of the IMF once the changed assumptions are incorporated. The EDSM assumes significant privatization receipts whereas the IMF assumes none; and the EDSM baseline also assumes slightly higher growth. These two effects more than offset the EDSM incorporation of discovered debt associated with aid to euro area countries.

Appendix 6D
EDSM Baseline Projections through 2020

Table 6D.1   Ireland

	2011	2012	2013	2014	2015	2016	2017	2018	2019	2020
Percent of GDP:										
Debt	104.1	117.4	123.8	120.7	118.4	115.1	111.7	108.0	104.3	100.8
Net debt	85.1	92.8	99.0	100.8	99.2	97.1	94.6	91.6	88.7	85.9
Net interest		3.4	4.1	4.4	4.4	4.5	4.5	4.5	4.5	4.4
Amortization		8.8	9.3	8.0	12.3	16.2	12.7	16.5	18.2	21.5
Billions of euros:										
Nominal GDP	162.6	163.9	165.0	169.0	175.0	181.2	188.7	196.5	204.6	213.1
Primary deficit			4.5	0.5	−3.5	−4.9	−6.0	−7.3	−7.6	−7.9
Total deficit			11.2	8.0	4.3	3.3	2.5	1.5	1.6	1.5
(+) bank recapitalization			0.0	0.0	0.0	0.0	0.0	0.0	0.0	0.0
(−) privatization receipts			0.0	1.0	1.0	1.0	0.0	0.0	0.0	0.0
Net borrowing requirement			11.2	7.0	3.3	2.3	2.5	1.5	1.6	1.5
(+) financial asset purchase			0.7	−7.3	−0.2	−1.0	−0.2	−0.2	−0.2	−0.2
Amortization			15.4	13.5	21.5	29.3	24.0	32.4	37.2	45.7
IMF			0.0	0.0	0.6	2.6	3.4	3.8	3.8	3.8
EFSM			0.0	0.0	5.0	0.0	0.0	3.9	0.0	0.0
EFSF			0.0	0.0	1.3	4.2	0.0	0.0	0.0	0.0
EU bilateral			0.0	0.0	0.0	0.0	0.0	0.0	1.7	1.7
Private ST			10.2	10.2	10.2	10.2	10.2	10.2	10.2	10.2
Private MLT (pre-2013)			5.2	2.7	3.6	10.2	6.4	9.3	14.5	20.9
Private MLT (new)			0.0	0.5	0.8	2.1	4.0	5.2	7.0	9.1
Gross borrowing requirement			27.3	13.2	24.6	30.6	26.3	33.7	38.6	47.0
Debt	169.3	192.5	204.4	204.1	207.1	208.4	210.8	212.1	213.5	214.8
IMF	12.6	19.0	22.5	22.5	21.9	19.3	15.9	12.0	8.2	4.3
European Union	22.0	36.8	45.1	45.1	38.8	34.6	34.6	30.7	29.1	27.4

(continues on next page)

Table 6D.1   Ireland *(continued)*

	2011	2012	2013	2014	2015	2016	2017	2018	2019	2020
Billions of euros:										
Central bank notes/bonds		25.0	25.0	25.0	25.0	25.0	25.0	25.0	25.0	25.0
ST	4.4	10.2	10.2	10.2	10.2	10.2	10.2	10.2	10.2	10.2
MLT (pre-2013)	102.0	101.5	96.3	93.5	89.9	79.7	73.3	64.1	49.6	28.8
MLT (new)		0.0	5.3	7.8	21.3	39.6	51.7	70.1	91.4	119.1
Net interest payments			6.7	7.5	7.8	8.2	8.5	8.8	9.1	9.4
IMF			0.4	0.8	0.8	0.8	0.6	0.5	0.3	0.2
European Union			1.3	1.6	1.6	1.4	1.2	1.2	1.1	1.0
Central bank notes/bonds			0.8	0.8	0.9	1.0	1.1	1.2	1.3	1.3
ST			0.2	0.3	0.2	0.2	0.2	0.2	0.2	0.2
MLT (pre-2013)			4.9	4.6	4.5	4.4	3.9	3.5	3.1	2.4
MLT (new)			0.0	0.2	0.4	1.1	2.1	2.7	3.7	4.8
(–) Financial assets			0.8	0.8	0.7	0.7	0.7	0.6	0.6	0.6
Financial assets	30.9	40.3	41.0	33.7	33.5	32.5	32.4	32.2	32.0	31.8
Net debt	138.4	152.2	163.4	170.3	173.6	175.9	178.4	179.9	181.5	182.9

EFSM = European Financial Stabilization Mechanism; EFSF = European Financial Stability Facility; IMF = International Monetary Fund; ST = short term; MLT = medium and long term

Source: Author's calculations.

Table 6D.2 Portugal

	2011	2012	2013	2014	2015	2016	2017	2018	2019	2020
Percent of GDP:										
Debt	108.2	124.1	126.9	126.7	126.2	124.4	121.9	119.2	116.6	114.0
Net debt	97.7	112.6	120.9	120.8	120.4	118.8	116.5	114.0	111.5	109.2
Net interest		4.2	4.0	4.5	4.4	4.7	4.7	4.7	4.6	4.6
Amortization		22.7	18.2	17.2	20.8	25.4	23.4	24.1	22.3	22.8
Billions of euros:										
Nominal GDP	171.1	165.1	165.6	168.4	172.6	178.5	185.0	191.7	198.7	205.9
Primary deficit			2.6	–0.5	–3.1	–4.3	–5.2	–5.9	–6.2	–6.4
Total deficit			9.3	7.1	4.5	4.1	3.5	3.1	3.1	3.1
(+) bank recapitalization			0.0	0.0	0.0	0.0	0.0	0.0	0.0	0.0
(–) privatization receipts			1.0	0.5	0.0	0.0	0.0	0.0	0.0	0.0
Net borrowing requirement			8.3	6.6	4.5	4.1	3.5	3.1	3.1	3.1
(+) financial asset purchase			–3.0	–3.3	0.0	0.0	0.0	0.0	0.0	0.0
Amortization			30.1	28.9	35.9	45.3	43.4	46.1	44.4	47.0
IMF			0.0	0.0	0.5	2.7	3.8	4.5	4.6	4.8
EFSM			0.0	0.0	0.0	4.8	0.0	0.6	0.0	0.0
EFSF			0.0	0.0	1.7	2.2	0.0	0.0	0.0	0.0
EU bilateral			0.0	0.0	0.0	0.0	0.0	0.0	0.0	0.0
ST			19.2	17.4	23.6	23.6	23.6	23.6	23.6	23.6
MLT (pre-2013)			10.9	10.7	9.2	9.7	11.3	10.9	7.7	8.6
MLT (new)			0.0	0.8	0.8	2.4	4.7	6.6	8.5	10.0
Gross borrowing requirement		53.2	35.4	32.2	40.4	49.4	46.9	49.2	47.4	50.2
Debt	185.1	204.9	210.2	213.4	217.9	222.0	225.5	228.6	231.6	234.8
IMF	13.1	21.3	24.7	27.4	26.8	24.2	20.4	15.9	11.3	6.5
European Union	22.2	42.6	49.1	54.3	52.6	45.6	45.6	45.0	45.0	45.0
ST	18.8	19.2	17.4	23.6	23.6	23.6	23.6	23.6	23.6	23.6
MLT (pre-2013)	131.1	121.8	110.9	100.2	90.9	81.3	70.0	59.1	51.5	42.9
MLT (new)			8.1	8.0	23.9	47.3	65.9	84.9	100.2	116.7

(continues on next page)

Table 6D.2   Portugal *(continued)*

	2011	2012	2013	2014	2015	2016	2017	2018	2019	2020
Billions of euros:										
Net interest payments			6.6	7.6	7.6	8.4	8.7	9.0	9.2	9.5
IMF			0.3	0.8	1.0	1.0	0.8	0.7	0.5	0.3
European Union			1.1	1.3	1.4	1.4	1.2	1.2	1.2	1.2
ST			0.1	0.4	0.4	0.6	0.3	0.3	0.3	0.3
MLT (pre-2013)			5.4	4.9	4.5	4.2	3.7	3.2	2.7	2.3
MLT (new)			0.0	0.5	0.5	1.5	2.9	3.8	4.7	5.6
(–) Financial assets			5.6	5.7	5.4	6.3	6.9	7.3	7.8	8.2
Financial assets	17.9	18.9	10.0	10.0	10.0	10.0	10.0	10.0	10.0	10.0
Net debt	167.2	186.0	200.1	203.4	207.9	212.0	215.5	218.6	221.6	224.8

EFSM = European Financial Stabilization Mechanism; EFSF = European Financial Stability Facility; IMF = International Monetary Fund; MLT = medium and long term; ST = short term

Source: Author's calculations.

Table 6D.3 Italy

	2011	2012	2013	2014	2015	2016	2017	2018	2019	2020
Percent of GDP:										
Debt	120.8	127.0	132.7	132.8	130.5	127.2	123.1	119.6	117.1	114.6
Net debt	99.7	103.2	107.8	108.0	106.1	103.4	99.9	97.0	95.0	93.1
Net interest		4.5	4.8	4.9	5.3	5.6	5.5	5.4	5.3	5.2
Amortization		20.0	18.3	19.5	21.2	15.9	18.3	15.4	16.0	15.9
Billions of euros:										
Nominal GDP	1,578.5	1,565.4	1,558.8	1,590.1	1,628.5	1,673.6	1,722.4	1,769.3	1,817.3	1,866.7
Primary deficit			−31.2	−52.5	−58.6	−75.3	−87.8	−99.1	−84.4	−86.7
Total deficit			44.3	25.6	26.9	17.7	6.2	−4.2	11.1	11.1
(+) bank recapitalization			20.0	22.0	0.0	1.0	1.0	0.0	0.0	0.0
(−) privatization receipts			0.0	11.0	16.0	17.0	17.0	0.0	0.0	0.0
Net borrowing requirement			64.3	36.6	10.9	1.7	−9.8	−4.2	11.1	11.1
(+) financial asset purchase			16.4	5.3	3.2	2.2	1.1	0.4	0.4	0.4
Amortization			285.9	309.3	345.3	266.3	314.5	271.8	290.6	297.3
ST			131.2	131.2	131.2	131.2	131.2	131.2	131.2	131.2
MLT (pre-2013)			154.7	154.5	170.9	73.4	113.9	60.7	73.8	71.9
MLT (new)			0.0	23.5	43.2	61.7	69.4	79.9	85.6	94.1
Gross borrowing requirement			366.6	351.2	359.5	270.2	305.8	268.0	302.2	308.8
Debt	1,906.8	1,988.4	2,069.1	2,111.0	2,125.1	2,129.1	2,120.3	2,116.5	2,128.1	2,139.6
ST	131.2	131.2	131.2	131.2	131.2	131.2	131.2	131.2	131.2	131.2
MLT (pre-2013)	1,775.6	1,857.1	1,702.4	1,547.9	1,377.0	1,303.7	1,189.8	1,129.1	1,055.3	983.4
MLT (new)			235.4	431.8	616.9	694.2	799.3	856.2	941.5	1025.0
Net interest payments			75.5	78.1	85.6	93.0	94.0	94.8	95.4	97.8
ST			4.5	1.9	2.2	2.4	2.5	2.5	2.5	2.5
MLT (pre-2013)			78.5	73.5	67.1	63.5	61.0	56.0	53.5	51.0
MLT (new)			0.0	10.5	24.2	35.2	38.5	44.4	47.5	52.3

(continues on next page)

Table 6D.3   Italy *(continued)*

	2011	2012	2013	2014	2015	2016	2017	2018	2019	2020
Billions of euros:										
(–) Financial assets			7.4	7.8	7.9	7.9	8.0	8.0	8.0	8.0
Financial assets	332.6	372.2	388.6	393.9	397.1	399.3	400.3	400.8	401.2	401.7
Net debt	1,574.2	1,616.2	1,680.5	1,717.1	1,728.1	1,729.8	1,720.0	1,715.7	1,726.8	1,737.9

MLT = medium and long term; ST = short term

Source: Author's calculations.

Table 6D.4   Spain

	2011	2012	2013	2014	2015	2016	2017	2018	2019	2020
Percent of GDP:										
Debt	69.1	84.2	92.1	97.7	102.4	106.2	108.4	109.2	110.1	111.2
Net debt	57.5	72.0	79.4	84.6	89.0	92.6	95.0	96.2	97.4	98.7
Net interest		2.7	3.2	3.6	4.1	4.6	4.9	5.1	5.2	5.3
Amortization		13.0	13.9	15.8	18.1	17.5	16.6	15.2	16.5	16.8
Billions of euros:										
Nominal GDP	1,063.4	1,049.5	1,043.1	1,051.5	1,065.2	1,083.4	1,105.1	1,131.8	1,159.2	1,187.1
Primary deficit			38.6	24.2	14.9	4.3	−6.6	−19.2	−19.7	−20.2
Total deficit			72.1	61.6	58.9	54.2	47.6	38.2	40.3	42.7
(+) bank recapitalization			0.0	0.0	0.0	0.0	0.0	0.0	0.0	0.0
(−) privatization receipts			0.0	0.0	0.0	0.0	0.0	0.0	0.0	0.0
Net borrowing requirement			72.1	61.6	58.9	54.2	47.6	38.2	40.3	42.7
(+) financial asset purchase			4.6	5.0	5.3	5.3	−0.0	0.0	0.0	0.0
Amortization			145.0	166.2	192.7	189.3	184.0	171.7	190.9	199.7
ST			84.6	84.6	84.6	84.6	84.6	84.6	84.6	84.6
MLT (pre-2012)			60.4	67.9	80.9	63.0	45.4	23.8	36.9	38.0
MLT (new)			0.0	13.7	27.2	41.7	53.9	63.2	69.4	77.1
Gross borrowing requirement			221.6	232.8	256.8	248.8	231.6	209.9	231.3	242.5
Debt	735.0	883.7	960.3	1027.0	1091.1	1150.6	1198.2	1236.4	1276.8	1319.5
ST	90.6	84.6	84.6	84.6	84.6	84.6	84.6	84.6	84.6	84.6
MLT (pre-2013)	644.4	799.1	738.7	670.9	589.9	526.9	481.5	457.6	420.7	382.8
MLT (new)			137.0	271.5	416.6	539.1	632.2	694.2	771.4	852.1
Net interest payments			33.5	37.5	44.0	49.8	54.3	57.4	60.0	62.9
ST			1.5	1.6	1.6	1.6	1.7	1.7	1.7	1.7
MLT (pre-2013)			34.5	32.4	30.0	27.3	25.6	23.6	22.8	21.4
MLT (new)			0.0	6.1	15.2	23.7	29.9	35.1	38.5	42.8

(continues on next page)

Table 6D.4 Spain *(continued)*

	2011	2012	2013	2014	2015	2016	2017	2018	2019	2020
Billions of euros:										
(–) Financial assets			2.6	2.6	2.7	2.9	3.0	3.0	3.0	3.0
Financial assets	123.7	127.7	132.3	137.3	142.6	147.9	147.9	147.9	147.9	147.9
Net debt	611.3	756.0	828.0	889.7	948.5	1,002.7	1,050.4	1,088.6	1,128.9	1,171.0

MLT = medium and long term; ST = short term

Source: Author's calculations.

Debt Restructuring and Economic Prospects in Greece

Greece has been at the epicenter of the European debt crisis.[1] It is the only industrial nation since the 1930s (excluding early postwar Germany) that has been forced to restructure public debt with forgiveness. Financial contagion from Greece contributed to debt stress in the euro area periphery, at first in Ireland and Portugal but eventually even in the large and stronger economies of Italy and Spain. Following the temporary specter of a Greek exit from the euro, in mid-2012 the sharp escalation of potential European Central Bank (ECB) support through the promise of purchases of government bonds in Outright Monetary Transactions (OMT), if needed and in the presence of adjustment programs, marked the turning point toward more normal sovereign borrowing conditions in the euro area periphery. By early 2014, Ireland had successfully exited from its adjustment program, and Portugal was near completion of its program as well. The jury is still out, however, on whether the debt restructuring already carried out for Greece will prove to be sufficient.

In April 2012 a successful exchange of Greek public debt conveyed 53.5 percent debt reduction for privately held debt.[2] However, much of the debt was excluded because it was held by the ECB, euro area official sector, and International Monetary Fund (IMF). Losses on the holdings by Greek banks necessitated recapitalization that offset a significant part of the debt reduction. In December 2012 an additional package of official sector relief (in the form of lower interest rates and support for a buyback of about half of

---

1. An earlier version of this chapter appeared in Cline (2013a).

2. Jeromin Zettelmeyer, Christoph Trebesch, and Mitu Gulati (2012) calculate the corresponding present-value reduction of the private sector involvement (PSI) exchange at 60 percent from the standpoint of Greece and 65 percent from the standpoint of creditors (central estimates).

the restructured privately held debt) helped consolidate the conditions for managing the remaining debt over the next few years if reasonable growth and fiscal expectations are achieved.

Over the longer term, however, it is unclear that Greece will be able to reenter private capital markets in substantial volume for long-term bonds by 2020 even if its debt level is down to the range of about 120 percent of GDP. The damage to its credit reputation from restructuring with a large haircut seems likely to leave it in a more difficult borrowing position than other euro area sovereigns even if it achieves comparable debt levels. Nonetheless, the interest burden would be lower than usually associated with this range of debt because of dominant official sourcing, and in April 2014 the government successfully issued a modest amount of medium-term debt. On balance, further relief on official sector claims may or may not be needed in the future. Such relief is not urgent at present, however, because almost all of Greece's borrowing needs should already be covered for the next several years. Eventual official debt forgiveness would appropriately be linked to demonstrated performance on fiscal consolidation.

Initial Programs and Deteriorating Prospects

In May 2010, Greece entered into an economic adjustment program with €110 billion in official support from the IMF (€30 billion) and European governments (€80 billion in the Greek Loan Facility [GLF]). In comparison, Greek public debt at the end of 2009 stood at €298 billion, or 127 percent of GDP (IMF 2011a, 37). The official program was premised on a return to government borrowing from private markets in 2012, in amounts reaching about €70 billion annually in 2014 (IMF 2011a, 49). The hope that Greece's debt problem could be resolved through official lending to tide it over during a liquidity problem turned out to be overly optimistic, however. By December 2012, efforts to resolve the problem had escalated to involve relatively deep debt forgiveness by private holders, a new round of large additional official support through the European Financial Stability Facility (EFSF), a major buyback, and initial variants of official sector debt relief in the form of lower interest rates on GLF debt and the option to capitalize interest on EFSF debt for 10 years. From the vantage point of early 2014, despite a modest April issuance of five-year bonds, there is little prospect of returning any time soon to much broader market access at longer terms and moderate spreads and considerable possibility that further official relief may lie ahead. The slide from the policy framework of solvency and refinancing to insolvency and forgiveness reflected in considerable part a progressive deterioration in prospects for growth and fiscal adjustment. Nominal GDP had initially been expected to rise by 13 percent from 2009 to 2015 (IMF 2010c); instead, by July 2013 the expectation was that it would fall by 18 percent over this period (IMF 2013k). Figure 7.1

Figure 7.1   Successive IMF projections for Greece, September 2010 through July 2013

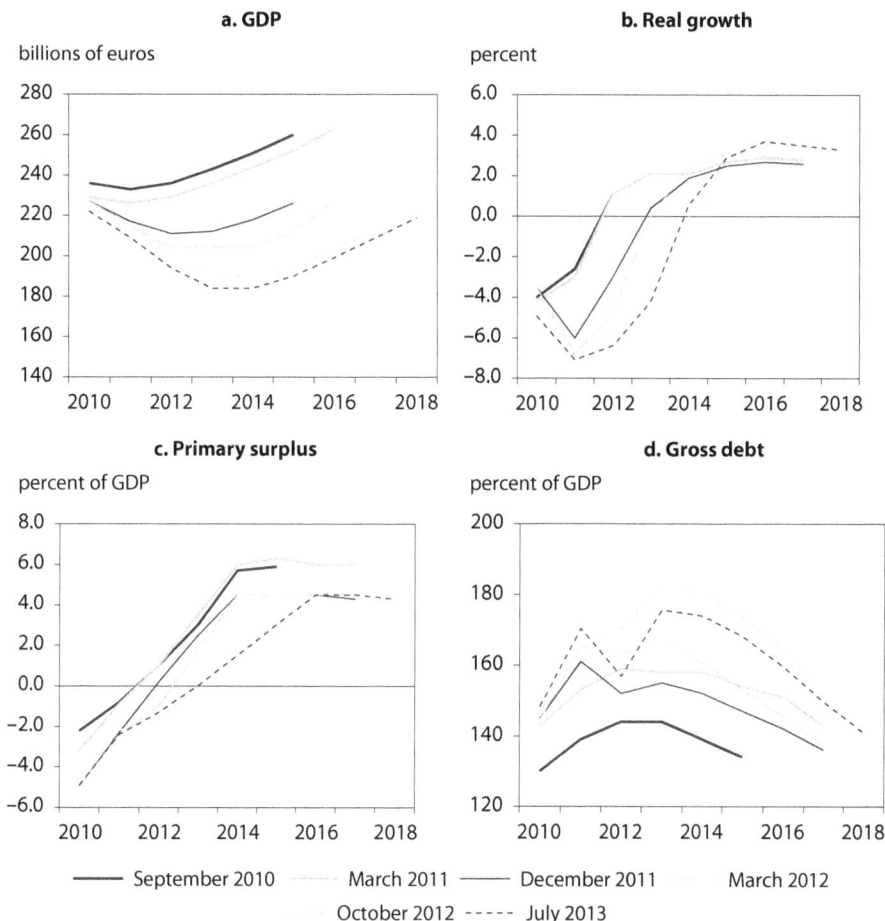

a. GDP

billions of euros

b. Real growth

percent

c. Primary surplus

percent of GDP

d. Gross debt

percent of GDP

——— September 2010 ········ March 2011 ——— December 2011 ········ March 2012
········ October 2012 ----- July 2013

IMF = International Monetary Fund

Sources: IMF (2010c, 2011a, 2011e, 2012c, 2012i, 2013k).

shows successive IMF program review projections for Greece.[3] In panel A, for example, the March 2012 report placed nominal GDP in 2015 at a level 16 percent lower than that projected in March 2011. Panel B shows the corresponding successive downgradings of projected economic growth. For 2012, for example, the first two IMF program reviews anticipated GDP growth of +1

---

3. The late-2012 set of projections, however, is from the IMF's October 2012 *World Economic Outlook* (IMF 2012i), because of the unusually long hiatus with no program review publication between March (IMF 2012c) and January (IMF 2013c).

percent; in December 2011 the outlook was for 2012 growth of –3 percent, and by October 2012 the outlook had fallen to –6 percent.

Similarly, panel C shows the successive downgradings in expectations for the primary surplus as a percent of GDP. At the outset the program had aspired to a medium-term surplus of 6 percent of GDP; by December 2011 this target had been cut to 4.5 percent; and by October 2012 the date of achieving this lower target had been delayed by two years. Despite shortfalls from initial fiscal goals, Greece carried out large fiscal adjustment in terms of reducing primary spending by 24 percent in real terms from 2009 to 2012. In its July 2013 program review, the IMF emphasized the progress on fiscal adjustment, stating: "steadfast fiscal adjustment by the Greek authorities since 2009 delivered an improvement in the cyclically-adjusted primary balance of over 15 percent of GDP" (IMF 2013k, 4).

Finally, panel D displays the successive IMF projections of the ratio of debt to GDP. The September 2010 projection was far more optimistic than the October 2012 projection, even though there had been substantial debt relief between the two reviews. The combination of lower primary surplus performance and much lower nominal GDP more than offset the debt relief. (The modest reduction in the projected debt ratio for 2012 from the March 2011 report to the December 2011 report reflects the limited impact of the restructuring of privately held debt, discussed below.)

As noted, despite the slippage on the primary balance, Greece carried out large fiscal adjustment in terms of reducing primary spending. Following a decline of 24 percent in real terms from 2009 to 2012, real primary spending is scheduled to fall an additional 7 percent from 2012 to 2017 (IMF 2013k, 51). A sharp decline in revenue associated with recession meant that the progress in reducing the fiscal deficit was moderated. Even so, the primary deficit fell from a peak of 10.4 percent of GDP in 2009 to 1.3 percent of GDP in 2012 and swung to a small surplus in 2013. The improvement by 9.1 percent of GDP through 2012 was three-fifths of the way toward the goal of a total adjustment of 15 percent of GDP from 2009 to 2017. As noted, in cyclically adjusted terms, the primary balance had already improved by 15 percent of GDP from 2009 to 2012.

From Stretchout to Debt Reduction

In October 2011, I prepared projections (Cline 2011) that indicated that Greece should be able to sustain its debt on the terms that had been arranged in the July 2011 package of official support combined with private sector involvement (PSI), even though the PSI amounted to a stretchout of maturities with minimal debt forgiveness. Even so, achievement of ambitious fiscal targets (a 6 percent of GDP primary surplus by 2014) and reasonable growth performance were crucial to that possibility. In addition to the earlier €110 billion program of support from the IMF and euro area, the euro area pledged further support of €109 billion. For its part, PSI was supposed to provide refinancing of €135 billion over 2011–20.[4] I emphasized four features that made Greek debt more sustainable than might be inferred from the ratio of gross debt to GDP: large privatizations were planned, providing funds to retire debt; Greece held relatively large public financial assets, making net debt considerably lower than gross debt; there would be a misleading surge in gross debt offset by a corresponding rise in assets as a consequence of the collateralization needed for the PSI; and a large share of the debt was from official sources at relatively low interest rates (Cline 2011, 2).[5]

My baseline projection called for gross debt to peak at 175 percent of GDP in 2012 and fall to 113 percent by 2020; net debt would fall from 121 percent of GDP in 2011 to 69 percent by 2020. Noting that the net debt ratio by 2020 would be about the same as the level for US federal debt held by the public in 2011, I concluded that with the July 2011 support package in hand, Greek public debt should be sustainable.[6] However, the arrangement was not given an opportunity to materialize. German authorities in particular pressed for much deeper debt forgiveness by private sector holders.[7] Yet the scope for gains from private holder forgiveness was limited because by then only about half of the debt was held by the private sector (in part because about €50 billion in government bonds had been purchased from the market by the ECB in its Securities Markets Programme [SMP]). By late October 2011 euro area authorities reached agreement with representatives of banks and insurers that they would accept a 50 percent reduction in the face value of debt.

As discussed in chapter 5, in June 2013 the IMF issued a report concluding that there should have been earlier, preemptive debt haircuts in Greece (IMF 2013h). However, as suggested by the mid-2011 projections in Cline (2011),

---

4. The mid-2011 PSI converted claims to 30-year par bonds at moderate interest rates (about 4.5 percent) or "discount" bonds forgiving 20 percent of face value but bearing somewhat higher interest rates (about 6.5 percent) (Cline 2012a, 201). The main effect of the PSI agreement was to provide long-term rollover of maturities otherwise coming due, without conveying much real relief gauged against the original terms of the debt.

5. Specifically, at end-2010 Greece held a reported €101 billion in financial assets, placing its net debt at 110 percent of GDP, far lower than the gross debt ratio of 143 percent (Cline 2011). Regarding collateral, the July 2011 PSI deal would have involved setting aside AAA zero-coupon bonds to collateralize the (far less concessionary) bond exchange then envisioned. The funds for this collateral, on the order of €30 billion to €40 billion, would reasonably have been seen as an asset, given the expectation that the exchanged bonds would be fully serviced and the collateral not called (Cline 2011, IIF 2011).

6. A prominent Greek economist who would soon become prime minister, Lucas Papademos, reached the same conclusion, and argued that further forced debt relief would be counterproductive. See "Forcing Greek Restructuring Is Not the Answer," *Financial Times*, October 21, 2011. The more conventional opinion was that "Greece, which is unambiguously insolvent, ought to have a hard but orderly write-down." See "How to Save the Euro," *Economist*, September 17, 2011, 11.

7. See for example Ambrose Evans-Pritchard, "German Push for Greek Default Risks EMU-wide Snowball," *Telegraph*, October 10, 2011.

there was a plausible case at that time that Greece could avoid debt forgiveness if it marshaled the political will to take the needed fiscal adjustment. The 53 percent haircut eventually forced on private creditors will leave a legacy of tainted credit reputation that will haunt Greek access to capital markets for a long time, and it made sense in 2010–11 to seek to avoid a shock of this nature if possible.

Restructuring Private Claims

In April 2012, Greece successfully exchanged approximately €200 billion in debt held by the private sector for 10- to 30-year exchange bonds with a face value of 31.5 percent of the original bonds and paying 2 to 4.3 percent interest, plus an up-front payment of 15 percent of original face value over two years (Zettelmeyer, Trebesch, and Gulati 2012, 6). The direct reduction in gross debt was €107 billion (€200 billion less €137 billion forgiven, but plus the €30 billion up-front "sweetener"), representing a 53.5 percent cut in the nominal value of Greek debt held by private investors and exchanged (and 51.9 percent of total eligible privately held debt).[8]

However, the €200 billion exchanged accounted for only 56.2 percent of the end-2011 debt total. Almost all of the rest was exempt, including importantly about €21 billion held by the IMF, €53 billion held by euro area governments in the GLF, and €57 billion held by the ECB from its SMP purchases as well as by national central banks (table 7A.1). In addition, losses by Greek banks on their holdings as a result of the debt exchange required recapitalization of €22 billion, necessitating this amount in new public borrowing (IMF 2013c, 6). The net debt reduction was thus €85 billion, or 23.9 percent of total public debt at the end of 2011.[9] The overall effect of the large PSI of April 2012 was thus to reduce total Greek debt by slightly less than one-fourth. It is perhaps not surprising that once the country had plunged into insolvency mode, a debt reduction by only one-fourth would not have been sufficient to reestablish solvency decisively.

Political Turmoil, "Grexit" Risk, and Outlook by Late 2012

In the second quarter of 2012 political uncertainty escalated. The main parties (New Democracy and Pasok) fared badly in May elections, and the absence of a coalition required a second election in June. A key opposition coalition (Syriza) condemned the economic adjustment program, and market

---

8. Of the total eligible private holdings of €206 billion, €6 billion was not exchanged (Zettelmeyer, Trebesch, and Gulati 2012, 5).

9. Other bank losses brought the total amount of bank recapitalization needed to €50 billion (IMF 2012c, 28).

expectations of a possible Greek exit from the euro ("Grexit") escalated.[10] After New Democracy won in the follow-up June elections, and affirmed Greece's commitment to the adjustment program, fears about an exit from the euro eased but delays in euro area and IMF financing persisted in view of shortfalls in fiscal performance.

Prospects for economic performance appeared much grimmer by late 2012 than a year earlier. Thus, whereas my October 2011 study had anticipated GDP growth of −3.8 percent in 2011, +0.6 percent in 2012, and +2.1 percent in 2013, the new baseline for growth by October 2012 showed −6.9 percent for 2011, −6 percent for 2012, and −4 percent for 2013 (IMF 2012i). The growth deterioration alone meant that the projected debt-to-GDP ratio would now be almost 20 percent higher than before. The delay of achievement of the 4.5 percent of GDP primary surplus for two years meant still further escalation in the debt ratio.

To make matters worse, the IMF apparently no longer considered the sizable public financial assets to be worth anything. Whereas the *World Economic Outlook* (WEO) in October 2010 had estimated end-2010 public financial assets at €49 billion, or 22 percent of GDP, a year later it placed the value of these assets at zero and by the October 2012 issue the assets were still at zero (IMF 2010d, 2011c, 2012i).[11]

In October 2012, the IMF's WEO projected that for Greece the ratio of gross public debt to GDP would rise from 165 percent of GDP at the end of 2011 to 171 percent at the end of 2012, peak at 182 percent in 2013, and then decline to 153 percent by 2017 (IMF 2012h). The corresponding absolute level for projected debt was €344 billion, down only €12 billion from the level at the end of 2011. In principle it was surprising that the debt ratio was scheduled to rise in 2012, considering that in 2012 there was a restructuring with a nominal haircut of 53.5 percent for private holders. Similarly, it was surprising that the absolute debt reduction was expected to amount to only €12 billion after a net cut of €85 billion (discussed above) and with the 2012 fiscal deficit then projected at only €9.5 billion. One reason for the paradox of a rising debt ratio was that GDP was falling, by a nominal decline of 7 percent. But it also appears that the IMF's October 2012 WEO overstated the baseline end-2012 debt ratio by about 10 percent of GDP.[12] An official

---

10. In February 2012, Citigroup's chief economist had raised the probability of a Grexit in the next 18 months from between 25 percent and 30 percent to 50 percent (Buiter and Rahbari 2012). He later raised the probability to 90 percent. Kate Mackenzie, "Buiter's Now Predicting Grexit Probability of 90%," FT Alphaville, July 26, 2012.

11. Government financial assets equal the difference between gross debt and net debt.

12. Actual end-2012 debt was €304 billion. The buyback had extinguished about €20 billion net, so without the December package the end-2012 debt would have stood at about €324 billion, significantly below the October WEO figure of €344 billion (IMF 2012b). Zsolt Darvas (2012) had noted at the time that the WEO's projected end-2012 debt buildup could not be fully explained.

sector outlook for a rising debt ratio even after the deep PSI cut undoubtedly contributed to a policy environment favoring further debt reduction, this time by the euro area public sector.

December 2012 Official Relief Package

By the third quarter of 2012, the IMF was increasingly pressing for a sufficient easing of the terms of euro area official support to bring the 2020 debt ratio down to a sustainable level of 120 percent of GDP or less.[13] In late November 2012, euro area finance ministers and the IMF agreed on what amounted to a new round of debt relief, this time for official sector creditors. The package involved four elements of relief: lower interest rates on GLF loans; support for a buyback of debt; scope for deferring and capitalizing interest due on EFSF lending; and passing on of ECB profits on Greek debt purchased in the market to Greece.[14]

Interest rates on the bilateral (GLF) loans were to be cut by 100 basis points, to 50 basis points above interbank rates. Interest payments on the second round of euro area support (through the EFSF) were eligible to be "deferred" (i.e., capitalized) over the next decade, although such capitalized interest in turn would be subject to interest payments. Some €10 billion in support would be used to buy back some €30 billion in government debt at about 33 cents on the euro of face value. Some €9 billion in prospective profits from ECB receipts on Greek government bonds acquired at a discount in the SMP that would have devolved to member country central banks would instead be passed along to Greece.[15] Altogether some €40 billion would be cut from the debt, placing the debt-to-GDP ratio at no more than 124 percent by 2020 and 110 percent by 2022. In December 2012, the Greek government successfully repurchased debt with a face value of €31.9 billion for €11.29 billion (Ministry of Finance 2012b).[16]

---

13. Matthew Dalton and Costas Paris, "IMF Pushes Europe to Ease Greek Burden," *Wall Street Journal*, August 6, 2012; Dina Kyriakidou and Lesley Wroughton, "Exclusive: IMF, EU Clash over Greece's Bailout," Reuters, September 26, 2012.

14. Peter Spiegel, "Eurozone Agrees Greek Aid Deal," *Financial Times*, November 27, 2012; James Kanter, "European Finance Ministers and I.M.F. Reach Deal on Greek Bailout Terms," *New York Times*, November 26, 2012; EC (2012).

15. Prior to the PSI debt exchange the ECB exchanged at full face value its holdings of Greek public debt acquired in the SMP at market prices. SMP profit returns to Greece are placed by the IMF at €9.3 billion through 2020 (IMF 2013c, 87). At the end of 2011, the ECB and euro area national central banks (NCBs) held €56.5 billion in Greek public bonds (Darvas 2012, 4; Reserve Bank of Australia 2012, 31). The Greek Ministry of Finance provides a narrower measure of the holdings of the ECB itself at the end of 2011, amounting to €42.7 billion (Ministry of Finance 2012a). In appendix table 7A.1 the time profile of maturities on the narrower ECB estimate during 2012–20, as reported in the latter source, is applied to the broader ECB-NCB total for end-2011 to obtain stocks and flows through 2020.

16. The corresponding IMF figures were €31.8 billion and €10.8 billion, respectively (IMF 2013c, 87).

Prospects for 2014–20

In mid-January 2013, the IMF issued its long-delayed review under the Extended Arrangement that had been agreed in March 2012, with its new assessment incorporating the effects of the December 2012 official relief package (IMF 2013c). By June 2013, the Fund's updated program review broadly left unchanged the baseline macroeconomic assumptions of the January review. The assumptions of the June review (IMF 2013k, 57, 60, 65, 68) are used as the baseline for the European debt simulation model (EDSM) simulations of this chapter (scenario "2" of table 7.1).[17] For growth, the IMF's baseline envisions a return to significant growth averaging 3.2 percent annually in 2015–20. In the alternative scenarios, the favorable case adds 0.5 percent per year to the baseline.[18] The unfavorable scenario uniformly reduces the growth rate by 1 percentage point below the baseline for 2014 and after. For the primary surplus, the IMF baseline calls for an already relatively ambitious plateau of almost 4.5 percent of GDP on average in 2016–20. In the alternative scenarios, the favorable case adds 1 percent of GDP to the baseline targets. The unfavorable case subtracts 1 percent in 2014–15 and limits the primary surplus to 3 percent of GDP in 2016–20 (about 1.5 percent below the baseline). For bank recapitalization and other discovered debt, the largest amount was already included in the 2012 outcome (€41 billion). The IMF projections called for an additional €7.2 billion in 2013, used as the estimated actual outcome in table 7.1.

Appendix table 7A.1 sets forth details of the resulting baseline projection of the EDSM. For the ratio of gross debt to GDP, figure 7.2 shows the baseline as well as the favorable 25th percentile in the distribution, unfavorable 75th percentile, and probability-weighted average path. The baseline debt ratio rises from 157 percent of GDP in 2012 to 175 percent in 2013 and then declines steadily to 127 percent by 2020. The distribution of the outcomes across the scenarios is relatively narrow, with the 2020 debt-to-GDP ratio at 122 percent in the favorable 25th percentile and at 135 percent in the unfavorable 75th percentile.

It is important to recognize that by now the predominantly official sector sourcing of Greek public debt means that interest rates are moderate, aiding debt sustainability. Table 7A.1 reports interest payments by creditor.[19] Not only are the GLF rates modest (for example, at about 1 percent in 2013–15 and 2 percent by 2016) but interest rates on the EFSF debt are also moderate,

---

17. For 2013, the growth estimate is from Consensus (2014). The primary surplus is from Reuters, "Greek PM Says Budget Surplus Tops Forecast, Allows Spending," February 15, 2014.

18. Note that adopting the 60th percentile of annual growth in 1990–2012, as in chapter 6, would set the high benchmark at 3.4 percent, no different than the baseline range in 2015–18. Given the severity of the Greek recession/depression, stronger snapback growth is a reasonable premise for the favorable scenario.

19. Effective interest rates can be calculated by comparing these payments against the stock of debt outstanding at the end of the previous year.

Table 7.1   Scenario assumptions for Greece

Scenario	2013	2014	2015	2016	2017	2018	2019	2020
	Real GDP growth (percent)							
1	—	–0.4	1.9	2.7	2.5	2.3	2.0	1.6
2	–3.7	0.6	2.9	3.7	3.5	3.3	3.0	2.6
3	—	1.1	3.4	4.2	4.0	3.8	3.5	3.1
	Primary surplus (percent of GDP)							
1	—	0.5	2.0	3.0	3.0	3.0	3.0	3.0
2	0.8	1.5	3.0	4.5	4.5	4.3	4.3	4.2
3	—	2.5	4.0	5.5	5.5	5.3	5.3	5.2
	Bank recapitalization and contingent debt recognition (billions of euros)							
1	—	0	0	0	0	0	0	0
2	7.2	0	0	0	0	0	0	0
3	—	0	0	0	0	0	0	0
	Privatization (billions of euros)							
1	—	2.5	1.0	1.2	1.3	2.2	2.6	2.6
2	1.6	3.5	2.0	2.2	2.3	3.2	3.6	3.6
3	—	4.5	3.0	3.2	3.3	4.2	4.6	4.6

Scenarios: 1 = unfavorable; 2 = baseline; 3 = favorable

Sources: IMF (2013k); author's calculations.

at about 1.5 percent for 2013–14 and 3 percent by 2016 and after.[20] Interest payments to the IMF are also moderate, at an effective rate of 3.7 percent in 2014 for example.

Overview

Whereas Ireland exited from its official support program in December 2013, and Portugal will complete its program in May 2014 either with a "clean exit" or some form of follow-up precautionary program, Greece's official support program lasts through March of 2016.[21] Total official disbursements under the two support programs were scheduled to reach approximately €240 billion, of

20. Detailed projections for interest payments and other elements of debt flows and stocks during 2013–16 were kindly made available by IMF experts.

21. The first IMF program for Greece in the euro area debt crisis was a three-year Stand-By Arrangement beginning in May 2010. The second program was an Extended Fund Facility program for four years beginning in March 2012.

Figure 7.2 Debt projections for Greece

gross public debt as percent of GDP

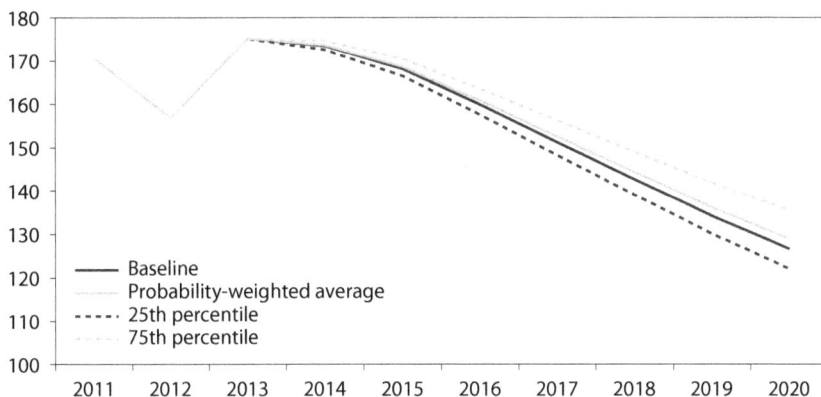

Source: Author's calculations.

which all but about €20 billion had been disbursed by early 2014.[22] The large official support has effectively taken Greece out of the need for private market access for most of the next decade.[23]

In view of the IMF projections and those here, more relief may be needed in the future for Greece to regain full market access by 2020 and after. For a country that has gone through debt restructuring with deep forgiveness forced on private creditors, it is difficult to believe that the euro area benchmark of 120 percent of GDP debt ratio that has become the target for creditworthiness would be sufficiently low to induce investors to reenter the long-term debt market in volume and at moderate spreads. Essentially the markets are likely to impose a higher sovereign risk premium on a country that has defaulted than on others that have consistently honored their debt.

At the same time, it is important to recognize that the debt ratio somewhat overstates the debt burden because of low interest rates on debt held by the euro area official sector. However, the GLF component with its particularly low rates constitutes only a minority of the debt outstanding. In the projections set forth in appendix 7A, the ratio of interest payments to GDP is still as high as 4.3 percent by 2020. In comparison, net interest payments in 2020 in the base cases of EDSM projections stand at 4.4 percent of GDP in 2020

---

22. Harry Papachristou and Lefteris Papadimas, "Greece resumes protracted bailout talks with lenders," Reuters, February 24, 2014. See appendix table 7A.1 for annual disbursements of IMF and euro area official lending.

23. The exception is about €9 billion in residual borrowing needs in 2014–15 (table 7A.1). This modest financing gap is of the same general magnitude as the cumulative €10.9 billion in "unidentified" financing projected for 2014–15 in the IMF program projections (IMF 2013k, 60).

for Ireland, 4.6 percent for Portugal, 5.3 percent for Spain, and 5.2 percent for Italy (chapter 6). So even taking account of some interest rate concessionality, Greece would be on a broadly equal footing with other sovereigns in the area with respect to debt burden but not on an equal footing with regard to credit history. The most optimistic interpretation would then be that markets would be sophisticated enough to look through the debt ratio to the interest burden as the meaningful measure of debt sustainability, but even so would charge some extra risk spread not because Greek public debt was "high" but because the sovereign credit reputation had been tarnished. With the passage of several years of successful achievement of fiscal targets, the size of this reputational risk premium might be manageable.[24]

The principal argument for a more optimistic view of prospective market access is that Greece already managed to issue €3 billion in new five-year debt on private markets in April 2014, at a yield of 4.95 percent.[25] However, this successful issue may not represent a sign of strong reentry to the capital market. It seems likely that investors were taking the bet that unrestructured private debt is far too small to provide much relief to the sovereign through a new round of haircuts. In effect, the small amounts of new private holdings may be seen as having de facto seniority, a status that would disappear if the government were to attempt to borrow large amounts of long-term debt.

Prior to the April issuance, the IMF had emphasized that additional relief may be needed. It noted that if the debt ratio is to be brought down to 110 percent of GDP by 2022, as agreed in principle in the December 2012 package, doing so "in all likelihood will necessitate either large reductions in EFSF interest rates or principal haircuts on the GLF" (IMF 2013c, 84).[26]

The present study reinforces the IMF diagnosis that further official debt

---

24. Optimists might see the decline of spreads on restructured 10-year bonds to the range of 500 basis points in March 2014 (from 2,000 basis points immediately after the restructuring and 1,000 basis points by end-2012; Datastream) as evidence that Greece is already poised to reenter the market. However, although Greek authorities apparently plan to rebuild the yield curve relatively soon through modest issuances of three- to five-year obligations, it would be misleading to interpret the spreads on restructured 10-year obligations as indicative of rates at which Greece could place sizable amounts of new long-term bonds. The restructured debt is relatively small, seems unlikely to be restructured again, and has special characteristics such as UK rather than domestic legal jurisdiction. These differences also mean that the spreads on the restructured obligations are not directly comparable with spreads on Greek obligations in 2010–11 prior to the restructuring. They are thus not included as representing Greek sovereign risk after 2011 in figure 1.1 (chapter 1) showing sovereign spreads for euro area periphery economies.

25. Robin Wigglesworth and Elaine Moore, "Greek €3 billion Bond Sale Snapped Up," *Financial Times*, April 10, 2014.

26. The IMF baseline implies some market access beginning by 2018 and full reliance on the market after 2020. It suggests that if the debt level were down to 115 percent of GDP, Greece could borrow at a spread of 450 to 600 basis points, based on recent high-debt European country experience plus a premium for Greece's debt restructuring, with the spread rising by 10 basis points for each percentage point increase in the debt-to-GDP ratio (IMF 2013c, 87).

relief may be needed.[27] The probability distribution of outcomes across the scenarios places even the favorable 25th percentile ratio of gross debt to GDP at 119 percent in 2020. The baseline projection here tracks almost identically with that of the IMF once allowance is made for the Fund's assumption of 4 percent of GDP further relief by 2020. The bulk of any future relief would seem likely to have to come from official creditors, both because they will account for 80 percent of the total stock of debt outstanding in 2020 (excluding that held by Greek public subsectors), and because the private holders have already experienced deep reductions in the restructuring.[28]

In view of likely political resistance in Germany and other partner countries to outright reduction of debt principal, it is useful to gauge the maximum extent of relief that might be achieved in what has come to be called "OSI" (official sector involvement, the parallel of private sector restructuring). If the euro area official sector were to eliminate all interest payments on debt owed by Greece (but excluding the ECB's holdings), the cumulative effect would be to reduce the debt-to-GDP ratio by 2020 by 15 percentage points, bringing it down to 112 percent. Conceivably that reduction could suffice to reestablish market access, especially if a strong track record of achieving fiscal targets has been built by then. It would be important, however, for policymakers to exclude the already restructured private debt from yet another haircut in the event of such OSI. Restructured private claims amount to only about 10 percent of public debt (table 7A.1), and a second round of haircuts would provide minimal relief while causing a shock to sovereign risk spreads for future borrowing.

For the next several years, nonetheless, Greek public debt should now be relatively manageable even without additional OSI, thanks to the private restructuring and easing in official sector terms. As shown in table 7A.1, official sources should almost fully cover borrowing needs through 2020, albeit with the help of capitalizing interest in amounts that cumulate to €26 billion by 2020, or 11 percent of GDP in that year. With debt dynamics manageable over this period, Greece should be able to avoid an exit from the euro and/or a severe new round of falling output. Successful adherence to the baseline of the revised adjustment program would go a long way to removing the Greek crisis from its earlier pivotal role in contributing to a broader debt crisis in the euro area.

---

27. If political constraints limit the primary surplus to a ceiling of 2.5 percent of GDP, as in the final exercise considered in chapter 6, the need for relief could be greater, because by 2020 the debt-to-GDP ratio in the adjusted baseline would stand at 135 percent instead of 127 percent.

28. Baseline debt holdings in 2020 are: private, €80 billion (short term, exchange bonds, pre-2014 debt); official, €246 billion (IMF, GLF, EFSF, EFSF interest capitalization, ECB); and Greek official subsectors, €18.7 billion (table 7A.1).

Appendix 7A

Table 7A.1 EDSM baseline projections through 2020 for Greece

	2010	2011	2012	2013	2014	2015	2016	2017	2018	2019	2020
Percent of GDP:											
Debt	147.9	170.6	156.8	175.1	173.4	168.1	159.9	151.3	142.7	134.3	126.6
Net debt	147.9	170.6	156.8	175.1	173.4	168.1	159.9	151.3	142.7	134.3	126.6
Net interest		7.3	3.4	4.6	5.3	5.4	5.6	5.1	4.8	4.6	4.3
Amortization		17.9	12.6	15.8	20.6	16.0	10.4	10.2	8.9	11.0	9.1
Billions of euros:											
Nominal GDP	222.2	208.5	193.8	184.6	184.9	191.1	200.3	210.0	220.0	230.4	240.5
Primary deficit	10.7	4.8	2.5	−1.5	−2.8	−5.7	−9.0	−9.5	−9.5	−9.9	−10.1
Total deficit	10.7	20.0	9.5	7.0	6.9	4.5	2.2	1.3	1.2	0.7	0.3
(−) privatization receipts		−1.0	0.0	−1.6	−3.5	−2.0	−2.2	−2.3	−3.2	−3.6	−3.6
(−) ECB profit return			0.0	−2.7	−2.5	−2.0	−1.7	−0.1	−0.1	−0.1	−0.1
(+) bank recapitalization	8.4	−3.0	41.0	7.2	0.0	0.0	0.0	0.0	0.0	0.0	0.0
(+) other debt discovery			2.4	7.5	0.0	0.0	0.0	0.0	0.0	0.0	0.0
(+) buybacks			11.3								
(+) PSI-related operations			34.5								
(+) deposits			−1.0	3.0	−3.7	3.3	−1.8	0.0	0.0	0.0	0.0
(+) other			0.0	1.9	1.4	−1.7	4.2	0.0	0.0	0.0	0.0
Net borrowing requirement			97.7	22.3	−1.4	2.1	0.7	−1.1	−2.1	−3.0	−3.4
Subsectors debt change			10.6	−3.0	−1.1	−1.6	−1.6	−1.6	−1.6	−1.6	−1.6
Amortization		37.3	24.5	29.1	38.1	30.6	20.9	21.5	19.6	25.5	21.9
IMF		0.0	0.0	1.7	7.4	8.6	3.1	0.9	2.1	3.4	4.5
ECB		0.0	11.9	8.2	10.5	6.8	2.0	4.9	1.7	6.4	1.5
ST		9.2	11.8	18.4	15.0	15.0	15.0	15.0	15.0	15.0	15.0
MLT (pre-2013)		28.1	0.8	0.8	5.2	0.0	0.0	0.0	0.0	0.0	0.0
Exchange bonds		0.0	0.0	0.0	0.0	0.0	0.0	0.0	0.0	0.0	0.0
MLT (new)				0.0	0.0	0.2	0.9	0.8	0.8	0.7	0.9
Gross borrowing requirement		53.3	122.2	51.4	36.7	32.7	21.6	20.4	17.5	22.5	18.5

(continues on next page)

Table 7A.1   EDSM baseline projections through 2020 for Greece *(continued)*

	2010	2011	2012	2013	2014	2015	2016	2017	2018	2019	2020
Billions of euros:											
Total financing	40.6	53.7	128.3	51.5	34.3	29.0	17.1	15.8	15.0	17.6	15.0
IMF	10.3	9.9	1.6	8.6	8.9	7.1	1.8	0.0	0.0	0.0	0.0
EA: GLF	21.1	32.0	0.0	0.0	0.0	0.0	0.0	0.0	0.0	0.0	0.0
EA: additional	0.0	0.0	108.3	27.9	8.6	0.0	0.0	0.0	0.0	0.0	0.0
EA: interest capitalization				−0.1	2.4	3.7	4.5	4.7	2.5	4.9	3.5
Private ST	9.2	11.8	18.4	15.0	15.0	15.0	15.0	15.0	15.0	15.0	15.0
Private MLT				0.0	1.8	6.9	0.3	0.8	0.0	2.6	0.0
Debt	328.6	355.7	303.9	323.2	320.7	321.3	320.4	317.7	314.0	309.4	304.4
IMF	10.3	20.7	22.3	29.2	30.7	29.2	27.9	27.1	24.9	21.6	17.1
EA: GLF	21.1	53.1	53.1	53.1	53.1	53.1	53.1	53.1	53.1	53.1	53.1
EA: additional	0.0	0.0	108.3	136.2	144.8	144.8	144.8	144.8	144.8	144.8	144.8
EA: interest capitalization				−0.1	2.4	6.0	10.5	15.2	17.7	22.6	26.0
ECB	20.0	56.5	44.6	36.4	25.9	19.1	17.1	12.3	10.6	4.2	2.7
ST	9.2	11.8	18.4	15.0	15.0	15.0	15.0	15.0	15.0	15.0	15.0
MLT (pre-2013)	268.0	213.6	32.3	31.5	26.3	26.3	26.3	26.3	26.3	26.3	26.3
Exchange bonds			29.9	29.9	29.9	29.9	29.9	29.9	29.9	29.9	29.9
MLT (new)			0.0	0.0	1.8	8.6	8.0	7.9	7.2	9.0	8.1
Intragovernment holdings				−5.0	−8.0	−9.1	−10.7	−12.3	−13.9	−15.5	−17.1	−18.7
Interest payments				6.6	8.5	9.7	10.2	11.2	10.8	10.6	10.6	10.4
IMF				0.6	0.9	1.2	1.1	1.1	1.0	1.0	0.8	0.7
EA: GLF				0.8	0.4	0.5	0.7	1.0	1.1	1.1	1.1	1.1
EA: additional				0.0	1.3	2.4	3.6	4.3	4.3	4.3	4.3	4.3
EA: interest capitalization					0.0	0.1	0.2	0.3	0.5	0.5	0.7
ECB				2.8	2.2	1.8	1.3	1.0	0.9	0.6	0.5	0.2
ST				0.6	0.9	0.8	0.8	0.8	0.7	0.8	0.9	0.9
MLT (pre-2013)				8.1	1.2	1.2	1.0	1.0	1.0	1.0	1.0	1.0
Exchange bonds				0.6	0.6	0.6	0.9	0.9	0.9	0.9	0.9
MLT (new)				0.0	0.0	0.1	0.6	0.6	0.6	0.5	0.6
Accrual adjustment				0.9	1.3	1.0	0.4				
Financial assets		0.0	0.0	0.0	0.0	0.0	0.0	0.0	0.0	0.0	0.0

EA = euro area official sector; ECB = European Central Bank; EDSM = European debt simulation model; GLF = Greek Loan Facility; IMF = International Monetary Fund; MLT = medium and long term; PSI = private sector involvement; ST = short term

Sources: IMF (2013k); Ministry of Finance (2012a); author's calculations.

Appendix 7B
Comparison to IMF Projections and Impact of the December 2012 Relief Package

Figure 7B.1 shows the EDSM baseline and the corresponding IMF (2013k) baseline projections for the ratio of gross debt to GDP. The two projections are extremely close, as should be expected in view of identical assumptions for the key macro inputs (growth, primary surplus, privatization, and bank recapitalization). By 2020 the EDSM debt ratio stands at 127 percent of GDP versus 124 percent in the IMF projection. The divergence by 2020 can be fully explained, however, by the fact that the IMF assumes further official relief of some type. The January 2013 IMF review stated that "measures delivering roughly 4.1 percent of GDP by 2020 will be needed to bring debt to 124 percent of GDP by 2020" (IMF 2013c, 84). By implication, in the absence of such measures the IMF baseline would also place gross debt at around 128 percent of GDP in 2020.

Figure 7B.2 shows the impact of the December 2012 package of official relief. The revised baseline for the ratio of gross debt to GDP was lower than the prerelief baseline by about 10 percentage points of GDP in 2012, reflecting the debt buyback. The difference widens to 20 percentage points by 2020, reflecting the cumulative effect of lower GLF interest rates and the effect of the return of ECB profits from the SMP.[29] Taking the average of 15 percent and applying it to the level of GDP in the middle of this period, the implicit debt reduction from the official support package was about €30 billion, or 35 percent of the size of the €85 billion net debt savings from the April private sector involvement.

---

29. The outlook prior to the December official relief package was for debt to peak at 192 percent of GDP in 2013 and then decline to 148 percent by 2020. Note that the IMF (2013c, 84) places the corresponding impact of the December package at 17.2 percent of GDP by 2020, composed of 10 percent for the buyback, 2 percent for interest rate reductions, 0.6 percent for elimination of EFSF fees, and 2.8 percent for remittance of SMP profits. Note further that figure 7B.2 is from Cline (2013a) and reflects the postrelief outlook as of early 2013. Its baseline for the period 2013–18 is slightly more pessimistic than in the updated estimates of appendix 7A and figure 7B.1, but the comparison between pre- and postrelief paths remains unchanged.

Figure 7B.1   Baseline debt projections: IMF and EDSM

gross public debt as percent of GDP

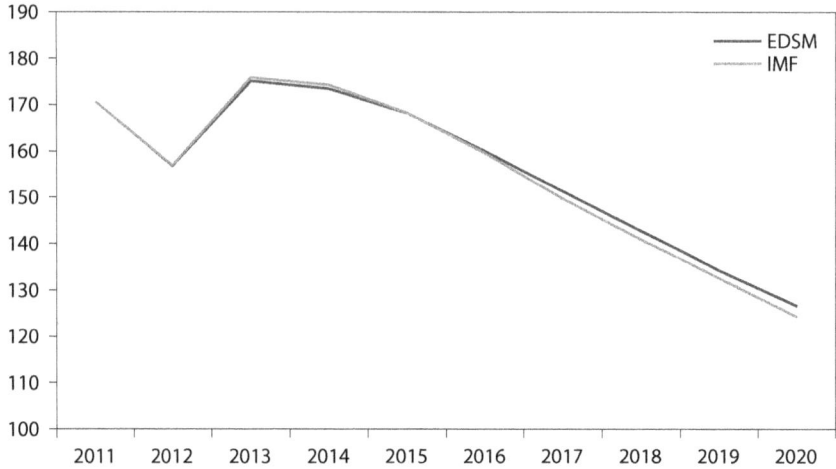

EDSM = European debt simulation model; IMF = International Monetary Fund

Source: IMF (2013k); author's calculations.

Figure 7B.2   Baseline projections for Greek public debt before and after December 2012 package of official relief and buyback

gross public debt as percent of GDP

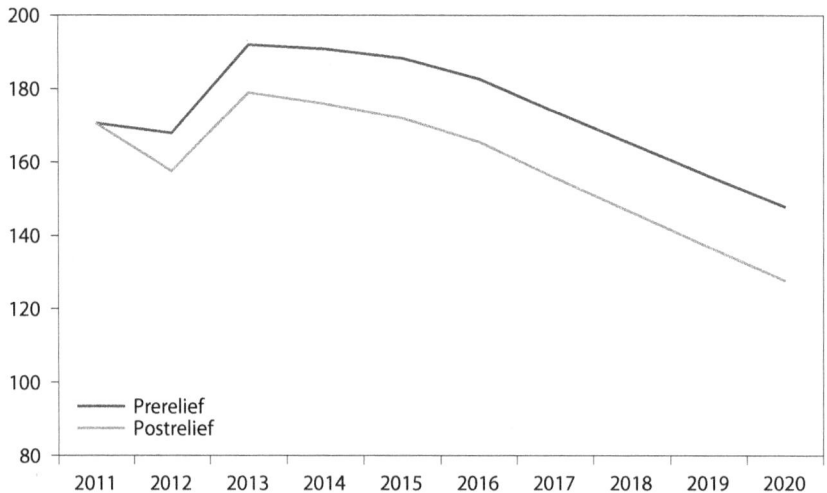

Source: Author's calculations.

References

Acharya, Viral V., and Sascha Steffen. 2014. *Falling Short of Expectations? Stress-Testing the European Banking System.* CEPS Policy Brief 315 (January 15). London: Centre for Economic Policy Research.

Ahearne, Alan. 2012. Political-Economic Context in Ireland. In *Resolving the European Debt Crisis,* ed. William R. Cline and Guntram B. Wolff. Special Report 21. Washington: Peterson Institute for International Economics and Bruegel.

Alesina, Alberto, and Roberto Perotti. 1995. Fiscal Expansions and Fiscal Adjustments in OECD Countries. *Economic Policy* 10, no. 21: 205–48.

Alvarez & Marsal. 2013. *Investigation Report: Bank of Cyprus—Holdings of Greek Government Bonds.* Athens: Alvarez & Marsal. Available at http://cdn.cyprus-property-buyers.com/wp-content /uploads/2013/04/April04_2013_AM.pdf.

Åslund, Anders. 2012. *Why a Breakup of the Euro Area Must Be Avoided: Lessons from Previous Breakups.* Policy Brief 12-20 (August). Washington: Peterson Institute for International Economics.

Auer, Raphael. 2013. Rapid Current-Account Rebalancing in the Southern Eurozone. VoxEU, May 7. Available at www.voxeu.org.

Auerbach, Alan J., and Yuriy Gorodnichenko. 2010. *Measuring the Output Responses to Fiscal Policy.* NBER Working Paper 16311. Cambridge, MA: National Bureau of Economic Research.

Barnett, Jeffrey L., and Phillip M. Vidal. 2013. *State and Local Government Finances Summary: 2011.* Washington: US Census Bureau.

Bi, Ran, Marcos Chamon, and Jeromin Zettelmeyer. 2011. *The Problem that Wasn't: Coordination Failures in Sovereign Debt Restructurings.* IMF Working Paper 11/265. Washington: International Monetary Fund.

BIS (Bank for International Settlements). 2013. *BIS Effective Exchange Rate Indices.* Basel. Available at www.bis.org/statistics/eer/index.htm.

BIS (Bank for International Settlements). 2014. *Consolidated Banking Statistics.* Basel. Available at www.bis.org/statistics/consstats.htm.

Blanchard, Olivier, and Daniel Leigh. 2013. *Growth Forecast Errors and Fiscal Multipliers.* IMF Working Paper WP/13/1 (January). Washington: International Monetary Fund.

Bofinger, Peter, Lars P. Feld, Wolfgang Franz, Christoph M. Schmidt, and Beatrice Weder di Mauro. 2011. A European Redemption Pact. VoxEU, November 9. Available at www.voxeu.org.

Bootle, Roger. 2012. *Leaving the Euro: A Practical Guide*. Wolfson Economics Prize MMXII. London: Policy Exchange. Available at www.policyexchange.org.uk/images/WolfsonPrize/wolfson%20economics%20prize%20winning%20entry.pdf.

Brunnermeier, Markus K., Luis Garicano, Philip R. Lane, Marco Pagano, Ricardo Reis, Tano Santos, Stijn Van Nieuwerburgh, and Dimitri Vayanos. 2011a. European Safe Bonds (ESBies). Processed (September 26). Available at www.euro-nomics.com.

Brunnermeier, Markus K., Luis Garicano, Philip R. Lane, Marco Pagano, Ricardo Reis, Tano Santos, Stijn Van Nieuwerburgh, and Dimitri Vayanos. 2011b. ESBies: A Realistic Reform of Europe's Financial Architecture. VoxEU, October 25. Available at www.voxeu.org.

Buchheit, Lee C. 2012. Sovereign Debt Restructuring: The Legal Context. In *Resolving the European Debt Crisis*, ed. William R. Cline and Guntram B. Wolff. Special Report 21. Washington: Peterson Institute for International Economics and Bruegel.

Buchheit, Lee C., Anna Gelpern, Mitu Gulati, Ugo Panizza, Beatrice Weder di Mauro, and Jeromin Zettelmeyer. 2013. *Revisiting Sovereign Bankruptcy*. Committee on International Economic Policy and Reform (October). Washington: Brookings Institution.

Buiter, Willem, and Ebrahim Rahbari. 2012. Rising Risks of Greek Euro Area Exit. *Global Economics View* (February 6). New York: Citigroup Global Markets.

Buti, Marco, and Nicolas Carnot. 2013. *The Debate on Fiscal Policy in Europe: Beyond the Austerity Myth*. ECFIN Economic Brief Issue 20 (March). Brussels: European Commission.

CBO (Congressional Budget Office). 2011. *Improving CBO's Methodology for Projecting Individual Income Tax Revenues* (February). Washington.

Central Bank of Ireland. 2013. *Money and Banking Statistics: April 2013*. Dublin.

Chen, Ruo, Gian-Maria Milesi-Ferretti, and Thierry Tressel. 2012. *External Imbalances in the Euro Area*. IMF Working Paper 12/236. Washington: International Monetary Fund.

Claessens, Stijn, Ashoka Mody, and Shahin Vallée. 2012. *Paths to Eurobonds*. IMF Working Paper WP/12/172 (July). Washington: International Monetary Fund.

Cliffe, Mark, and Martin Leen. 2010. *EMU Break-up*. ING Financial Markets Research (July). London: ING.

Cliffe, Mark, Peter Vanden Houte, and Martin van Vliet. 2012. *EMU: Fixing It Is Far Cheaper than Breaking It*. ING Financial Markets Research (August). Available at www.markcliffe.com.

Cline, William R. 2003. *Restoring Economic Growth in Argentina*. World Bank Policy Research Working Paper 3158 (October). Washington: World Bank.

Cline, William R. 2006. International Debt: The Past Quarter Century and Future Prospects. In *C. Fred Bergsten and the World Economy*, ed. Michael Mussa. Washington: Peterson Institute for International Economics.

Cline, William R. 2010a. A Note on Debt Dynamics. Washington: Peterson Institute for International Economics. Processed (May).

Cline, William R. 2010b. *Financial Globalization, Economic Growth, and the Crisis of 2007–09*. Washington: Peterson Institute for International Economics.

Cline, William R. 2011. *Sustainability of Greek Public Debt*. Policy Brief 11-15. Washington: Peterson Institute for International Economics.

Cline, William R. 2012a. Alternative Strategies for Resolving the European Debt Crisis. In *Resolving the European Debt Crisis*, eds. William R. Cline and Guntram B. Wolff. Special Report 21. Washington: Peterson Institution for International Economics and Bruegel.

Cline, William R. 2012b. *Interest Rate Shock and Sustainability of Italy's Sovereign Debt*. Policy Brief 12-5 (February). Washington: Peterson Institute for International Economics.

Cline, William R. 2012c. *Sovereign Debt Sustainability in Italy and Spain: A Probabilistic Approach*. Working Paper WP 12-12 (August). Washington: Peterson Institute for International Economics.

Cline, William R. 2012d. The Multiplier, Sovereign Default Risk, and the US Budget. Washington: Peterson Institute for International Economics. Processed (February).

Cline, William R. 2013a. *Debt Restructuring and Economic Prospects in Greece*. Policy Brief 13-3 (February). Washington: Peterson Institute for International Economics.

Cline, William R. 2013b. The Misleading Allure of Delaying Adjustment in the Euro Area Periphery. RealTime Economic Issues Watch, March 19. Washington: Peterson Institute for International Economics.

Cline, William R. 2013c. The Multiplier, Sovereign Default Risk, and the US Budget Deficit: An Overview. In *Public Debt, Global Governance and Economic Dynamism*, ed. Luigi Paganetto. Dordrecht, Netherlands: Springer.

Cline, William R. 2013d. *Estimates of Fundamental Equilibrium Exchange Rates, November 2013*. Policy Brief 13-29 (November). Washington: Peterson Institute for International Economics.

Cline, William R., and John Williamson. 2008. *New Estimates of Fundamental Equilibrium Exchange Rates*. Policy Brief 08-7 (July). Washington: Peterson Institute for International Economics.

Cline, William R., and John Williamson. 2011. *Estimates of Fundamental Equilibrium Exchange Rates*. Policy Brief 11-5 (May). Washington: Peterson Institute for International Economics.

Cline, William R., and Guntram B. Wolff, eds. 2012. *Resolving the European Debt Crisis*. Special Report 21. Washington: Peterson Institute for International Economics and Bruegel.

Coenen, Günter, Matthias Mohr, and Roland Straub. 2008. *Fiscal Consolidation in the Euro Area*. Working Paper 902 (May). Frankfurt: European Central Bank.

Committeri, Marco, and Francesco Spadafora. 2013. *You Never Give Me Your Money? Sovereign Debt Crises, Collective Action Problems, and IMF Lending*. IMF Working Paper WP/13/20 (January). Washington: International Monetary Fund.

Consensus. 2014. *Consensus Forecasts* (February 10). London: Consensus Economics.

Corsetti, Giancarlo. 2012. Has Austerity Gone Too Far? VoxEU, April. Available at www.voxeu.org.

Darvas, Zsolt. 2012. *The Greek Debt Trap: An Escape Plan*. Policy Contribution 2012/19. Brussels: Bruegel.

de Grauwe, Paul, and Yuemei Ji. 2013. Panic-Driven Austerity in the Eurozone and Its Implications. VoxEU, February 21. Available at www.voxeu.org.

Delpla, Jacques, and Jakob von Weizsäcker. 2010. *The Blue Bond Proposal*. Bruegel Policy Brief 2010/03 (May). Brussels: Bruegel.

Deo, Stephane, Paul Donovan, and Larry Hatheway. 2011. *Euro Break-Up—The Consequences*. UBS Investment Research: Global Economic Perspectives. London: UBS. Available at http://bruxelles.blogs.liberation.fr/UBS%20fin%20de%20l'euro.pdf.

Eaton, Jonathan, and Mark Gersovitz. 1981. Debt with Potential Repudiation: Theoretical and Empirical Analysis. *Review of Economic Studies* 48, no. 2: 289–309.

EC (European Commission). 2012. Eurogroup Statement on Greece. Brussels. Available at www.consilium.europa.eu/uedocs/cms_Data/docs/pressdata/en/ecofin/133857.pdf (accessed on January 30, 2013).

EC (European Commission). 2013a. Commissioner Barnier welcomes trilogue agreement on the framework for bank recovery and resolution. Memo/13/1140 (December 12). Brussels.

EC (European Commission). 2013b. *Financial Assistance to Greece*. Brussels. Available at http://ec.europa.eu.

EC (European Commission). 2013c. *Intergovernmental Support Mechanisms*. Brussels. Available at http://ec.europa.eu/economy_finance/assistance_eu_ms/intergovernmental_support/index_en.htm.

EC (European Commission). 2014. *Real Effective Exchange Rates Based on Unit Labor Cost (Total Economy)*. Brussels. Available at http://ec.europa.eu/economy_finance/ameco/user/serie /ResultSerie.cfm.

ECB (European Central Bank). 2009. *Withdrawal and Expulsion from the EMU: Some Reflections*. Legal Working Paper Series 10. Frankfurt.

ECB (European Central Bank). 2011. The European Stability Mechanism. *ECB Monthly Bulletin* (July): 71–84.

ECB (European Central Bank). 2012. Technical Features of Outright Monetary Transactions. Press release, September 6, Frankfurt.

ECB (European Central Bank). 2013a. *Survey on the Access to Finance of Small and Medium-sized Enterprises in the Euro Area: April 2013 to September 2013* (November). Frankfurt.

ECB (European Central Bank). 2013b. *Corporate Finance and Economic Activity in the Euro Area: Structural Issues Report 2013*. Occasional Paper 151 (August). Frankfurt.

ECB (European Central Bank). 2014a. *Consolidated Banking Data*. Frankfurt. Available at www.ecb .int/stats/money/consolidated/html/index.en.html.

ECB (European Central Bank). 2014b. *MFI Interest Rates*. Frankfurt. Available at www.ecb.europa .eu/stats/money/interest/interest/html/index.en.html.

ECB (European Central Bank). 2014c. *MFI Balance Sheets*. Frankfurt. Available at www.ecb.europa .eu/stats/money/aggregates/bsheets/html/index.en.html.

EFSF (European Financial Stability Facility). 2011. *EFSF Guideline on Precautionary Programmes*. Brussels. Available at www.efsf.europa.eu/attachments/efsf_guideline_on_precautionary_ programmes.pdf.

EFSF (European Financial Stability Facility). 2013. *Transactions*. Brussels. Available at www.efsf. europa.eu/investor_relations/issues/index.html (accessed on January 29, 2013).

Eichengreen, Barry. 2010. The Euro: Love It or Leave It? VoxEU, May 4. Available at www.voxeu.org.

ESM (European Stability Mechanism). 2013. *Financial Assistance for Spain*. Luxembourg. Available at www.esm.europa.eu/pdf/FAQ%20Spain%2011022013.pdf.

EU (European Union). 2012. *Treaty Establishing the European Stability Mechanism (ESM)*. D/12/3 (February). Brussels.

EU (European Union). 2013. Council Regulation (EU) No. 1024/2013. *Official Journal of the European Union* (October 29): I287/63-89.

Eurogroup. 2013a. Eurogroup Agrees to the Main Features of a Direct Bank Recapitalisation Instrument and Welcomes Latvia's Progress towards Joining the Euro (June 26). Brussels: Eurozone Portal.

Eurogroup. 2013b. ESM Direct Bank Recapitalization Instrument (June 20). Luxembourg. Available at www.eurozone.europa.eu/media/436873/20130621-ESM-direct-recaps-main-features.pdf.

European Council. 2011. *European Council 2/25 March 2011: Conclusions*. EUCO 10/1/11 Rev. 1 (April 20). Brussels. Available at www.consilium.europa.eu/uedocs/cms_data/docs/pressdata /en/ec/120296.pdf.

European Council. 2012. *Treaty on Stability, Coordination and Governance in the Economic and Monetary Union*. Available at http://european-council.europa.eu/media/639235/st00tscg26_en12.pdf.

Eyraud, Luc, and Anke Weber. 2013. *The Challenge of Debt Reduction during Fiscal Consolidation*. IMF Working Paper WP/13/67 (March). Washington: International Monetary Fund.

Federal Constitutional Court (Germany). 2014. Principal Proceedings ESM/ECB: Pronouncement of the Judgment and Referral for a Preliminary Ruling to the Court of Justice of the European Union. Press release 9/2014, February 7. Available at www.bundesverfassungsgerichte.de/en /press/bvg14-009en.html.

Federal Reserve. 2014a. *Selected Interest Rates (Weekly)*. H.15. Available at www.federalreserve.gov /releases/h15.

Federal Reserve. 2014b. *Factors Affecting Reserve Balances*. H.4.1. Available at www.federalreserve.gov /releases/h41/current/h41.htm#h41tab1.

Finnish Government. 2012. Joint Statement of the Ministers of Finance of Germany, the Netherlands and Finland. Helsinki: Ministry of Finance.

Gagnon, Joseph E., and Marc Hinterschweiger. 2011. *The Global Outlook for Government Debt over the Next 25 Years: Implications for the Economy and Public Policy*. Policy Analyses in International Economics 94 (June). Washington: Peterson Institute for International Economics.

Gagnon, Joseph E., and Marc Hinterschweiger. 2013. Responses of Central Banks in Advanced Economies to the Global Financial Crisis. In *Responding to Financial Crisis: Lessons from Asia Then, the United States and Europe Now*, ed. Changyong Rhee and Adam S. Posen. Washington: Peterson Institute for International Economics and Asian Development Bank.

German Council of Economic Experts. 1981. Sachverstandigenrat zur Begutachtung der Gesamtwirtschaflichen Entwicklung, vor Kurskorrekturen: zur finanzpolitischen und währungspolitischen Situation im Sommer 1981. Available at www.sachverstaendigenrat-wirtschaft.de/fileadmin/dateiablage/download/gutachten/0901061.pdf.

Giavazzi, Francesco, and Marco Pagano. 1990. *Can Severe Fiscal Contraction Be Expansionary? Tales of Two Small European Countries*. NBER Working Paper 3372. Cambridge, MA: National Bureau of Economic Research.

Goyal, Rishi, Petya Koeva Brooks, Mahmood Pradhan, Thierry Tressel, Giovanni Dell'Ariccia, Ross Leckow, and Ceyla Pazarbasioglu. 2013. *A Banking Union for the Euro Area*. Staff Discussion Note 13/01. Washington: International Monetary Fund.

Greenlaw, David, James D. Hamilton, Peter Hooper, and Frederic S. Mishkin. 2013. Crunch Time: Fiscal Crises and the Role of Monetary Policy. Paper prepared for the US Monetary Policy Forum, New York, February 22. Available at http://dss.ucsd.edu/~jhamilto/USMPF13 _final.pdf.

Gros, Daniel. 2011. The Euro Crisis Reaches the Core. VoxEU, August 11. Available at www.voxeu. org.

Gros, Daniel. 2013. Foreign Debt Versus Domestic Debt in the Euro Area. *Oxford Review of Economic Policy* 29, no. 3: 502–17.

Guajardo, Jaime, Daniel Leigh, and Andrea Pescatori. 2011. *Expansionary Austerity: New International Evidence*. IMF Working Paper WP/11/158 (July). Washington: International Monetary Fund.

Guerrieri, Paolo. 2012. *Intra-European Imbalances: The Need for a Positive-sum-game Approach*. International Economics Briefing Paper 2012/03 (December). London: Chatham House.

Hellwig, Christian, and Thomas Philippon. 2011. Eurobills not Eurobonds. VoxEU, December 2. Available at www.voxeu.org.

Hutchison, Michael M., and Ilan Noy. 2005. How Bad Are Twins? Output Costs of Currency and Banking Crises. *Journal of Money, Credit and Banking* 37, no. 4: 725–52.

IGCP (Portuguese Treasury and Government Debt Agency). 2013a. *Emissões da Dívida Direta de Estado*. Agência de Gestão da Tesouraria e da Dívida Pública. Available at www.igcp.pt/ gca/?id=87.

IGCP (Portuguese Treasury and Government Debt Agency). 2013b. *Portugal: Dívida Pública*. Boletim Mensal, Julho 2013. Agência de Gestão da Tesouraria e da Dívida Pública. Available at www .igcp.pt/fotos/editor2/2013/Boletim_Mensal/07_Boletim_Mensal.pdf.

IIF (Institute of International Finance). 2011. *The July 21, 2011 Support Package for Greece*. Washington. Available at www.iif.com/download.php?id=l4CaNrPkuFY (accessed on January 30, 2013).

IMF (International Monetary Fund). 1995. *Guidelines for Fiscal Adjustment.* Pamphlet Series 49. Washington.

IMF (International Monetary Fund). 2001. *Government Finance Statistics Manual 2001.* Washington.

IMF (International Monetary Fund). 2009. *Global Financial Stability Report, October 2009.* Washington.

IMF (International Monetary Fund). 2010a. *Global Financial Stability Report, April 2010.* Washington.

IMF (International Monetary Fund). 2010b. *Global Financial Stability Report, October 2010.* Washington.

IMF (International Monetary Fund). 2010c. *Greece: First Review under the Stand-By Arrangement.* IMF Country Report 10/286 (September). Washington.

IMF (International Monetary Fund). 2010d. *Greece: Second Review under the Stand-By Arrangement.* IMF Country Report 10/372 (December). Washington.

IMF (International Monetary Fund). 2010e. Will It Hurt? Macroeconomic Effects of Fiscal Consolidation. In *World Economic Outlook* (October). Washington.

IMF (International Monetary Fund). 2010f. *World Economic Outlook Database* (April). Washington.

IMF (International Monetary Fund). 2010g. *World Economic Outlook Database* (October). Washington.

IMF (International Monetary Fund). 2010h. *World Economic Outlook Report* (April). Washington.

IMF (International Monetary Fund). 2011a. *Greece: Third Review under the Stand-By Arrangement.* IMF Country Report 11/68 (March). Washington.

IMF (International Monetary Fund). 2011b. *Portugal: Request for a Three-Year Arrangement under the Extended Fund Facility.* IMF Country Report 11/127 (June). Washington.

IMF (International Monetary Fund). 2011c. *World Economic Outlook Database* (September). Washington.

IMF (International Monetary Fund). 2011d. *Ireland: First and Second Reviews under the Extended Arrangement.* IMF Country Report 11/109 (May). Washington.

IMF (International Monetary Fund). 2011e. *Greece: Fifth Review under the Stand-by Arrangement.* IMF Country Report 11/351 (December). Washington.

IMF (International Monetary Fund). 2012a. Are We Underestimating Short-Term Fiscal Multipliers? In *World Economic Outlook* (October). Washington.

IMF (International Monetary Fund). 2012b. *Fiscal Monitor* (October). Washington.

IMF (International Monetary Fund). 2012c. *Greece: Request for Extended Arrangement under the Extended Fund Facility.* IMF Country Report 12/57 (March). Washington.

IMF (International Monetary Fund). 2012d. *Ireland: 2012 Article IV and Seventh Review Under the Extended Arrangement.* IMF Country Report 12/264 (September). Washington.

IMF (International Monetary Fund). 2012e. *Ireland: Sixth Review under the Extended Arrangement.* IMF Country Report 12/147 (June). Washington.

IMF (International Monetary Fund). 2012f. *Portugal: Fifth Review under the Extended Facility.* IMF Country Report 12/292 (October). Washington.

IMF (International Monetary Fund). 2012g. *Spain: 2012 Article IV Consultation.* IMF Country Report 12/202 (July). Washington.

IMF (International Monetary Fund). 2012h. *World Economic Outlook Database* (April). Washington.

IMF (International Monetary Fund). 2012i. *World Economic Outlook Database* (October). Washington.

IMF (International Monetary Fund). 2012j. *Portugal: Third Review under the Extended Arrangement.* IMF Country Report 12/77 (April). Washington.

IMF (International Monetary Fund). 2013a. *Cyprus: Request for Arrangement under the Extended Fund Facility*. IMF Country Report 13/125 (May). Washington.

IMF (International Monetary Fund). 2013b. *Global Financial Stability Report, April 2013*. Washington.

IMF (International Monetary Fund). 2013c. *Greece: First and Second Reviews under the Extended Arrangement under the Extended Fund Facility*. IMF Country Report 13/20 (January). Washington.

IMF (International Monetary Fund). 2013d. *International Financial Statistics*. Washington.

IMF (International Monetary Fund). 2013e. *Ireland: Ninth Review under the Extended Arrangement*. IMF Country Report 13/93 (April). Washington.

IMF (International Monetary Fund). 2013f. *Portugal: Seventh Review under the Extended Arrangement*. IMF Country Report 13/160 (June). Washington.

IMF (International Monetary Fund). 2013g. *World Economic Outlook Database* (April). Washington.

IMF (International Monetary Fund). 2013h. *Greece: Ex Post Evaluation of Exceptional Access under the 2010 Stand-By Arrangement*. IMF Country Report 13/156 (June). Washington.

IMF (International Monetary Fund). 2013i. *Sovereign Debt Restructuring—Recent Developments and Implications for the Fund's Legal and Policy Framework* (April). Washington.

IMF (International Monetary Fund). 2013j. *Ireland: Tenth Review under the Extended Arrangement*. IMF Country Report 13/163 (June). Washington.

IMF (International Monetary Fund). 2013k. *Greece: Fourth Review under the Extended Arrangement*. IMF Country Report 13/241 (July). Washington.

IMF (International Monetary Fund). 2013l. *Spain: 2013 Article IV Consultation*. IMF Country Report 13/244 (August). Washington.

IMF (International Monetary Fund). 2013m. *Italy: 2013 Article IV Consultation*. IMF Country Report 13/298 (September). Washington.

IMF (International Monetary Fund). 2013n. *World Economic Outlook Database* (October). Washington.

IMF (International Monetary Fund). 2013o. *Germany: 2013 Article IV Consultation*. IMF Country Report 13/255 (August). Washington.

IMF (International Monetary Fund). 2013p. *Ireland: Twelfth Review under the Extended Arrangement*. IMF Country Report 13/366 (December). Washington.

IMF (International Monetary Fund). 2013q. *Portugal: Eighth and Ninth Reviews under the Extended Arrangement*. IMF Country Report 13/324 (November). Washington.

IMF (International Monetary Fund). 2013r. *Fiscal Monitor* (April). Washington.

IMF (International Monetary Fund). 2014. *International Financial Statistics* (monthly). Washington.

Isaacs, Kate P. 2013. *Federal Employees Retirement System: Budget and Trust Fund Issues* (June). Washington: Congressional Research Service.

Lourtie, Pedro. 2012. Understanding Portugal in the Context of the Euro Crisis. In *Resolving the European Debt Crisis,* ed. William R. Cline and Guntram B. Wolff. Special Report 21. Washington: Peterson Institute for International Economics and Bruegel.

Meade, James E. 1951. *The Theory of International Economic Policy: Volume I—The Balance of Payments*. London: Oxford University Press.

Merler, Silvia, and Jean Pisani-Ferry. 2012a. Hazardous Tango: Sovereign-Bank Interdependence and Financial Stability in the Euro Area. In *Financial Stability Review—Public Debt, Monetary Policy and Financial Stability,* no. 16 (April). Paris: Banque de France.

Merler, Silvia, and Jean Pisani-Ferry. 2012b. *The Simple Macroeconomics of North and South in EMU*. Bruegel Working Paper 2012/12. Brussels: Bruegel.

Merler, Silvia, and Jean Pisani-Ferry. 2012c. *Who's Afraid of Sovereign Bonds?* Bruegel Policy Contribution 2012/02. Brussels: Bruegel.

Ministério das Finanças. 2012. *Anúcio do Ministro das Finanças sobre o Programa de Recapitalização para as Instituíçoes de Crédito Portuguesas* (June 4). Lisbon.

Ministero dell' Economia e delle Finanze. 2013. *Economic and Financial Document 2013*. Rome.

Ministry of Finance (Greece). 2012a. *Decision on Exchange of Greek Treasury Bonds* (original in Greek). Protocol no. 2/13203/0023A. Athens.

Ministry of Finance (Greece). 2012b. Hellenic Republic Announces Exchange Offer Transaction Results. Press release. Athens.

Mody, Ashoka, and Damiano Sandri. 2011. *The Eurozone Crisis: How Banks and Sovereigns Came To Be Joined At the Hip*. IMF Working Paper 11/269. Washington: International Monetary Fund.

Nordvig, Jens. 2012. The Probability of a Greek Exit, Revisited. VoxEU, December 17. Available at www.voxeu.org.

NTMA (National Treasury Management Agency Ireland). 2013. *NTMA Issues Eight New Floating Rate Treasury Bonds in Exchange for Promissory Notes* (February 8). Dublin.

OECD (Organization for Economic Cooperation and Development). 2012. *OECD Economic Outlook*. 2012/2. Paris.

OECD (Organization for Economic Cooperation and Development). 2013. *OECD Economic Outlook*. 2013/1. Paris.

Ostry, Jonathan D., Atish R. Ghosh, Jun I. Kim, and Mahvash S. Qureshi. 2010. *Fiscal Space*. IMF Staff Position Note SPN/10/11 (September). Washington: International Monetary Fund.

Parker, Jonathan A. 2011. On Measuring the Effects of Fiscal Policy in Recessions. *Journal of Economic Literature* 49, no. 3: 703–18.

Pisani-Ferry, Jean, and Guntram B. Wolff. 2012. *The Fiscal Implications of a Banking Union*. Bruegel Policy Brief 2012/02. Brussels: Bruegel.

Ramey, Valerie A. 2011. Can Government Purchases Stimulate the Economy? *Journal of Economic Literature* 49, no. 3: 673–85.

Reserve Bank of Australia. 2012. Statement on Monetary Policy. Canberra.

Romer, Christina D., and David H. Romer. 2010. The Macroeconomic Effects of Tax Changes: Estimates Based on a New Measure of Fiscal Shocks. *American Economic Review* 100, no. 3: 763–801.

Schoenmaker, Dirk, and Toon Peek. 2014. *The State of the Banking Sector in Europe*. OECD Economics Department Working Paper 1102 (January). Paris: Organization for Economic Cooperation and Development.

Sinn, Hans-Werner, and Akos Valentinyi. 2013. European Imbalances. VoxEU, March 9. Available at www.voxeu.org/article/european-imbalances.

SSA (Social Security Administration). 2014. *Social Security Income, Outgo, and Accounts*. Washington. Available at www.ssa.gov/oact/progdata/assets.html.

Stiglitz, Joseph E., and Andrew Weiss. 1981. Credit Rationing in Markets with Imperfect Information. *American Economic Review* 71, no. 3 (June): 393–410.

Swan, Trevor W. 1955. Long-Run Problems of the Balance of Payments. Written but unpublished in 1955, later published in *Australian Economy*, 1963, ed. Heinz Wolfgang Arndt and Warner Max Corden. Melbourne: Cheshire.

Ubide, Ángel. 2013. *How to Form a More Perfect European Banking Union*. Policy Brief 13-23 (October). Washington: Peterson Institute for International Economics.

US Treasury. 2013. *Report to Congress on International Economic and Exchange Rate Policies* (October). Washington.

van Rixtel, Adrian, and Gabriele Gasperini. 2013. *Financial Crises and Bank Funding: Recent Experience in the Euro Area*. BIS Working Paper 406. Basel: Bank for International Settlements.

Véron, Nicolas. 2013. *A Realistic Bridge Towards European Banking Union.* Policy Brief 13-17. Washington: Peterson Institute for International Economics.

Véron, Nicolas, and Guntram B. Wolff. 2013. *From Supervision to Resolution: Next Steps on the Road to European Banking Union.* Bruegel Policy Contribution 2013/04 (February). Brussels: Bruegel.

Williamson, John. 2006. Meade's Analysis and Today's Global Imbalances. Lecture delivered at Cambridge University, November 21. Available at www.piie.com/publications/papers /williamson1106.pdf.

Wolff, Guntram B. 2012. The Euro Area Crisis: Policy Options Ahead. In *Resolving the European Debt Crisis,* ed. William R. Cline and Guntram B. Wolff. Special Report 21. Washington: Peterson Institute for International Economics and Bruegel.

World Bank. 2013. *Bank Capital to Assets Ratio (%).* Washington. Available at http://data.worldbank .org/indicator/FB.BNK.CAPA.ZS.

Zettelmeyer, Jeromin, Christoph Trebesch, and Mitu Gulati. 2012. *The Greek Debt Exchange: An Autopsy.* London: Centre for Economic Policy Research. Processed.

Zoli, Edda. 2013. *Italian Sovereign Spreads: Their Determinants and Pass-Through to Bank Funding Costs and Lending Conditions.* IMF Working Paper WP/13/84. Washington: International Monetary Fund.

Index

GPSR Authorized Representative: Easy Access System Europe, Mustamäe tee
50, 10621 Tallinn, Estonia, gpsr.requests@easproject.com

www.ingramcontent.com/pod-product-compliance
Lightning Source LLC
Chambersburg PA
CBHW072118020426
42334CB00018B/1637